Buddhist Tantra

A Philosophical Reflection and Religious Investigation

By the same author

- Tantra : Its Mystic and Scientific Basis

About the Author

Professor Lalan Prasad Singh spent about two decades as a mendicant in search of truth and salvation. During this period he went through the rigours of Tantra Sādhanā. He came to a conclusion that Tantra is neither a lifeless ritual nor a religious dogma. It is an intuitional science which rids the practitioner from the snares of false subjectivity and takes him to the state of spiritual sublimity and divine effulgence. After going through test and turmoil of life of mendicant he returned back to active academic life. In January 1996 he retired as a Professor of Philosophy from Magadh University, Bodh Gaya and in February of the same year be became Senior Fellow of Indian Council of Philosophical Research, Government of India. In 2000 A.D. Professor Singh was awarded Fellowship of Indian Institute of Advance Studies, Shimla. He bacame a Visiting Research Professor in 2004 at the Catholic University of America, Washington D.C. He was also awarded Indo-French Cultural Fellowship in 1994. During his sojourn at Paris, he delivered series of lectures on Tantra at the Department of Philosophy, Soubourn University IV, Paris (France). He also addressed the students and staff members of Department of Philosophy of Nihon and Toyo University, Tokyo in 2006. He presented many papers at the National and International Seminars and Symposia such as World Philosophical Congress 1975, International Congress of Orientalists, Mexico City 1976, First Sanskrit Symposia, Mexico City, World Sanskrit Congress, Lieden, Holland. Prof. Singh is a distinguished Professor of Philosophy and a Social Activist. Currently he is a Visiting Fellow at Department of Boddhist Studies, University of Delhi.

Buddhist Tantra

A Philosophical Reflection and Religious Investigation

Lalan Prasad Singh
M.A., D. Litt.

CONCEPT PUBLISHING COMPANY PVT. LTD.
NEW DELHI-110059

ISBN-13-978-81-8069-647-3 **ISBN-10-81-8069-647-2**

First Published 2010

Published and Printed by

Concept
Since 1974

Concept Publishing Company Pvt. Ltd.
Regd. Office:
A/15-16, Commercial Block, Mohan Garden
New Delhi-110059 (India)
Phones : 25351460, 25351794, *Fax* : 091-11-25357109
Email: publishing@conceptpub.com,
Website: www.conceptpub.com

Editorial Office:
H-13, Bali Nagar, New Delhi-110 015, India.

Cataloging in Publication Data--*Courtesy:* D.K. Agencies (P) Ltd. <docinfo@dkagencies.com>

Singh, Lalan Prasad, 1936-
Buddhist tantra : a philosophical reflection and religious investigation / Lalan Prasad Singh.
p. cm.
Includes bibliographical references (p.).
Includes index.
ISBN 13: 9788180696473
ISBN 10: 8180696472

1. Tantric Buddhism. 2. Buddhist philosophy. I. Title.

DDC 294.3925 22

To

Amitabh and Chiyako

With best of my love and blessings

Foreword

Verification is the most acceptable criterion of truth today. The principal criticism of religion arises from the fact that it is a system of faith which is held to be wholly unverified. This is the position generally held by western theologians and philosophers of religions. They believe that, insofar as there is truth in religion, it has been revealed once and for all. On the other hand *Yoga* and *Tantra* claim to be sciences which enable a man to realize spiritual truth directly. The content of this direct realization of truth cannot be formulated as a theological or philosophical doctrine. All discursive, all doctrinal formulation relate only to what is phenomenal. Logic and language arise from a pragmatic and empirical context. Kant pointed out that the most abstract systems of conceptual truth exemplified by Mathematics and Physics presuppose *a priori* forms of sensibility and thought. Where sensibility is transcended, the theory is also transcended. There is no doubt that there are no limits to philosophical reflection, but this reflective activity serves the purpose of indicating the limits of positive and theoretical knowledge. In doing so, it necessarily indicates what lies beyond it, or underlies it, its transcendental or noumenal bases. This vaguely glimpsed reality, beyond the ken of definitive knowledge, is the horizon in which spiritual or noumenal truth has to be searched. It requires a reorientation and transfiguration of consciousness, which is what *Tantra* helps one to achieve. Human consciousness is ordinarily extrovert and discursive, a flow of images and words. Human life is another name for the ceaseless striving after the shadowy world constructed by delusive thought.

Buddhist philosophy considers human life to be a process of ceaseless suffering. This suffering cannot be removed by the progress of material well-being and scientific knowledge because it is rooted in existential delusion. As a conscious being, man identifies himself with transient objects like the body and the mind. He regards what is impermanent as permanent; he holds the non-self as the self. This basic delusion produces in him ceaseless craving for things that are themselves nothing but appearances and constructs. A mere intellectual knowledge of these philosophical principles does not enable one to reach a new state of consciousness. For that transformation one needs the practical science of *Tantra*. Now the fact is that basic elements of *Tantra* are found widespread in all religions. All religions contain various Tantric practices that are included in their systems of worship. In all systems, the worship of man is required to turn his mind and will towards the object of worship which is always given a name, and also associated directly or indirectly with some symbolic form. Very often, however, such worship, prayer or rememberings of some holy names, or the contemplation of God is brief, occasional or formal. Prolonged spiritual exercises carried on over a long period of time are rare and rerer still is their practice with unflagging zeal and hope. If prayer, contemplation and remembrance are carried on with an alert and detached mind, forgetful of its worldly interests and worries, and even forgetful of the body and its external environment, undistracted by the distractions of memories, images, desires and inner speech, and centered wholly in the idea taken up for remembrance or contemplation, one enters the portals of yogic practice. If this conscious process follows a definite *pranic* rhythm and the echoing vibration of the affrmation of spontaneous self-consciousness, it would be the beginning of Tantric yoga. In the practice of *Tantra* the mind has to enter the channel of emptiness without losing itself in the inactivity of sleep. This is possible only through the awakening of *Mantra.* The concept of *Boddhi-chitta* is of central importance in this context.

Buddhist Tantra is not an escape from the world nor a pursuit of personal experiences. it is a way to realize Transcendental Wisdom in its innate union with Universal Compassion. From the experience of enlightenment Buddha returned to the world to liberate mankind. He is the preeminent model for *Tantra-Sadhana.* It is unfortunate that many misconceptions have grown about Tantra. About Hindu Tantra, some eminent authors such as John Woodroffe and Swami Pratyagātānand and Gopinath Kaviraj have helped to clarify this tradition. On the Buddhist Tantra, Benoytosh Bhattacharya and S.B. Dasgupta have written valuable works. A spate on recent works on Buddhist Tantric literature and practice has served to spread much obscurity and misunderstanding. Perplexing technicalities, textual contradictions and mistranslation make such work highly dengerous. I am glad that Dr. L.P. Singh has sought to present in this work a short philosophical and practical account of Buddhist Tantra. He has been a Professor of Philosophy and practitioner of *Tantra.* This work should be of help to those who seek the spiritual guidance of Buddhist Tantra.

G.C. Pande
Former Vice Chancellor
Allahabad University
& Rajasthan University

Preface

Lord Buddha, after the attainment of *Nirvana* under Bodhi-Tree at Bodh Gaya through the practice of Tantra Sadhana reflected on the nature and significance of *Nirvana* which resulted into the birth of a new School of Philosophy and a new religious order known as Buddhism.

Buddhist Tantra is the sublime and profound form of spirituality. It is monotheistic. It presents the highest form of monism. In Buddhist Tantra, *Advaya* means the eternal co-existence of *Prajñā vāda and Upāya* which constitute the infinite unity and transcendental reality (*Boddhicitta*). Buddhist Tantra has made great contribution to the speculative metaphysics in the form *of Vajñān vāda* (Yogācāra) and *Śunyavāda* (Mādhyamika)

Buddhist Tantra is not based on false asceticism. The symbolism of sex and wine under some esoteric discipline is supposed to sublimate the baser instincts. Tantra recognizes that sex and hunger are inherent in man, but they can be sublimated. In the recognition of the gradual development and transformation of human consciousness Tantra takes cognizance of the baser and crude aspects of human nature and introduces spiritual discipline and esotericism to sublimate them into higher forms of divine life.

The Mantra is not constituted of a nonsensical syllable. The practice of Pañcsmakāra take morbid forms of sexo-yogic practice. However, those who get initiation from the proper Guru, the incantation of Mantra creates acoustic vibration that awakens the dormant spiritual energy (Kuṇḍaliṇī) and the practice of *Pañcsmakāra Sadhana* helps the Sadhaka in liberating the initiate from the fetters of mundane and supra mundane existence. Its goal is the enlightenment (*Nirvana*). Tantra Sadhana moves man from the dualism of subject and object to the higher and sublime state of the oneness (*Samarastā*) of infinite unity and pure consciousness.

Āgama and Nigama, Tantra and Veda consitute the warp and woof of Indian culture. Tantra forms the esoteric basis of all the major world religions. A thorough study of Tantricism is *sine-qua-non* for proper understanding of different religious orders in general and Indian culture in particular. Unfortunately, Tantra is still regarded as black magic and degenerated form of religious practices. The practice of Pañcsmakāra Sadhana has been greatly scandalized. The whole Tantirc literature is written in Sandhyābhāṣā. It is full of symbolism. The romantic field and significance of the mystic symbolism of Tantra cannot be understood without one's initiation (*abhiṣeka*) into its intuitional science. The significance of the five M's i.e. *Māṁsa, Matysas, Mudrā, Madya* and *Māithuna* is metaphysical. It cannot be grasped in its manifest form. The *Maithuna* refers to the union fo Śiva and Śakti or Prajñā and Upāya in the Sasrāra Cakra or Uṣnisa-Kamala. The esoteric significance of the *Madirā* is the pineal nectar that emanates from the *Uṣniṣa-Kamala.*

Philosophers and scientists have been pondering on truth and reality since time immemorial. Western Civilization is proud of its monumental achievements in natural science and technology. Eastern civilization specially that of India have made profound contribution in the form of their intuitional science and mysticism. The most profound ontological doctrine is considered to be the *Mādhyamika* which claims *Śunyatā* to be an intrinsic nature, to be the ultimate mode of existence of phenọmenon. One can experience *Śunyatā* only when the mind is liberated from all kinds of reification. However, Buddhist Tantra is aware of the futility of speculative philosophy and hence it recommends the practice of intuitional science and esotericism for the realization of ultimate reality. In this intuitive experience of *Prajñā* and *Upāya,* essence and existence become identical. Western philosophy has to acknowledge that Tantra and Yoga have made enormous discoveries and achievements in the terms of intuitional science and mysticism which have a sound metaphysical, epistemological and sotoreogical basis.

Tantra has a rich spiritual heritage and a highly developed forms of cultural history. It has not received the attention it deserves. But due to incisive intellectual interpretation, by Swami Pratyagatanand, M.M. Gopinath Kaviraj, M.M. Haraprasad Sastri, Sir John Woodroffe, Benoytosh Bhattacharya, Pt. Lakshman Joo, Jaidev Singh, G. Tucci, Alexy Wayman, D.L. Snellgrove, and G.C. Pande it was placed in a proper spiritual and philosophical perspective. His Holiness Dalai Lama has done a pioneering work in propagating and propounding Tantra philosophy and practice and presenting Buddhist Tantra in its proper esoteric perspective to the present world.

This book has grown out of fellowship awarded to me by the Indian Institute of Advanced Study, Shimla to make indepth study of Buddhist Tantra.

I would like to put on record my profound gratitude to Shri Chandra Shekhar, the former Prime Minister and the Renaissance Man of Modern Indian Politics. He has been the greatest solace of my life.

I would like to record my indebtedness to my preceptor G.C. Pande. It would not be out of place to mention here that Professor Pande is the greatest living indologist and an original thinker. He has been the source of my intellectual and spiritual inspiration for more than four decades. I am thankful and grateful to my friend and benefactor a statesman, leading philanthropist, Industrialist Shri Kamal

Morarka. I am thankful to Prof. K.T.S. Sarao, Professor Ven. Bhikshu Satyapal and Dr. H.P. Gangnegi of the Department of Buddhist Studies, University of Delhi.

My thanks are due to Shri Ambitabh Verma IAS and his wife Dr. Anita; Shri Rajiv Gauba IAS, and his wife Dr. Pammi; Shri R.K. Singh IAS, and his wife Jugnu; Shri Anurag Gupta IPS and Thakur D.P. Singh for their constant help and cooperation.

I am indebted to Venerable Marcel Bertels, Director, Maitreya Project for supplying me some valuable books on Tantra . I would like to record my sincere thanks to Professor H.S. Gill who made my stay at Shimla pleasant and meaningful. My sincere thanks are due to my children, Mili, Arvinda, Ambitabha, Ashutosh, Varsha and Anand Vijaya whose help and affection have been quite invaluable in completing this research work. I am specially thankful to my youngest daughter Varsha without her help and affection this research project would not have been completed. I would like to express my love and affection to my grand children Janu, Shanu, Kishu and Rakshu who are the source of my pure joy. I express my sincere thanks and gratitude to the authorities of National Museum, New Delhi for providing some rare photographs on Tantric Art for publication in this book. Last but not the least, I am thankful to Shri Ashok Kumar Mittal, the owner of Concept Publishing Company and his loving wife Mrs. Usha Mittal and sons Shri Nitin and Shri Devashish for their invaluable love and affection without whose help and cooperation this book would not have been before the reader. I express my thank to Shri Rajendra Prasad Shah who has helped me in editing and proof reading.

4th January, 2009
New Delhi

Lalan Prasad Singh

Contents

List of Illustrations

1 Introduction to Buddhist Tantra

Tantra forms the esoteric basis of all major religions. It stands for the awakening of dormant divinity. It is a mystic technique to invoke the spirituality of man and woman. Every entity has a characteristic vibrations. This vibration is a serial name or *mantra*. *Śabda* is used in three senses. (i) *Śabda* is a symbol or sign. (ii) *Śabda* is a concept or construct. (iii) According to Tantra *Śabda* is an expression of vibrational creative energy. It is totally opposed to all modern philosophical or linguistic conception or view about *Śabda*. Words are esoteric names. Really speaking *manṭras* are divine commands and these commands are not universal rather personal. Even Berkeley has stated that things are nothing but meanings in the cosmic mind. And hence *Tantra* is invocation of this divine command and esoteric practice to realise the ultimate truth and meaning of existence and being. This ultimate reality and meaning is known in Hindu *Tantra* as *Ātaman* or *Brāhman*, in Buddhist Tantra it is called *Bodhicitta*. *Bodhicitta* is bereft of all existence. It is beyond all thought-categories as subject and object. It is without a beginning and is of the nature of *Śūnya*. *Guhyasamāja Tantra* defines *Bodhicitta* as "Neither the perception of the absence of existence in non-existence can be called perception, nor the perception of non-existence in existence can be discovered."[1]

Buddhist Tantra reveals the mysterious nature of *Bodhicitta*. *Bodhicitta* can be experienced only through the esoteric practice of *mantra*, *maṇḍala* and *Herukā*. This mystic experience is attainable only by the *yogis* who have attained the state of choiceless awareness and spiritual perfections. "All the misinterpretations of *Tantra* centre round this one fact, and all the abuses that have been most vehemently poured forth by scholars are due to their not comprehending this one point of supreme importance."[2]

There is a controversy over the origin and development of Buddhist Tantra. According to traditional belief Aṣaṅga, the founder of the *Yogācāra* School, is an exponent of Buddhist Tantra. In *Mahāyāna-Sūtra-Lāṅkāra* of Aṣaṅga, there is a clear reference and evidence to Tantricism.

Some scholars think that Nāgārjuna, the founder of *Mādhyamikā* School, is the real exponent of Buddhist esotericism. There is a general belief that he was initiated into the *Tantra Sādhanā*, by Buddha Vairacana, with the grace of *Boddhi-Sattva* at the 'iron tower' in South India. But according to a Tibetan accounts, Nāgārjuna was imparted Tāntric initiation by Siddhācārya Sarahapāda and he attained *Vajra Kāya Siddhi.*[3]

To my view it is the Buddha himself, who is the founder of Tantricism in Buddhism. It is a well-known fact that *Tantra-Sādhanā* is performed in cremation ground or a lonely place. When it is performed under a *kula*-tree, the progress is accelerated. According to accepted *Tāntric* belief the Banyan tree is one of the five trees recognised as *kula*-tree. It is, therefore, not without any reason that Siddhāratha performed his *Sādhanā* under the famous banyan tree at Boddh Gayā and attained *Nirvāṇa.*

It is further confirmed by a characteristic occult power which the Buddha obtained along with *Nirvāṇa,* which is manifestly of *tāntric* origin. *Tantra-Sādhanā* is kept secret and is imparted only to its rightful claimants. It is evident that the Buddha himself practiced *asphanaga-yoga*[4] (Yoga of psychic expansion), when he was in the search of eternal truth. *Vinaya Pīṭaka*[5] says that Buddha's own disciple Bharadvāja rose into the air and brought down the begging bowl which was held high above by *Setthi.* Dr. B. Bhattacharya, writes "Buddha recognised *ṛddhis* or supernatural powers and mentioned four *iddhipadas*[6] continuously to the attainment of supernatural powers.[7] The Tāntric account is further supported by the concept of *Bodhi-Maṇḍala* or the mystic circle around the famous tree beneath which the Buddha practiced meditation and attained *bodhi.* This belief and cult of *Bodhi-Maṇḍala* is a necessary practice to draw circles or other mystic diagrams in a place selected for *tāntric* practice. The *maṇḍala* of Buddhist *tantra* is nothing but *yantra* of Hindu *tantra.* Even the formulas of refuge and worship which were current of all times and in all the countries of Theravāda Buddhism possesses a mantric character. Their perfect parallelism of sound, rhythm and ideation, their concentration of highest symbols like Buddha, *Dhamma* and *Saṁgha* and their underlying devotional attitudes in which *Śraddhā* (devotion) and *Mettā* (love) occupies the first place, and made their *mantra* in the best sense. *Mantra, mudrā* and *maṇḍala* are the basis of Buddhist tāntric *sādhanā* from their very inception and thus a new introduction was made to revive and resuscitate the lost science of *tantra* by the Buddha.

There has been two great traditions of development of Buddhism, that of the *sūtra* and that of *tantra. Sūtra* is comparatively well known in the general course of its progress. *Sūtra* and its commentaries and philosophical treatises with their commentaries created the vast literatures of Buddhism. This part of development is known as Theravāda Buddhism of Pāli text. The whole conception of origin and development of Buddhist Tantra, namely, its authority in the *sūtra,* has not yet been logically and fairly applied to the *tantra.* There is a misunderstanding over *tantra.* It is considered to be something corrupt[8] and belonging to the twilight of Buddhism. There is misunderstanding that tāntric culture which regulated the life in olden days did not prove very helpful for the Buddhism. This is due to the fact that *Mahāyāna sūtras* and their commentaries were little known in the academic world before the end of the nineteenth century.

Dr. S. Radhakrishnan writes "Buddhism does not like the idea of basing the reality of Brahman on Vedic authority, for whom once we admit the evidence of revelation, there is no end to it. So, in the *tevijja suttas* Buddha compares those, who believe in Brāhman or the authority of Vedas and seek union with Him to those who built the staircase at the junction of four roads to mount up to high mansion as to which they can neither see nor know whether it exist at all."[9]

To my mind it is certainly not the ethical obsession of the Buddha which is responsible for his indefiniteness on metaphysical problems. Buddha had a firm faith in meditation and esotericism. His conviction of barrenness of intellectual flapping of wings in the vacuum prevented him from becoming a pseudo metaphysician. The Buddha was aware of the antinominal character of reason. He was aware of the interminable nature of metaphysical conflict and he was also aware that this conflict can be resolved only by rising to the higher state of criticism Criticism is freedom of the human mind from all kinds of entanglements. Criticism is freedom and this heralded the new era of questioning and dialectic reasoning.

The dormant divinity when awakened with the ideation, incantation of *mantra* opens the gate of *Bhūmi* (consciousness). This divine power is known in Buddhist Tantra as *Herukā, Vajra-Tārā, Vajra-Yoginī, Vajra-caṇḍikā. Herukā* is known in Hindu Tantra as *kulakuṇḍalinī*.

The central objective of *tantra* is to attain Buddhahood or *Nirvāṇa* during this human life. All qualities of Buddhahood is characterized by four bodies of the Buddha — Emanation body *(nirmāṇakāya)*, Enjoyment body *(sambhoga-kāya)*, Dharma body *(dharma-kāya)*, and Pure body *(sahaja-kāya)*. These bodies refer to four states of awakening *(jāgrata)*, dream *(svapna)*, deep sleep *(suṣupti)* and fourth (*tūrya*). The four letters of word *Kāla-cakra* symbolizes these four bodies. These states of Buddhahood is the supreme unchanged bliss which is also known as the supreme unchanged gnosis. According to Buddhist Tantra this gnosis is attained by the practice of *mahā-mudrā*. The accomplishment of *mahā-mudrā* is beyond the reach of concept or thought. According to the *Kāla-cakra* tradition there are 11 kinds of initiations. First 10 of which are the mundane (*laukika*) initiations and the last one is spiritual *(alaukika)*. According to the usual classification in the *Anuttarayoga tantra*, the mundane initiations are all clubbed together in three; therefore, the supermundane one is called 'the fourth' *(caturtha)*. The mundane initiations lead to the accomplishment of the mundane *siddhis*, while the supermundane initiation is instrumental in accomplishing the supermundane *siddhi*, the supreme unchanging gnosis. The mundane *siddhis* are obtained by the *maṇḍala* and other practices and the supermundane *siddhi* is obtained by the practice of *Mahāmudrā*.[10]

Tantricism, both Hindu and Buddhist, represents a special aspect of the religious and cultural life of India. A thorough study and deeper understanding of Tantricism is necessary for understanding the subtaranean cultural flow and is indispensable for understanding the Indian mind and culture. Tantricism has been the target of serious criticism charitable and uncharitable from scholars both oriental and occidental.

The word *tantra* has been used in many senses in Sanskrit. It connotes a system and refers to some *śastras.* M.M. H.P. Shastri says, "Tantra deals with the problem of *tattva,* i.e. study of the absolute. *Tattva* means pertaining to *thatness.* Hence, Tantra is that branch of esoteric cult which brings the realization of *tattva* (Absolute) with the help of *Mantra Sādhanā. Tantra* stands for the application of the esoteric science for the attainment of spirituality. In esoteric sense Tantra means the spiritual cult by which divine knowledge is unfolded. It is a spiritual discipline in a wide sense, and, when used in a limited sense, it is a mystic form of spiritual *Sādhanā.*

The mystic definition of Tantra is that it is a spiritual cult which liberates from the bondages of crudeness and ignorance. The word *ta* is the *Bīja-mantra* (acoustic root) of crudeness (*jaḍatā*). Tantra is a process of *Sādhanā* which relieves one from the fetters of crudeness (*ta*). Thus, Tantra is an intuitional science which stands for the progressive realization of the divine. It liberates one from the cimmerian darkness and leads unto the divine effulgence. It is a path of salvation. It is a science of the consciousness.

Tantra deals with both the theoretical and the practical aspect of spiritual life. The former is known as *Nigama* and the latter is called *Āgama.* Some scholars have tried to prove that Tantra is the developed form of the *Sāṅkhya* and *Vedānta* systems, that the science of *Sāṅkhya* and *Vedānta* philosophy has been culminated into the Tāntric cult, that, thus, Tantra is a part of the *Vedas.* P.C. Bagchi says, "The Tantra is regarded as a *Śruti* or *Āgama,* revelation, as opposed to a *Smṛti* or *Nigama,* 'tradition'. It is thus classed with the *Vedas.* It is usually defined as Śrutiśākhāviśeṣaḥ", a particular branch of the *Vedas.* This contention is untenable. By no logic or cultural evidence can it be proved that Tantra is a branch of the *Veda. Tantra* and *Veda* are two different currents of Indian cultural life.

The Buddhist Tantra belongs to Mahāyāna tradition. *Sādhanamālā,* the canonical literature of *tantra* believes that Buddhist tantra was developed from Yogācārya School. Yogācārya School evolved out of the *Śūnyavāda* of the *Mādhyamikā. Sādhanāmālā* belongs to Vajrayāna school and throws immense light on the ends, objects and practices of Buddhist Tantra. In *Sādhanāmālā,* the word *Mahāyāna,* occurs twice and from these references we can assume the Buddhist Tantra was an outcome of *Mahāyāna* tradition. The *Mahāyāna* in the view of Buddhist Tantra is co-extensive and synonym of *Dharma.* The word *Śūnya* occurs almost on every page of the *Sādhanamālā.* However, there is philosophical and esoteric difference between the concept of *Śūnya* as conceived by *Mādhyamikā* and as conceived by the Vajrayānist. For the *Mādhyamikā* both the concept and the object are *Śūnya* in essence. There is no reality either of mind or of the phenomenal world. Its philosophical position is not acceptable to Vajrayānist. For the Buddhist *vijñāna* is absolutely necessary. There is a little controversy whether the Tantra is based on Yogācāra or to *Śūnyavāda* as a philosophical treatise of Yogācāra has been formal and explained in many places in the book and according to some this leads to infer that the *Vajrayāna* is a direct development of Yogācāra School.[11]

The *Vajra* stands for adamantine path or *Śūnya*-vehicle. *Śūnya* is used in an esoteric sense to represent *Vajra*. *Śūnyatā* is described as *vajra* because it cannot be changed, cannot be burnt and cannot be destroyed.

There is a great philosophical difference between the Mahāyāna and Hīnayāna School of Buddhism on the concept of *Śūnyatā*. Though both of them agree that the realization of *Śūnyatā* leads to the cessation of suffering but the method and the technique followed by these two traditions of Buddhism are widely different. The Theravāda Buddhism believes in obtaining liberation for himself by his own efforts without caring much for the condition of suffering humanity. One obtains *Nirvāṇa* and cessation from suffering and, however, by obtaining *Nirvāṇa* one cannot know the perfect truth or remove the veil which conceals the transcendental nature of truth.

The ideal of the Mahāyānist is not to attain his or her individual liberation. Ideal of Mahāyānist is to become *Boddhi-sattva*. The Mahāyānists are not afraid of *saṁsāra, i.e.* the cycle of birth and death in some sense as the Hīnayanists are, but they are prepared to undergo any suffering if these lead to the spiritual upliftment of sentient beings. The condition for the sufferings of humanity actuates and forces them to abandon even their salvation but thereby they will be in a position to remove the veil covering the transcendental nature of truth.

The *Mādhayamika* concept of *nirvāṇa* is *śūnya*. *Śūnya* is a state which is neither existence, nor non-existence, nor a combination of the two either, nor negation of the two. The Yogācāra School enriched the concept of *Śūnya* by affirming the positive aspect of the *Vijñāna* (consciousness), which is in the state of flux. The *Vijñāna* of the previous moments gives rise to the *Vijñāna* of the next moment and this process goes on until *Vijñāna* attains *Nirvāṇa* after having eliminated of all impurities, but the sublimity and the profundity of Yogācāra lies in the concept that the consciousness will not strive further for *Nirvāṇa* but will continue itself in the spiritual upliftment of all beings. The *Yogācārī* would attain liberation only when the whole human beings would be free from snares of false subjectivity. On the analysis and the elucidation of the concept of *Nirvāṇa* we feel there are two distinct elements, *i.e. Vijñāna* and *Śūnya*. The Buddhist tantra introduced a new element of *mahāsukha* or eternal bliss. It introduces further the Theory of Five *Dhyāni Buddha* which preside over all the five *skandhas*. It introduces the element of *Śakti* in Buddhism for the first time and it has created a vast pantheon of gods and goddesses.

It is very difficult to come to any conclusion regarding the scripture from which *tāntricism* drew its inspiration. However, it is believed that Padma-vajra's *Guhya-siddhi* throws some light on the origin and the development of Buddhist Tantra. Padma-Vajra has dealt with in detail about the doctrine, tenets and the esoteric significance embodied in *Guhyasamāja*. Padma-vajra has written a treatise which is known as *Śrīsamāja*. The other eminent scholars like Indrabhauti in his great commendable work entitled *Jñāna-siddhi* accepts *Guhyasamāja* as work of great authority and he gives summary of some of the basic teachings of this work.

The Buddhist tantra are in the form of *saṅgitis* and it has rightly said that they have been delivered by the Buddha in an assembly of the faithful.[12] It is in the *saṅgiti* form that all new ideas were introduced into Buddhism. Orthodox followers of the *saṁgha* were opposed to any new ideas. The orthodox followers were never in a mood to accept anything which had not been stated by the Buddha. The original Tantras of Buddhism are in *saṅgiti* form wherein it is inculcated and incorporated doctrine and ideas, practices which were dramatically opposed to some teachings of Buddha. The Buddha's teachings are pregnant with great philosophical import and these teachings have been interpreted by different *Ācāryas* at the different periods of history in a different way and which has given rise to the different schools and traditions of Buddhism. This does not show any weakness but it speaks of the profundity, the richness and the sublimity of the Buddha's teachings.

There is a clear distinction between empirical and the absolute, *saṁvṛti* and *paramārtha* in the original doctrine of the Buddhism. Hence, Buddhism retained in some form in the *Abhidharma*. The transient and gross objects of common sense could not be identified from other objects. Such a distinction is the result of *Abhidharma metaphysical* and according to G.C. Pande, it does form part of the original Buddhism.[13]

There has been shifts in the metaphysical stand in *Yogācāra* School where spiritual reality is conceived as infinite beyond empirical flux attainable only to transcendental wisdom. Professor G.C. Pande rightly observes, 'Hīnayanic philosophy aims at providing the self-absorbed and ascetical monk with an analytical tool which would enable him to objectify his mental states and detach himself from them, and is thus an essentially unworldly and cloistered philosophy which could be charged with encouraging soteriological egoism and an exaggerated attention to the myriad forms of suffering to be abandoned rather than to what is most real and worthwhile. For if every man is totally alone, drowning in a flood of tears, and it proposes to save him by telling him that there is no real person who could be called the drowning man but only an inexorable flood with the taste of tears. Perhaps the Hīnayānist could retort by saying that the Mahāyānist proposes to save the man by telling him that he has been either the drowning man or the flood. In a way the retort would be well taken for Mahāyāna does declare all empirical objects or *Dharmas* to be unreal and unborn like the objects of a dream but it concedes them a phenomenal and pragmatic reality. The way it suggests is not simply that of analytic withdrawal *(nivṛtti)* but of positive perfection *(Pāramitā)* culminating in transfiguration or *Parāvṛtti*.[14] The mystic and esoteric culture of Mahāyāna which resulted in Buddhist Tantra is more spiritual and catholic than

Theravāda Buddhism which is reflected in its meditational practice, ethical idealism and religious devotionalism.

The Tibetan Canon, consists of two branches. The first is known as *Kanjur*. It comprises thirteen volumes of rules of monastic life *(vinaya)*, twenty-one volumes of revealing teachings concerning the doctrine of perfection of wisdom *(Prajñāpāramitā)*. *Prajñāpāramitā* became both the philosophical and esoteric basis of later Buddhist philosophy and practice. The forty-four volumes of *Mahāyāna-sūtra*, extol the infinite merits that accrued from the devotion and thought and commend the career of living the life of self-nagation of Bodhisattva. Twenty-two volumes *tantras* deal with ritual and the esoteric practices. It is a part of the contents of some of these last works that have become known as Buddhist tantra.

The second part of the canon is known as *Tanjur* (translation of treatises) and comprises works of Bodhisattva and Buddhist Patriarch. Normally, these treatises are not considered as *buddhavacana*. It consists of commentaries on the *sūtras* and the commentaries on the *tantrās*.

Unfortunately, the scholars did not pay much attention on the development of earlier Mahāyāna which has its authority and the scholars did not go into the depth of the *tantra*. There is still a tendency to regard *tantra* as something corrupt. This was due to the fact that the scholars were not aware of the philosophical import of *Mahāyāna sūtras* and their commentaries and treatises associated with them were little known till the end of the nineteenth century.

As far the charge that Buddhism ceases to be distinguishable from certain other types of Indian religious practice at this time, this was now no more true than it had ever been. It is indeed true that Buddhist and non-Buddhist *tantrās* are based upon similar ideas and often contain similar material, and that many parallels may be obvious, but one may well ask at what previous stage of the doctrine was this not true. The followers of the non-Buddhist tantrās may well have been as dependent upon them who called themselves Buddhists, as the Vedantists were probably dependent upon the *mādhyamikas*. These are questions which can only gradually be resolved as these works become better known.[15]

There has been another misunderstanding about the *tantra*. John Woodroffe has rightly observed that one can reasonably dispute the fact that the basic text of the *tantrās* is murky and macabre appearances and does not excuse to say that it is open to anyone to sit down and write *tantra*.[16]

Śiva and *Śakti* are inseparable in *tantra*. *Śakti* is immanent principle. Without *Śakti* one cannot attain the state of Buddhahood. To my view the fundamental position of Hindu and Buddhist *tāntric* pantheon is the same. Men and women are *upāya* and *prajñā* in their ultimate nature according to *Hevajra Tantra*.

In *Hevajrā* Tantra, *prajñā* is addressed as *yuvati* (young woman), *janani* (mother), *bhagani* (sister), *rajaki* (washer woman), *nartaki* (dancing girl), *duhita* (daughter), *dombi* (doma girl). *Prajñā* is called *janani* because she is the cause of creation. She is called *nartaki* because the manifest universe is but a cosmic dance of *prajñā* and every object is in a dancing posture (*nṛtaratā*). She is *dombi* because she is beyond the touch of human mind and senses. In the *Atharva Veda* Brahman is called *Vrātya* (untouchable). It is so called because it cannot be grasped by the senses and the mind.

In *Guhyasamāja Tantra Śakti* has been introduced. But one should not be mistaken that before this there was no element of *Śaktism* in Buddhist Tantra. *Śakti* has been the inevitable principle of practice for obtaining liberation since the origin of Tantra. *Guhyasamāja Tantra* has only introduced the new idea of five *Dhyāni Buddhas* presiding over the five *skandhas* or factors of which the universe is composed along with *Śakti*. These five *skandhas* are: *Rūpa* (form), *Vedenā* (feeling), *Saṁjñā* (name), *Saṃskāra* (impression) and *Vijñāna* (consciousness). *Sādhanamālā* describes the names, colours and symbols of the different *Dhyāni Buddhas*. The names *are: Vairocana, Ratna Sambhava, Amitābha, Amoghasiddhi* and *Akṣobhya*. Their colours are : white, yellow, red, green and blue, and they are depicted in different *mudrās*, namely, *Bodhyāṅgi* (teaching), *Varada* (grace), *Dhyāna* (meditation), *Abhaya* (protective) and *Bhūmisparsa* (earth-touching).

The female (*Śakti*) counterparts of the, five *Dhyāni Buddhās* are: *Locana, Vairadhatviśvari, Pandārā, Māmaki* and *Tārā*. These five consorts of *Dhyāni Buddhās* belong to the five families of *dveṣa, moha, rāga, cintāmaṇi* and *samaya*. The names of the five *Bodhisattva* of the *Dhyāni Buddhas* are: *Vajrapāṇi, Samantabhadra, Padmapāṇi, Ratnapāṇi and Viśvapāṇi*.[17]

In *Caryāpāds* of the *Siddhācāryas* the divine love of *yogin* and *yoginī* has been symbolically expressed in the form of a metaphor of ordinary courtship and sex union of lover and beloved. Here the individual self is male or lord and the *Śūnyatā* is female or lady. Kakkurloda says in his divine intoxication, "Desireless am I and the void-mind is my husband". Tilopāda says, "The mind is the lord, and vacuity (*Śūnyatā*) is the lady". This would always keep united in the *sahaja*. Like Sri Ramakrishna, Kanhupāda says that when the Lord's mind merges himself in his wife-vacuity, he becomes one with her and as salt after dissolving in water.

Tantra is full of symbolism. The concept of *Dhyānī Buddha* is great esoteric significance. All *Dhyāni Buddhās* are consorting amorously at every *padma* or *cakra*. Like Hindu tantra these *Dhyāni Buddhās* have been described with colour, form and *bāhana*. Those who are adept in practical *Sādhanā* can alone understand the deeper meaning of the mystic symbols which have been employed in both Hindu and Buddhist Tantra.

Tāntric Buddhism is based on the philosophy of non-duality. The five *Dhyāni Buddhās* have been wrongly represented by five primordial gods which certainly smack of polytheism. In accordance with the monotheistic spirit and tradition of tāntricism, the concept of *Ādi Buddha*, the Supreme deity like *Ādinātha* and *Sadā Śiva* of Hindu tantra, came into being. According to Dr. B. Bhattacharya, this theory of *Ādi Buddha* or *Vajra-dhara* (the primordial monotheistic Buddha) was originated in the Nālandā monastery in about tenth century.[18] According to Alexander Csoma de Koros, also the theory of *Ādi Buddha* was introduced at Nālandā in the beginning of the tenth century.[19] There are some disputes and controversy regarding the place and the concept of *Ādi-Buddha*. The identification of *Vajra-dhara* with *Ādi-Buddha* is not acceptable to the world of scholarship. According to some scholars *Bodhi-Sattvas* such as *Samantabhadra* and *Vajrapāṇi* are *Ādi-Buddhas*. Only those who are initiated into Tāntrism can understand the non-dualistic significance and profound importance of the esoteric symbolism of *Ādi Buddha* and *Dhyāni Buddha* which are one in essence. *Ādi Buddha* in his *yab-yum* pose remains the same except that he has locked in love with *Śakti* which is known as *Prajñāpapārmitā*. *Śakti* is richly dressed and profusely jewelled. She carries the *karatri* (knife) which symbolizes the cutting of the veil of nescience, and the *kapāla* (skull) which stands for the absolute union. The *Yab-yum mudrā* represents non-dualism in dualism.

The central objective of *tantra* is the transformation of energy into the transcendental experience of deep penetrative awareness. Through its method of mystic transformation and sublimation, *tantra* demonstrates that as a human being we are hybernated cosmic beings. We have, the capacity to enjoy limitless, blissful happiness while at the same time remaining free from the delusions that normally contaminate our mind, Buddhist tantra has taken a very revolutionary stand on the concept of enjoyment. Contrary to what some people think, there is nothing wrong with having pleasures and enjoyment. What is wrong is the motivation and the perspective that transform our ordinary pleasure into misery. With proper understanding and transformation and esoteric practice whatever we do can bring us closer to our goal of totality and enlightenment. With proper transformation all our actions can lead to the path of spirituality and enlightenment.

Perhaps all this sounds impossible. Certainly other more gradual spiritual approaches, including those of the *Sūtra* path of Buddhism itself, stress that desire, jealousy and the other delusions of our daily life are always impure and should be treated as poisons. We are constantly reminded of their dangerous effects and are instructed to avoid their influence as much as possible. But, as has been pointed out already, *tantra* takes a different approach. Although it also insists that delusions such as desirous attachment are the source of our delusion and suffering and, therefore, must be overcome, it teaches skillful ways of using the energy of these delusions to deepen our awareness and speed our spiritual progress. Just as those with skill can take poisonous plants and turn them into powerful medicine, so the skillful and well-trained tāntric practitioner manipulate the energy of desire and even anger to advantage. This is definitely possible.[20]

The Buddha was antagonistic to all sorts of sacrifices, necromancy, sorcery or magic. However, it is said that he has given instructions concerning *mudrās*, *maṇḍalas* and *tantrās*, so that the prosperity 'in this world could be attained by less advanced disciples, who seemed to care more for this world than for *nirvāṇa*. However, Dr.

Benoytosh Bhattacharya holds the view of contentions that India in Buddha's time was so steeped in superstitions that no religion could dare to forbid all kinds of magic, sorcery and necromancy. Dr. Benoytosh Bhattacharya writes: "A clever organizer, as Buddha was, he did not fail to notice the importance of incorporating magical practices in his religion to make it popular from all points of view and attract more adherents thereby. Up till now we were ignorant of Buddha's attitude towards the Tāntric practices, excepting a few meagre references in Pāli literature, and were unable to determine the time of their introduction in Buddhism. But Śāntarakṣita (A.D. 705-762) and his disciple Kamalaśila brought out this connexion very forcibly in the *Tattvasaṁgraha* and its commentary, stating fully the reasons which made Buddha to incorporate them in this system."[21]

Dr. Bhattacharya agrees that *tantra* and *mantra* have been practiced by the Buddhists since the time of Buddha. He has given detailed account of practice of *dharaṇis* which are said to confer great merits when muttered repeatedly. Then comes the worship of Buddha in *Prajñāpāramitā*. We find the recensions of *Prajñāpāramitā*, the *sūtras*, the *Hṛdayasūtra*, with its *Dhāraṇis* and *mantrās*, recitations of those *mantrās* use to confer great merits. *Prajñāpāramitā* and its contemporaneous with *Mañjūsrīmūla-kalpa* where *Mañjūśrī* is in princely form is worshipped in *maṇḍalas* with the esoteric discipline and process. However, I do not agree with Dr. Benoytosh Bhattacharya that the Buddha introduced and incorporated magical practices in his religion to make it popular. There is another contention which would not be acceptable to the world of scholarship. According to M.M. Haraprasad Shastri *tantra* came from outside India, most probably it came with Magi priests of Scythian. The Magi priests' origin of *tantra* is a brilliant suggestion according to Benoytosh Bhattacharya. Dr. Bhattacharya considers *Aṣaṅga* the originator of *tantra* in Buddhism and he thinks that he was *ghandarian* and it is no wonder that he drew inspiration from the Magi priests of Scythian origin.

Tantra has been originated in ancient India. From the excavation of Mohenjo-daro and Harappa we find the historical evidence of a developed urban life. The word *Harrappa* is composed of *hara* and *appa* which means Śiva and father respectively. The Harrappan civilization is the gift of Śaivism or Tantrism. The only male god of the Harrappan civilization is god Śiva. Śiva is characterized by a horned headdress, the symbol of great occult power. A seal showing Śiva seated on a raised throne in the posture of yoga was discovered at Mohenjo-daro. From the excavation of the Harrappan culture, it is quite evident that both *Śakti* cult and the Śaivism constituted the spiritual faith of non-Āryans. While writing about the religion of the Indus Valley civilization Sir John Marshall says "Śiva worship was of great antiquity in India, it originated out of the Mother Goddess, and, it was closely connected with the cult of Śiva."[22]

Śaivism and Śaktism are the two aspects of the Tantra. Śaktism represents the beginning of the *Tantra Sādhanā* and Śaktism is the culminating point of the spiritual march. Prof. Surendranath Dasgupta while discussing the origin and development of theistic schools, says: "In addition to the work of these *Vaiṣṇava* thinkers there sprang up another class of theistic works which were of a more eclectic nature. These also had their beginnings in periods as old as the *Upaniṣads*. They are known as the Śaiva and Tantra thought..."[23]

Śavisim and Śaktism, two schools of Tantra metaphysics, were the official religions of the non-Āryans of the Indus Valley Civilization. Among the aniconic objects of worship are the *liṅgas* and *yonīs* together with their dactylic forms. The *liṅga* (phallus) worship was prevalent among the classes of non-Āryans. E.H. Hartland in a detailed and informative article on phallism deals with the subject from the broader view.[24]

The central theme is to trace sex-worship as part of the history of religion which has been prevalent in different strata of culture. Sex worship was a customary practice and was considered to be part of the religious sacrament by the Indian people belonging to different faiths. With advancement of civilization it was transformed into Higher religious symbolism. The primitive people who were mostly engaged in war, the preservation of progeny was their greatest problem. The sex-worship, therefore, reasonably stands for procreation and not for any sexual indulgence. *Tantra* of Buddhist or Hindu import does not encourage sexual indulgence. It lays down very strict rules and severe discipline. The *tantra* offers an esoteric process known as *Ṣoḍaśī Sādhanā* for the sublimation of sex instincts. It is based on the principle that poison that kills, becomes an elixir of life when it is treated properly by able physician.

According to Buddhist *tantra*, *Śūnya* is highest spirit and inexhaustible store house of energy. The Buddhist *tantra* does encourage the practice of *Prajñā* and *upāya*. *Upāya* represents the experience of great bliss while *Prajñā* is the symbol of non-dual wisdom. The mystic union of *Prajñā* and *Upāya* has nothing whatsoever to do with the gratification of the senses rather it represents the complete transformation of ordinary sense desires. This is known as *Anuttara-yoga*. The object of *Anuttara-yoga* is to attain emancipation by purifying the mind. It is evident that highest degree of intellectual power is necessary to walk on the path of *Anuthara yoga*. The Buddha preached two kinds of path. The one, was for common man which is known as *Theravāda Buddhism*, and the other was "for few fortunate persons who were placed by high degree of intellectual refinement and power and this is mostly known as *Mahāyāna path*.

The chief complaint against the *tantra* is that it permitted women to enter into its fold for the *tāntric* practice and as a result encouraged corruption and immorality. Such misconception and misunderstanding about the *tantra* speaks of the complete ignorance about *tantra*.

Dr. Benoytosh Bhattacharya writes: "It has already been pointed out that the *Tantra* was divided into various sections, both in Hinduism as well as in Buddhism. With the Hindus *Dakṣiṇācāra*, or the right-hand path, is to be followed first, after which *Vāmācāra*, or the left-hand path, is permitted. In *Dakṣiṇācāra*, strict celibacy, restriction of food, drink, etc., are of primary importance, and when the neophyte is sufficiently advanced he is initiated into the mysteries of *Vāmācāra*, when women are permitted for the purpose of practising the Yoga together. Similarly, in Buddhism, *Tantra* is divided into four sections. In the two earlier sections, namely the *Kriyātantra* and the *Caryātantra*, strict celibacy and restrictions of food, drink, etc., are enjoined. When this course is complete, the neophyte then can be initiated into the mysteries of *Yogatantra*, in which women become necessary for the purpose of practising Yoga. It has been frequently seen that there is a class of neophytes whose *Kuṇḍalinī* is not roused without association with women, and for such disciples the great preceptors prescribed association with women. But it must be remembered that both in *Vāmācāra* and *Yogatantra*, complete control over the air that is continued within the body is essential, and this is obtained after a long continued practice of *Haṭhayoga*, *Prāṇāyāma*, and so forth, so that the association with women produce nothing but help initiates in rousing the *Kuṇḍalinī* power which is contained within the body. It is for this reason that the *Tantra* are to be taken recourse to when perfection is reached in practising *Haṭhayoga*, or, in other words, *Tant; as* begin where *Haṭhayoga* ends."[25]

The basic objective of Buddhist *tantra* is not to create or define any system of metaphysics. It is mainly concerned with esoteric practices. The central objective of *tantra* is to bring enlightenment through esoteric methods. S.B. Dasgupta writes: "We have said that Tāntric Buddhism was a growth within the province of Mahāyāna (the great vehicle), and as such, in aim and ambition Tāntric Buddhism imbibed the spirit of Mahāyāna in a marked way. As for the final goal the Mahāyānists believed that every man—nay, every being of the world is a potential Buddha; he has within him all the possibilities of becoming a Samyak-sambuddha, *i.e.*, the perfectly enlightened one. Consequently, the idea of Arhathood of the Hīnayānists was replaced by the idea of Boddhi-sattvahood of the Mahāyānists."[26]

According to Buddhist Tantra the *nirvāṇa* means the realization of *śūnyatā* which is not in any way absolute denial of any reality. It is the negation of subjectivity and objectivity. According to Buddhist *tantra* consciousness is *(vijñāpati-mātratā)* is the supreme reality. In the state of *nirvāṇa*, *grāhaka* and *grāhya* are eliminated but the power of consciousness is retained. Thus in Buddhist tantra, *nirvāṇa* admits of positive interpretation. *Nirvāṇa* is conceived as infinite bliss which has been introduced by *Vajrayānist* and *Sahajayānist*. *Nirvāṇa* is identified with *Mahāsukha*. In Buddhist Tantra *nirvāṇa* is considered as infinite bliss and it is considered as above, both enjoyment as well as liberation.

Tantra was wrongly downgraded to the class of black magic and condemned as a burial ground of all the dead and obsolete religious rites. If we try to go deeper into its philosophical and mystic import than we will be in a position to understand *tantra* as the scientific system of spiritual discipline based on human psychology. There cannot be any denying the fact that elements of magic and auto-suggestion are contained in the body of *tantra*. If the word magic and autosuggestion are understood in a proper scientific and psychological connotations. The scientific study of human mind has proved that it has a para-psychological power. The practice of autosuggestion is prescribed by *tantra* establishes one's rapport with divine consciousness. The Sādhaka establishes rapport with the supreme power, the *Hevajra,* the giver of all boons. With the establishment of divine rapport the *yogin* contains occult powers. Patañjali has analyzed and elucidated in detail about these occult powers attained by yogis in *vibhūtipāda.*

So-called reprehensible practices associated *tantra* are used to take control and sublimate the sensual desires. It results in the elevation of consciousness from the crude to the subtle state. Tantra Sādhanā is the mystic technique to transform the physical existence into the divine existence.

Pañcamakāra Sādhanā which is employed both in Hindu and Buddhist *tantras* is, esoteric process for the transformation of desire. Hunger and sex are innate biological instincts. They cannot be ignored. The suppression and the repression of these desires and instincts lead to abnormal human behaviour. The modern psychologists had accepted that suppression and repression of desires makes a man neurotic. The principle behind *Pañcamakāra Sādhanā* is that man must rise with the aid of that *Śakti* which if misused will cause his fall. Man has to work out his own salvation, not by incorporating his desire and suppressing the biological instincts but by sublimating and channellising them into higher forms of spiritual life.

The attainment of occult powers has created completely wrong message to the Western minds. A close and scientific analysis of such para-psychological powers would prove beyond any doubt that they have a sound scientific basis. Our knowledge of mind and consciousness is very limited and incomplete. The multi-dimensional and deeper aspects of human consciousness are yet to be understood. The science of *tantra* can help one to experience deepest consciousness and become aware of the immense power of mind. According to Buddhist *tantra* through esoteric practice one can rise higher and higher state of perfection till he becomes enlightened one. *Tantra* is a spiritual and esoteric science and it is not a religion.

We are aware that the scientific and the technological advancements are getting out of balance with our social and moral performance. Unless and until we arrest the decline of the moral values and enthrone them once again to the wills and minds of people there is no future for mankind. We need no science and technology, to arrest the decline of moral degeneration but spirituality and mystic techniques. The *tāntric mantras* are not mere words, they are mass of divine energy. The incantation of these *mantras* awakens the spiritual power of a man. We cannot stop the degeneration of humanity through institutionalized religion and hollow speculative philosophy. The vulgarization of human society in the name of progressive ideology and technological advancement has endangered the very existence of human civilization. The whole human society is at a cross road. Arnold

Toynbee has rightly defined society as a sum-total network of human relations. The constituents of the society are not individuals but their relations. Unless and until, society is based on spiritual philosophy of humanism, society is bound to disintegrate and degenerate. The spiritual humanism of *tantra* is definitely to provide sound ethical and the spiritual foundation for the harmonious blendings of materialism with spirituality, science with religion, and philosophy with mysticism.

The *Upaniṣad* has also warned against the wanton practice of spirituality without observing certain conditions and disciplines. In *Upaniṣads* it has been stated that path of spirituality is like walking on razor's edge. The *Kaṭha Upaniṣad* says:

उत्तिष्ठत जाग्रत प्राप्य वरान्निबोधत।
क्षुरस्य धारा निशिता दुरत्यया दुर्गं पथस्तत्कवयो वदन्ति।।

I agree with Dr. Benoytosh Bhattacharya, when he says: "It now remains to be said that the Tāntric culture is the greatest of all cultures, because it aims at the spiritual perfection and psychic development of man, and as such no one can deny that the Tāntric culture is the greatest contribution made by India towards the world's civilization. Whenever in future man awakens to the necessity of psychic, development or spiritual advancement, or of stimulating his latent magical faculties, all eyes must turn towards this branch of Sanskrit literature, and to those few Yogins India still possesses, for the most minute, thorough, accurate, easy and practical system of psychic exercises ever conceived by man in any country or in any time in history."[27]

REFERENCES

1. अभावे भावनाभावो भावना नैव।
   इति भावो न भावः स्यात भावना नोपलभ्यते।। *Guhya Samāja Tantra*, p. I 1. Oriental Institute, Baroda, 1931.
2. *Ibid.*, p. xxii.
3. *'A Tibetan Account of Nagarjuna'* an article by S.C. Sarkar in the *Sino-Indian Journal*, December, 1948.
4. *Lalita vistāra*, edited by Rajender Lal Mitra, p. 315.
5. *Book of the East*, volume XX, p. 9.
6. Their *Chandu* (will), *Viriyam* (effort), Cittam (thought), *Bimalsa* (investigation), CRC Childers *Dictionary of Pāli Language*, p. 157.
7. *The Cultural Heritage of India*, volume 4th, Ramakrishna Mission Institute of Culture, p. 260.
8. Kern, *Indian Buddhism*, p. 133.
9. *Indian Philosophy*, 7th Impression, volume 1, page 467, London, 1956.
10. *Vimala Prabha*, p. 19, Central Institute of Higher Tibetan Studies, Saranath, Varanasi, 1994.
11. *Sādhanamālā*, vol. 11, p. xxiv, Gaekwad's Oriental Series, no. 41, Baroda, 1968.
12. *Ibid.*, p. xxix.
13. Prof. G.C. Pande, *Studies in Mahayana*, p. 45.
14. *Ibid.*, p. 39.

15. D.L. Snellgrove, *The Hevajra Tantra*, part 1, p. 7, Oxford University Press, London, 1959.
16. John Woodroffe, *Shakti and Shakta*, p. 557. Ganesh & Co., Madras.
17. Lalan Prasad Singh, *Tantra: Its Mystic and Scientific Basis*, p. 37, Concept Publishing Company, 1987.
18. *Cultural History of India*, volume 1, p. 530.
19. *Journal of Asiatic Society of Bengal* (1883), 11, p. 57 ff.
20. Lama Yeshe, *Introduction to Tantra*, p. 30. Wisdom Publication, Boston, 1987.
21. Benoytosh Bhattacharya, *An Introduction to Buddhist Esotericism*, pp. 48-49. Chowkhamba Sanskrit Series, Varanasi, 1964.
22. Sir John Marshall, *Mohenjo-daro and the Indus Civilization*, p. 107. Arthur Probsthian, Great Russell Street, London, 1931.
23. Surendranath Dasgupta, *A History of Indian Philosophy*, vol. 1, p. 8, Cambridge University Press, 1963.
24. *Encyclopedia of Religion and Ethics*, vol. IX., pp. 815 -31.
25. Benoytosh Bhattacharya, *An Introduction to Buddhist Esotericism*, p. 169.
26. S.B. Dasgupta, *An Introduction to Tāntric Buddhism*, p. 5, University of Calcutta, 1958.
27. Benoytosh Bhattacharya, *An Introduction to Buddhist Esotericism*, p. 174.

2 Philosophical Basis of Buddhist Tantra

Philosophers and scientists have been pondering on truth and reality since time immemorial. Western civilization is proud of its monumental achievements in natural science and technology. However, the Eastern civilizations especially that of India have made profound accomplishment in forms of their intuitional science and esotericism. We propose to analyse and elucidate the Western realist position that natural science claims real approximation of truth and reality as it exists independently of human language and concept. On the other hand Eastern thinkers hold that there is no way of knowing truth and reality independently of our modes of investigation and linguistic framework. We propose to make indepth study of Buddhist philosophy, which forms the basis of Buddhist Tantra after examining incompatible theories concerning fundamental nature of reality as propounded by Western and Eastern traditions. The most profound ontological doctrine is considered to be the *Mādhyamikā*, which claims *śūnyatā* as an intrinsic nature to be the ultimate mode of existence of phenomenon. One can experience of *śūnyatā* only when mind is liberated from all kinds of reifications.

Nāgārjuna employed method of *reductio abasurdum* in analyzing the concept of emptiness, which is the core of *Mūlamādhya-makārikā* : According to Nāgārjuna and his followers all pheno-mena are empty and that their emptiness is also empty. Emptiness is the essence of all things. However, emptiness itself is empty. When you talk of phenomena and we ask a question, does it exist, we must be very careful in using the word "exist". Do we mean *exist* inherently that is a substance independence of its attributes or we mean *exist* conventionally. According to the Buddhist Tantra anything exists *nominally*, or conventionally. According to this school of thought emptiness forms the basis of all fundamental Buddhist stereological conceptions. From the ultimate standpoint, the entire world is non-existence. Buddha's teachings are so sublime and profound and enrich in metaphysical import that the different Ācāryas at the different period of history interpreted them differently out of which different philosophical schools of Buddhism originated. We would like to concentrate here on philosophical basis of Buddhist Tantra. Nāgārjuna says "Just as grammarian may teach even the first letters, so Buddha taught the *Dharma* to his disciples according to their capacity. Some he instructed in the *Dharma* which would turn them away from sins, some he instructed in the attainment of virtue, some he taught a dualistic doctrine, some he taught the non-dualistic, profound and frightful for the timid, he taught others the means of Bodhi, the matrix of emptiness and compassion."[1]

The basic problem or issue on which we would like to reflect upon is the important concern in the classical philosophical tradition of India. The issues, which have kept the Indian mind occupied, are the questions of ontology—the essential mode of existence of things. Different philosophical traditions gave different views. The philosophical pondering of ontological nature is strikingly different from the natural science, which results in two different kinds of approaches. But it does not mean the differing approaches invalidate one another. Eastern intuitional science and mysticism may compliment Western science and technology. The primary concern of doctrine of emptiness and Buddhist Tantra has been quite different than that of natural science. Buddhist Tantra and its philosophical doctrines have been concerned basically with the nature and problems of being and existence and unfathomed recourses of consciousness. Buddhist Tantra is an esoteric technique for awakening the dormant divinity, refining human awareness, balancing the mind and unveiling its latent powers. Buddhist Tāntric practice revealed beyond any doubt a number of cognitive powers, which have been discovered, and experienced in the state of spiritual awakening and enlightenment. We are aware that the modern Western scientific world view is quite skeptical of the Buddhist and Hindu Tāntric claims of heightened spiritual awareness and other mental powers. It is but natural for the Western civilization since its scientific revolution to denounce and be skeptical about potential of human mind which have been ignored and neglected by Western culture.

Even, the infallibility of natural science and the sensory experiences have been questioned by twentieth century Physics from Relativity Theory to Quantum Theory. It is accepted that there is an incongruity between the mode of existence of phenomena and their mode of appearance. Reality as a whole is a conceptual designation. An eminent Physicist Louis de Broglie says: "May it not be universally true that the concepts produced by the human mind, when formulated in slightly vague form, are roughly valid for Reality, but that when extreme precision is aimed at, they become ideal forms whose real content tends to vanish away. It seems to me that such is, in fact, the case.[2]

The central theme of Buddhist Tāntric philosophy is the Concept of Emptiness. Emptiness stands for the lack of independent existence or inherent existence. If we analyse the phenomena or processes that appear to exist independently, these phenomena are not non-existence rather they are conventionally real. The whole Mahāyana Buddhist philosophy depends upon the doctrine of two truths or two realities–a conventional and an ultimate truth. Nāgārjuna's greatest philosophical contribution lies on the formulation of the complex doctrine of two truths as a tool for understanding Buddhist metaphysics and epistemology. The Buddha was conscious about antinomical character of reason and he resolves it by rising to higher standpoint of criticism. Criticism itself is a philosophy. It is freedom from all kinds of entanglements, passions and mental reifications. It is freedom from all kinds of mental defilements. There has been great controversy and debate regarding Buddha's silence. Buddha's silence should not be misunderstood as agnosticism nor it should be misunderstood as his ignorance of metaphysics. He did not approve speculative metaphysics because of his preference to criticism. T.R.V. Murti rightly observes: "The rejection of theories (*ditthi*) is itself the *means* by which Buddha is led to the non-conceptual knowledge of the absolute, and not vice-versa. It is no accident then that Buddha concerns himself with an analysis of the various theories of reality and rejects them all. Buddha ascends from the conflict of Reason to the inexpressibility of the absolute. The consciousness in Reason and the attempt to resolve it by rising to a plane higher than reason is dialectic. And the dialectical method is the *Mādhyamikā* way".[3]

The Buddha was not nihilist. The doctrine of two truths that is a noumena and phenomena is implicit in all philosophy. The distinction between emptiness as real and phenomena as conventional reality vindicate the Buddhist standpoint. Buddhist makes a distinction between '*Paramārtha satya*' and '*Saṁvṛti Satya*'.

According to *Mādhyamikā Kārikā*, "Those that are unaware of the distinction between these two truths are incapable of grasping the deep significance of the teachings of Buddha."[4]

We would like to examine and elucidate Buddhist Tāntric philosophical standpoint in the context of Scientific Realism, Instrumentalism and Idealism. F.H. Bradley in his celebrated book, *Essays on Truth and Reality* writes, "Everything to philosophy is a consideration, in the sense that everything has a claim and a right to be considered. But how it is to be considered is the affair of philosophy alone, and here no external consideration can be given even the smallest hearing. . . . . . Philosophy, we saw, was a search, a search for that which in the end is true."[5]

Scientific realism is dominant ontological doctrine for understanding basic constituents of reality. However, when we analyse the claim of Scientific Realism, we are faced with diversity and inconsistency in physicists concept of reality. Does natural Science specially physics provides a sound concept of an independent physical reality? Are the foundations of Natural Science based on sound logical foundation? Does it give us the real picture of the nature of ultimate reality? Einstein, who is considered to be one of the greatest scientists that world has produced and who had life long commitment to Scientific Realism, says, "For the time being, we have to admit that we do not possess any general theoretical basis for Physics which can be regarded as its logical foundation."[6]

Descartes makes a seminal division between matter and mind. According to him the phenomenal is a proper field of study for Natural Science and he thinks cognitive realm as the proper domain for the study of philosophy. The soul, which does not have any physical dimension but it does influence the body through pineal gland. He does accept that the mind influences matter but his followers rejected any interaction between mind and matter. According to mechanistic view everything in the world both animate and inanimate things are independent. We can know the world of animate and inanimate through the scientific method and for understanding the objective world no philosophical postulation is required. It is a purely a matter of observation. Only verifiable statements and propositions have a place in science. According to this school of thought the natural world exists independently of human precepts and mental construct. Einstein who is considered to be one of the most leading light of modern Physics thinks that natural world exists independent of human mind and this basic scientific assumption is the foundation of all natural science. This ontological theory of independent objective physical world was questioned both by philosophers and scientific community. In the annals of human history various doctrines made claim to explain the nature of truth and reality. Aristotle's concept of natural science collapsed under the theoretical scrutiny at the advent of the modern Physics. The physicists claims that everything is made of atoms presents puzzlement. Richard Feynman says, "There is nothing that living things do that cannot be understood from the point of view that they are made of atoms acting according to the Laws of Physics".[7]

Feynman thinks that conservation of energy is a mathematical principle. He further states, "It is important to realise that in Physics today, we have no knowledge, of what energy is?"[8] Feynman raises a very basic issue whether energy is an abstraction or is a purely conceptual concept without having any independent physical existence. According to Einstein and Infield, "There is no essential distinction between mass and energy. Energy has a mass, and mass represents energy."[9] The question arises, if energy is a mathematical concept and not an objective physical reality it would not be true of mass. If atoms are composed of mass and energy then what would be their ontological basis? There is lot of controversy regarding the ontological status of atoms. Gribbin while elucidating the ontological status of atoms and sub-atomic particles writes, "If we cannot say what a particle does when we are not looking at it, neither can we say if it exists when we are not looking at it, and it is reasonable to claim that nuclei and positrons did not exist prior to the twentieth century, because nobody before 1900 ever saw one."[10] Another eminent American Physicist Henry Step presents a different viewpoint concerning particles of matter. He says, "An elementary particle is not an independently existing unanalysable entity. It is, in essence, a set of relationships that reach outward to other things."[11]

Werner Heisenberg makes a startlingly revolution by saying that, "atoms are not things."[12] Niels Bohr gives a revolutionary statement that, "There is no quantum world, there is only an abstract quantum description."[13] If we summarise the above discussion then we come to conclusion that both modern Physics and Philosophy question the fundamental nature of reality. In the words of Norwood Russell

Hanson, "There is no ultimate logical connection between the languages of classical Physics and Quantum Physics, any more than between a sense-datum language and a material object language."[14] There has been great change and revolution in the world of Physics with the formulation of General Theory of Relativity and Quantum Mechanics. In 1906 Sir J.J. Thomson was awarded Nobel Prize in Physics and stated that all mass and kinetic energy is composed of ether,[15] which was outrightly rejected few decades after by Einstein and Infeld who declared, "All assumptions concerning ether led nowhere!"[16]

Whether nature is the realization of mathematical concepts and these concepts while approachable to human mind and these concepts have grounding in objective reality, it is a matter of debate and discussion. In the words of Werner Heisenberg, "What we observe, is not nature in itself but nature exposed to our method of questioning."[17] Now, it is believed that quantity measured is the result of an interaction and measuring mind. If we accept the classical scientific view, the colour that we perceive with our sensory organs do not exist as an independent physical reality. There are only particles of mass, energy and when some of these particles known as photons interact with our sensory organs we have experience of colours. If we analyse this complex process of perception of colour we come to the conclusion that our sensory organs are designed in such a way when they interact with photons we have experience of the colour, but surprisingly these colours do not exist in the photons. Take for another example of touch sensation. When some photons interact with our skin we experience sensation of warmth but that warmth is not intrinsic to the photons. Thus, the postulation of the existence of independent physical reality as measured in quantity is questionable like independent status that we ascribed to a physical reality such as photons associated with quantity and mass. To make any claim of finality in the world of natural science would mean profound ignorance about ontological foundation of natural science. In general and history of Physics in particular scientific explanation and nature of ultimate truth can be summarized in the word of C.S. Pierce, "The conclusions of science make no pretence to being more than probable."[18] If we go through the history of original development of different doctrines of science we acknowledge that concept of truth and reality has undergone changes, transformation and modification with the growth of scientific knowledge. There was a time when Aristotle's mechanical celestial Physics was considered to be true. In the Seventeenth century conception of absolute space and time was acknowledged as great discovery of Physics on which Newton founded his classical Physics. Two centuries afterward ether was considered to be a physical reality. In the beginning of last century particles was considered to be definite having simultaneous velocity and position but all these concepts have been falsified by the recent scientific discoveries and assumptions.

In the recent years, the philosophical concepts and specially the intuitional science and mysticism have made great impacts on the scientific postulates and assumptions. Einstein has expressed grave doubts on some of the basic assumptions of Quantum Theory when he made a very bold statement, "That God does not play dice with the world." Another eminent Physicist Bohr says that we should not tell God what he can do. Philosophical issues like such as ultimate nature of reality, the *summum bonum* of life which gives meaning to human existence and being and the means of nature of *Nirvāṇa* have kept the mind of both philosophers, religious leaders and scientists engaged in search of finding a convincing answer to these age old problems. The concept of electrons is becoming a puzzlement like God of the religion. Whether electron is a wave or a particle has not yet been resolved. Whether it is a physical reality or a mental construct or a physical relation, is still unanswered question. A.N. Whitehead's, observation is very significant in this context, "European thought is represented as littered with metaphysical systems, abandoned and unreconciled."[19]

Nature does not speak itself at all. The phenomenal world of our experience is related to our mind. Language does exercise great impact. According to Buddhism, reality is an eternal flux. We experience only the point-instant. The conceptual construct of reality which is in the state of flux, which is expressed in linguistic frame is known as conceptualism. Prof. H.S. Gill, rightly observes, "The Buddhist thinkers, Dignāga and Dharmakīrti, argued that as the words of language are conceptual constructs created by human imagination and intellect, they are subject to interpretation and comprehension at the same human level. There are neither eternal pure sounds, nor eternal pure meanings. Language, like any other reality, is not a static entity. It is eternally in flux, and as such, the conceptual construct, the significations, are constantly being created. And, just like every other human creation, they are subject to construction and destruction."[20] Reification in Science and Philosophy is greatest impediment in understanding the nature of being and reality in their proper perspective. The reality exists in relation to our theoretical framework of language and consciousness. The basic question whether world exists the way it appears or whether its mode of existence is different from its mode of appearance. Thus, the physical reality does not define in terms of Scientific Realism. There is some truth in Schrodinger's observation that world is nothing but conglomeration of a "construct of our sensations, perceptions, memories."[21]

After close examination and analysis of the basic assumptions of Scientific Realism we feel that the physical reality lacks intrinsic existence independent of conceptual designation. According to Buddhist point of view the existence of the physical reality is dependence on mental construct and conceptual designation. All existence is conventional and not absolute. Existence is always contingent upon mental concepts and linguistic framework. Einstein who has been a committed realist acknowledges the inadequacy of natural science in presenting rational and logical account of scientific realism. He says, " For the time being, we have to admit that we do not possess any general theoretical basis for Physics which can be regarded as its logical foundation."[22]

Instrumentalism

Instrumentation is Pragmatic Theory of John Dewey, according to which thought exists as an instrument of adjustment to environment. Terms of thought and meaning are relative to the function they perform and that their validity or truth is determined by their efficacy. The puzzlement is the problem related to the ontological foundation of natural science led to according to some instrumentalists. The basic assumption of instrumentalism is that the ends justify the means, which is against the basic assumption of Indian culture. B. Alan Wallac writes "According to instrumenta-lism, one theory may still be superior to another if it serves as an effective leading principle for a more inclusive range of enquiries than does another, and if it supplies a method of analysis and representation. That makes possible more precise and detailed inferences than another. In short, a good theory is one that is broadly encompassed, simple, and precise in terms of its predications. Its approximation to reality is not an issue. Thus, Newton's account of the natural motion of bodies because Newton's Physics requires fewer *ad hoc* explanation."[23]

Instrumentalists argue that the postulates of mathematics are as arbitrary as the grammatical rules of language. Truth is conventional and mathematical doctrines are instruments. According to this view mathematical theories are old good because of their practical successful application. F.H. Bradley has examined in greater detail and made indepth study of Instrumentalism, which was published in *Mind* no. 51, July 1904. He says, "Not once again can I find anything new in the idea of instrumentalism. The degradation of the philosophy, science and fine art, to the rank of mere means, subserving an end falling outside themselves, is surely nothing novel. And we do not even gain a new attitude if, while denying intrinsic value of these things, we forget to ask what it is that, laying outside them, has its 39 self-intrinsic worth.[24]

It is argued that everything in our life may be regarded as a means so long the elements in our life and world have a value if it is conducive to benefit of the whole. Instrumentalism in this sense has a value so long it serves as welfare of the humanity. Bradley says, "The instrument in other words is such, only because it is not taken as a means to some end which fails to include itself as intrinsic and valuable. But surely instrumentalism, asserted in the above sense, would be equivalent to its own denial."[25]

If we analyse the complex process of our perception and if we like to retain our belief in an objective world existing independent of our experience then we have to accept that such world remains unknowable to us. Thus, the instrumentalism cannot be substitute of Scientific Realism as it led to solipsism. We do not know anything about physical world existing independent of our experience. Whatever we know about the world is our cognitive sensation. Democritus had made statement that the experience of colour observed by human mind are relational attributes that have no existence apart from human act of experience.

Philosophical Stand of Buddhist Tantra

Buddhist philosophy, which forms the basis of Buddhist Tantra, questions the basic assumptions that the world we experience exists independentally of our experience and concepts. The physical world is empirically knowable in relation to our modes of experience. The terms subjects and objects denote conventional duality. An absolute duality both subject and object exists in inter-independence and the distinction is conventional and not real. To elucidate this point further, let us take another example: the conceptual cognition of electromagnetic waves. Let us assume that such waves do in fact exist. In this case, the cognized event—electromagnetic waves—exists in relation to the conceptual awareness of it; and that conceptual awareness exists in relation to that event. That cognition concerns and its object via a generic idea of such waves, and that idea also exists only in mutually dependent relationship with corresponding conceptual awareness, we conceive reality which does not exist. The absolute space of classical science is living example but the generic idea of absolute space does exist. The central objective of Buddhist Tantra is to cultivate wisdom and compassion, which leads to the attainment of quiescence (*Nirvāṇa*). The mind is the only instrument through which we can know mind and consciousness. The consciousness is a continuum flow. This continuum flow can never be destroyed or be separated. In this state of pure continuum the duality of physical and mental does not exists. This *continuum* is known as emptiness.

According to Buddhism in the process of reification of our own personal identity we reify others which results in the objectification of our inanimate world. According to Buddhism self does not exist as the body, the mind, or the combination of the two. The simple negation of self is known as emptiness. The emptiness is the ultimate mode of the existence of the self. The experience of the emptiness liberates one from the reification of self as an intrinsic reality. It echoes the ancient precept that truth makes man free from all kinds of reifications and delusions. The realisation of emptiness is the fundamental liberation. The objective of philosophical contemplation, according to Buddhist Tantra, in concerning, metaphysical, epistemological, and stereological questions, is to rid the mind from reification and lead one to the experience of emptiness. The concept of emptiness and the relation between *nirvāṇa-saṁsāra* provides the ontological basis of the Buddhist Tantra. The central teaching of Buddhism is to penetrate into this original intuition of Buddha that doctrine of eternal self is a doctrine of fools. By negating the existence of eternal self the Buddha pulls down the very foundation of desire where it can rest.

Buddhist tantra does not believe in speculative metaphysics. According to Buddhist Tantra speculative metaphysics does not lead to knowledge rather the mental reification. It is closer to Mādhyamikā philosophical standpoint. However, Buddhist Tantra and Mādhyamikā have exercised great impact in the development of *Vijñānavāda* and *Vedānta*. One should be very clear that *Śūnyatā* should not be identified with non-existence. *Prajñā* is intuitional experience of the emptiness. We cannot experience the emptiness accept by negation. Intuition is the only mode of knowledge to experience the continuum, which removes the mental reification. Thus, the emptiness is both transcendental and immanent because it is beyond all categories of thought. It is immanent because it is not another thing besides the world. The purpose of philosophical deliberation is spiritual. It is to liberate mind from all kinds of reifications. *Prajñā* is *nirvāṇa*. It is a state of freedom and bliss. *Prajñā* is the consummation of moral and religious ideals. Buddhism affirms that state of *nirvāṇa* which cannot be put into linguistic expression but it is real. The function of *Prajñā* is not to transform the real but only to create change in our perspective. Change is epistemic and not ontological. It is considered that Nāgārjuna brought a Copernican revolution in Indian Philosophy. According to *Mādhyamikā Kārikā* "This leads to the other contention of the *Mādhyamikā* that there is no difference whatever between *nirvāṇa* and *saṁsāra*; Noumena and phenomena are not two separate sets of entities, nor are they two states of the same things. The absolute is only real; it is the reality of *saṃsāra*, which is sustained by false construction (*Kalpanā*). The absolute looked at through the thought-forms of constructive imagination is the empirical world; and conversely, the absolute is the word viewed *sub-specie acterntatis*, without these distorting media of thought."[26]

The *Prajñā* is nothing but the experience of continuum emptiness. It is an analytical knowledge of the empirical world as a transient, contingent and suffering. This knowledge leads to the eradication of the belief in intrinsic self and destroys the very foundation of egoism and passion.

If we analyse the simple form of quiescence, consciousness and choiceless awareness, the self can be identified as a mental state, which is devoid of intrinsic *I* or mind. With the practice of refining consciousness and other Buddhist esoteric practice, one attains a meditative state known as quiescence (*Nirvāṇa*). Kant in his *Critique* has shown that the presentation of a speculative philosophy is to provide pure knowledge. Nāgārjuana also holds the same view. There is an important distinction between Nāgārjuna's dialectic and Kantian Critique. For Nāgārjuna dialectic itself is a philosophy, it liberates man from ignorance which is the root cause of suffering. According to Kant the Critique paves path for the Practical Reason which provides noumenal values. It is a Practical Reason which provides freedom and immorality. The analysis and examination of both Kant's Critique and Nāgārjuna's dialectics prove that one cannot achieve freedom and enlightenment with the tools of philosophical reasoning and disputation. The Concept of Emptiness and *Prajñāpāramitā* provides the sound philosophical basis of Buddhist Tantra. Diṅnāga beautifully summarizes the concept of *Prajñāpāramitā*: "*Prajñāpāramitā* (Highest Wisdom) is non-dual knowledge, and that is the Tathāgata. The Treatise and the spiritual discipline as leading to this end, receive the same application."[27]

Prajñā (True Philosophy) is a non-dual experience of the reality. According to philosophical stand of Buddhist Tantra, this knowledge of reality cannot be attained, as by Hegel, through the process of synthesis but by negation. Negation is consciousness of its falsity. The awareness of falsity means the awareness of what appears as real is nothing but a bundle of contradiction. Buddhist Tantra is aware of the futility of a speculative philosophy and hence it recommends the practice of intuitional science and esotericism for the realization of the ultimate reality. In this intuitive experience of *Prajñā* and *Upāya* essence and existence becomes identical.

Buddhist Tantra is aware of the limitation of materialism and idealism, scientific realism and instrumentalism. The modern world has made a monumental achievement in science and technology. However, the modern world specially the Western civilization has to acknowledge that *Tantra* and *Yoga* have made enormous discoveries and achievements in terms of intuitional science and mysticism, which have a sound metaphysical, epistemological and soteriological basis.

REFERENCES

1. Ratnāvalī IV. C. 94-97: *Yathaiva Vaiyakarano Matrakamapi Pathayet/Buddhho Vadat tathā dharma vineyanaṁ yathā-kṣamāṁ Śūnyatā-karuṇa garbham ekesam.*
2. Louis de Broglie: *Matter and Light: The New Physics,* Trans. W.H. Johnston (New York: Norton, 1939), p. 280.
3. T.R.V. Murti, *The Central Philosophy of Buddhism*, George Allen and Unwin Ltd., London. 1960, p. 49.
4. *Ye' nayar na vijananti vibhagaṁ satyayor dvayoḥ; tetattvaṁ na vijananti gambhīraṁ Buddha-śāsane.* MK. XXIV. 9.
5. F.H. Bradely, *Essays on Truth and Reality*, Oxford University Press, London, 1914, p. 15.
6. Einstein, *The Fundamentals of Theoretical Physics, Out of My Later Years*, New York Philosophical Library, 1950, p. 110.
7. Richard P. Feynman, R.B. Leighton, M. Sands, The Feynman Lectures on Physics (Reading, M.A. Addition-Wesley, 1963), p. 1.
8. *Ibid.*, p. 4.
9. Albert Einstein and Leopold Infeld, *the Evolution of Physics* (New York: Simon & Schuster, 1966), p. 197.
10. John Gribbin, In Search of Schrodinger's Cat: *Quantum Physics and Reality* (New York: Bantam, 1984), p. 259.
11. Cited in Paul Davies, *Superforce* (New York: Simon and Schuster, 1985), p. 49.
12. Cited in Herbert, *Quantum Reality*, p. 22.
13. *Ibid.*, p. 22.
14. Hanson, *Pattern of Discovery*, p. 153.
15. Sir Oliver Lodge, *Ether and Reality* (New York: Doran 1925), p. 91.
16. Einstein and Infeld, *The Evolution of Physics*, p. 175.
17. Heisenberg, *Physics and Philosophy*, p. 58.
18. Cited in Medawar, Pluto's *Republic*, p. 120.
19. A.N. Whithead. *Process and Reality* (New York: Free Press, 1978), p. 14.
20. H.S. Gill, *Signification in Buddhist and French Tradition* (Harman Publication House), New Delhi, 2001, p. 3.
21. Erwin Schrodinger, *Mind and Matter*, (Cambridge: Cambridge University Press, 1958), p. 1.
22. Einstein, *Geometry and Experience, Ideas and Opinions*, p. 274.

23. B. Alan Wallac, *Changing Reality*, Snow Lion Publication, Ithaca, New York, p. 99, 1996.
24. *Essays on Truth and Reality* , p. 68.
25. F.H. Bradley, *Essays on Truth and Reality*, p. 69.
26. *Mādhyamikā Kārikās* of Nāgārjuna. Ed. by L. de La V. Roussin (Bub. Budd. IV). XXV. 9.
27. Prajñāpāramita Pindartha tacchabdyam Nirdeśa of Dignāga, quoted in Haribhadra's *Abhisamayālaṅkāraloka twice*. pp. 28, 153.

3 Vajrayāna

Vajrayāna is most scientific and positive approach to spiritual awakening and enlightenment. *Mañjūśrī Mūlakālpa, Sādhanāmālā* and *Guhyasamāja-Tantra* are the earliest canonical literatures on *Vajrayāna.* Apart from the method of worship of *Mudrās* (facial and finger expressions), *Maṇḍalas* (mystic diagrams) and *Mantras* (mystic spells), *Mañjūśrī-Mūlakālpa* lays down the ethical disciplines, to be strictly practiced, like *śīla* (moralism), *Cāryas* (do's of the disciple), *Kriyā* (rites), *Vrata* (vows), *Śaucācāra* (cleanliness in acts), *Niyama* (regulation of mind), *Japa* (incantation) and *Dhyāna* (meditation). *Guhyasamāja* deals with *yoga* (ordinary esoteric practice) and *Anuttarayoga* (Tantric forms of *Sādhanā*). Sentient being cannot attain the state of Buddhahood by starving his senses and desires. *Nirvāṇa* cannot be achieved by subjecting the mind and body to suffering, or by keeping aloof from all worldly pleasures and enjoyments. Vajrayāna is of the opinion that Buddhahood can be obtained by satisfying the unfulfilled desires and thereby exhausting them and not through processes, which are painful and suffering. The Buddha was against penance and physical suffering. Vajrayāna echoes the voice of Tathāgata. Vajrayāna is however not the Thunderbolt Vehicle. *Vajra* stands for *Śūnyatā,* which means that which is indestructible, which undergoes no change, i.e. which is eternal. The Reality is called *Śūnyatā* because it is beyond the dualism of subject and object. It is beyond the reach of the sense and mind. *Yāna* means path. However, *Śūnyatā* of Vajrayāna is quite different from the *Śūnya* of the Mādhyamikās or the *Vijñāna-vādins* (dialecticians) which is based on negativism and is opposed to any positive philosophy. The philosophy of both the Mādhyamikās and the *Vijñāna-vādins* is denial of all existence and non-existence and if we apply the same tenets to them, then they stand as philosophies denied by themselves. Whereas the *Śūnyatā* of Vajrayāna includes three principles, *viz.,* reality (*Śūnyatā*), consciousness (*Vijñāna*) and Bliss (*Mahā-Sukha*).

According to Sādhanamālā Vajrayāna is a development of *Vijñānavada* School The *Vijñāna* has evolved out of the *Śūnayavāda.* Benoytosh Bhattacharya writes, "the form or the branch of the Mahāyāna that was directly responsible in this matter seems to be a *tertium quid* which is known as Vajrayāna, and about which very little is known to the students of Buddhism."[1] The Hindu and Buddhist Tāntric canonical literatures have been written in the *Sandhyābhāṣā.* The *Sandhyābhāṣā* is a language, which seems to be full of nonsensical propositions for the layman, but for the initiates it is of great esoteric importance. According to the Tāntric tradition contents of the Tāntric texts could be explained only to the initiates and its meaning and the contents may be explained either by the light of the day, or by the darkness of the night. The famous songs of *Siddhācāraya* are all written in *Sandhyābhāṣā*, which are pregnant with profound mystic and metaphysical imports. Benoytosh Bhattacharya says, "It has been made abundantly clear that Vajrayāna was a direct development of the Yogācāra philosophy of Mahāyāna Buddhism, which was started by Maitreyanātha in the third century A.D. According to Yogācāra, the world, as we see it, has no existence. It is the creation of the mind or the momentary consciousness which is real. The worldly phenomena, according to Yogācāra, are like a dream or as if set up by magic. All individuals are composed of a chain of momentary consciousness, which passes through a series of births and rebirths until it is emancipated, when birth and rebirths cease".[2]

According to Yogācāra realization of *Śūnya* makes a man *Trikāladarśī*. There are two kinds of concealments, the first is known as *Kleśāvaraṇa* and the second is known as *Jñeyāvaraṇa*. *Kleśāvaraṇa* is obstruction of suffering and *Jñeyāvaraṇa* conceals the transcendental nature of reality. The first kind of obstruction like antipathy, attachment obstructs the sentient being in knowing a thing as it is. The second kind of obstruction is an impediment in the path of perfect knowledge. The first obstruction can be obliterated by the experience of *Śūnya*. The feelings of attachment and antipathy are the result of impure motivation, which are not caused by the external objects, but by the erroneous thinking of ego as real. The realization of non-self (*Nairātmya*) destroys the wrong thinking of ego as real and its relation with surrounding objects, which are unreal. The practice of Vajrayāna removes the veil and the Sādhaka experiences everything is *Śūnya*.

The Mahāyāna according to Vajrayāna is co-extensive with Dhamma.[3] In *Sādhanamālā*, the term *Śūnya* occurs almost on every page. However, there is conceptual difference between the *Śūnya* of Vajrayāna and that of the Mādhyamikā School. According to one *Śūnya* is conceived as:

अस्तिनास्तितदुभयानुभयचकुष्कोटिविनिमुक्तं शून्यरूपम्[4]

or, in other words,

न सन्नासन्न सद्सन्न चाप्पनुभयात्म्यकम् ।
चतुष्कोटिविनिर्मुक्तं शून्यं माध्यमिका विदुः ।।[5]

For Mādhyamikā's both subject and object are *Śūnya* in essence. There is no reality either of the mind or of the phenomenal world. Mādhyamikā's School has not been mentioned in *Sādhanamālā* except in one place, where it is in the form of an epithet, *Mahyamakaruceḥ* to one of Sādhanā's namely Dharmakuramati. Mādhyamikā philosophy is systematization of the *Prajñāpāramitā* treatise. Dignāga writes, "*Prajñāpāramitā* (Highest wisdom) is non-dual knowledge, and that is the Tathāgata. The treatise and the spiritual discipline, as leading to this, and receive the same appellation."[6] This is pregnant with implications.

For the *Yogācāra* illusion consists in the wrong objectification of consciousness (*Vijñāna*). The *Vedānta* and the *Vijñānavāda* are the victim of empirical illusion. For *Vedānta* illusion consists in mistaking the given being for something else. The rope-snake or dream-object of empirical illusion obstructs in experiencing the object as it is. According to Mādhyamikā liberation is possible only through *Śūnyatā*. T.R.V. Murti writes, "Kant comes nearest to Mādhyamikā conception of philosophy. His *Critique* shows the futility of all views, of reason itself, to reveal to us the unconditioned; like the Mādhyamikā dialect, it exposes the pretensions of dogmatic philosophy to give us pure knowledge. Like the Mādhyamikā, the *Critique* does not erect any view of its own on the criticism of other views, convinced as it is that all views belong to the phenomenal realm. There is, however, an important difference, almost a vital one, between the Mādhyamikā dialect and the Kantian Critique. For Kant the Critique has no value *per se;* it is intended to make the path safe for faith; and it is Practical Reason that secures for Kant his noumenal Values.[7]

According to Mādhyamikā dialectic itself is real metaphysics. It is philosophy *par excellence.* It liberates man from *Avidyā*, which is the root cause of suffering. Both according to Kant and Nāgārjuna criticism itself is a philosophy. Both Kant and Nāgārjuna brought Copernican revolution in philosophy.

However, Vajrayāna does not accept the Mādhyamikā's philosophical position in totality. For Vajrayāna the reality of *Vijñāna* is *sine qua non.* It is both metaphysical and mystical necessity. The word *Yogācāra* occurs in *Sādhanamālā*[8] twice only. However, the philosophy of *Vijñānavāda* has been discussed and formulated in *Sādhanamālā*. After the close examination of the contents and the subject matters which have been discussed in detail in *Sādhanamālā*, we come to the conclusion that Vajrayāna is the direct development of *Yogācāra* School.

The term *Vajrayāna* occurs twice[9] in *Sādhanamālā*. It stands for the esoteric practice which brings about supreme enlightenment. In Sanskrit supreme enlightenment is called *Anuttarasamya-kasambodhi.* According to Vajrayāna *Śūnya* is called *Vajra*. The concept *Vajra* has been used in its technical and esoteric sense. *Śūnya* is designated as *Vajra* because it is a firm and indestructible, and cannot be changed, cannot be pierced, cannot be penetrated, cannot be burnt, and cannot be destroyed.

दृढं सारमसौशीर्य्यमच्छेद्यभेद्यलक्षणाम्।।
अदाहि अविनाशि च शून्यता वज्रमुच्यते।।[10]

Buddhist Tāntric tradition belongs to Mahāyāna. There are conceptual difference between Mahāyāna and Theravāda. However, both of them believe that realization of *Śūnyatā* brings about the cessation of sufferings which is a philosophical imperative. Both the schools have employed different techniques for the cessation of sufferings. *Theravāda* believes in personal salvation, and its ideal is to become *Arahat*. According Theravāda one can attain *Nirvāṇa* and cessation of sufferings and the consequential freedom from rebirths. But according to Mahāyāna, if one attains *Nirvāṇa*, one cannot know the transcendental nature of truth, and one cannot decimate the profound philosophical wisdom to others.

According to Mahāyāna the *summum bonum* of life is to become Boddhisattva. The followers of Mahāyāna would not care for their own *Nirvāṇa*, but they would strive for the deliverance of their fellow-creatures, who are in the grip of constant suffering. The followers of Mahāyāna tradition would not care for cycle of birth and death, rather they would welcome to undergo any kind of sufferings and turbulence if it would help other in their spiritual upliftment. This lofty ideals of *Bodhisattva* has found profound expression in the *Karandavyūha*. Avalokiteśvara Bodhisattva refused to attain *Nirvāṇa* though he was fully entitled for it. He took spiritual resolution that he would attain *Nirvāṇa* only after all creatures of the world attain *Boddhijñāna*.[11]

According to *Daśabhūmikā Śāstra* Bodhisattva attains omniscience after he crosses the ten *Bhūmis*. The *Mādhyamikā* concept of *Nirvāṇa* is a state which is neither existence nor non-existence nor both and neither nor, it means neither the combination of existence and non-existence nor the negation of two can be predicated. However, the concept of *Nirvāṇa* according to *Yogācāra* is quite different from the *Śūnyavāda*. According to it the *Vijñāna* is present in addition to *Śūnya* in the state of *Nirvāṇa*. The Boddhi mind is a chain of consciousness, which is in the state of constant flux and change. The flux of constant change of consciousness becomes the cause of the next movement with the same memory, quality and conformation. This process of the flux of consciousness continues until the *Vijñāna* attains either omnisciences or *Nirvāṇa* after having eliminated all defilements.[12]

According to *Sādhanamālā*, "But once omniscience has been attained the chain of consciousness will not strive further for *Nirvāṇa* (extinction) but will engage itself in the spiritual uplift of all beings; it can only get rest or extinction when the whole world is delivered".[13]

There is a great controversy regarding origin and development of Tāntricism from the scripture *Guhyasiḍḍhi*. The close examination of Padmavajra's *Guhyasiḍḍhi* points out that *Guhyasamāja* should be considered as the canonical literature of Buddhist Tantra. Padmavajra has written a commentary on *Guhyasamāja*, which is known as *Śrīsamāja*. *Śrīsamāja is a* treatise and a profound digest of *Guhyasamāja* where he discusses the doctrines and theories, which were embodied in *Guhyasamāja*. Indrabhūti, who is one of the great exponent of Buddhist Tantra has discussed in detail in his work *Jñāna Siḍḍhi* and admits that *Guhyasamāja* is one of the great treatise on Tāntricism.

Some believe that *Guhyasamāja* is the original canonical literature of Tantricism. According to the tradition it has been delivered in an assembly faithful by *Sarvatathāgatakāyavākacitta*. The treatise written in a *Saṅgiti* is recognized as authoritative work belonging to *Vajrayāna* and is regarded as one of the nine *Dharma* of the Nepal.[14]

Some time *Aṣaṅga*, the brother of *Vasubandhu*, is acknowledged as the founder of Buddhist Tantra. It is said that he was initiated in esotericism by *Maitreya*, the future Buddha and he propagated Tantricism from *Tuṣita*. According to some scholars Nāgārjuna is considered as exponent of Buddhist Tantra. There is general belief that he was initiated into Tantricism by Buddhavairocāra at Iron Tower in South India, but from the Tibetan tradition it is believed that Nāgārjuna was initiated in Tāntricism by Siḍḍhācārya Sarahapāda and he attained *Vajrakāyasiḍḍhi*.[15]

L.P. Singh writes, "to our view that it is the Buddha himself who is a founder of Tāntricism in Buddhism. Further, it is a well-known fact that *Tantra* is performed in a cremation ground or at a lonely place. And when it is performed under a *Kula* tree, the progress is accelerated. According to the accepted Tāntric belief and usage, the banyan tree is one of the five trees recognized as *Kula* tree. It is, therefore, not without a reason that *Siddharatha* performed his *Sādhanā* under the famous banyan tree at Boddh Gayā and attained spiritual enlightenment (Buddhahood)."[16]

However, there is some misunderstanding about the origin of development of Buddhist Tantra. It is stated that the Buddha enjoined strict discipline for the *Bhikkhus*, which is known as *Patimokha* which is considered by some of Buddha's followers as unnatural. According to the historical accounts of the different Councils there had been great dispute and quarrels on different Buddhist concepts and disciplines. However, it would be wrong to assume that those *Bhikkhus* who thought *Nirvāṇa* could be attained through leading a natural life devised the original Tantra. It is now accepted that Buddha taught two kinds of truths, *Saṁvṛti* and *Parmārthic* truths for two different kinds of followers. Tāntric teachings were imparted to these who were morally and spiritually equipped with proper mental dispositions. These teachings, which are in the form of *Saṅgitis*, are known as Buddhist Tāntricism, which have been delivered by Buddha in an assembly of faithful.

From all accounts it could be stated that Buddha himself is the father of Tāntricism. This theory gets confirmation from the characteristic mystic power, which the Buddha attained alongwith *Parinirvāṇa*, which is manifestly of Tāntric origin. *Tantra Sādhanā* is kept secret, and is imparted only to the persons who are of high moral characters. It is said that Buddha himself practiced āsphanakā-yoga when he was in search of his own identity and destiny. The *Vinayapiṭaka*[17] says that Buddha's disciple Bharadvāja rose in the air and brought down begging bowl which was held high above by Setthi. Dr. B. Bhattacharya says, "Buddha recognised the *ṛḍḍhis* (supernatural powers) and mentioned four *Iddhipadas*,[18] conducive to attainment of supernatural power.[19] However, the Buddha had warned his disciple against the misuse of the occult powers.

This view is further confirmed by the practice of *Boddhimaṇḍala* (mystic diagram) around the famous *Boddhi* tree beneath which the Buddha practiced esoteric *Sādhanā* and attained Buddhahood. This belief cult of *Boddhimaṇḍala* is a necessary practice to draw mystic diagrams in a place chosen for *Tantra Sādhanā*. The *Maṇḍala* of Buddhist Tantra is nothing but the *Yantra* of Hindu Tantra. Even the formulas of refuse and worship, which were prevalent at all times and in all the countries of *Theravāda* Buddhism, speaks of *Mantric* character. The parallelism of sound rhythm, and idea and their invocations on the highest symbols like Buddha, *Dhamma* and *Saṁgha* and their underline devotional attitude, in which *Saddha* (devotion) and *Metta* (love) occupy the first place, make their *mantras* vibrant and alive. That their formal expression is as important as their ideas is emphasized by their threefold repetition and by the fact that some of these formulas are repeated twice, three times with a slightly different pronunciation within one and the same ceremony (be it *Pūjā, Paritta, Upasampadā, Patimokkha* recitals or at similar occasions) in order to be sure of proper form, the proper reproduction of the sound symbol, which is sanctified by tradition and, therefore, charged with psychic power.[20]

Mantra, mudrā, maṇḍala and the invocation of deities are the esoteric basis of *Tantra Sādhanā* from its very inception and Buddha revised and resuscitated the lost science of *Tantra*. There is a great controversy regarding the use of *Śakti* in Buddhism. *Anaṅgavajra* says, "Without *Prajñā-Pāramitā* emancipation is not possible, and *Prajñā-Pāramitā* resides in every women. Emancipation can only be obtained by coming in contact with any women whether of low origin or high or whether mother, sister or other near relatives."[21] But there is great confusion over the word *Parāvṛtti*. According to some scholars, "in the *Parāvṛtti* of sexual union supreme greatness is obtained". Sylvian Lēvi suggests that '*Parāvṛtti* of sexual act' means 'the mystic coupling of Buddhas and Boddhi-Sattvas' which have much important in Tāntrism. P.C. Bagchi is of the opinion that the Tāntric sexo-yogic practice means the enjoyment of bliss similar to that arising from the sexual act—which is evident in *Sūtra-Laṅkāra* itself.[22] He seems to be correct and we find that the word *Ātma-rati* is profusely used to convey the intensity of enjoyment which one experiences at the time of the unification of finite mind with the Infinite self. The Buddha revolted against the traditional rituals and religiosity of the Brahmanical school. He denounced the Vedic rituals as useless and a time-killing process and the chanting of Vedic verses without understanding as a fruitless labour.

Dr. S. Radhakrishnan says: "Buddha does not like the idea of basing the reality of Brāhman on Vedic authority, for whom once we admit the evidence of revelation, there is no end to it. So in the *Tevijja Sutta*, Buddha compares those who believe in Brāhmaṇa on the authority of the *Vedas* and seek union with Him to those who build a staircase at the junction of four roads to mount up to a high mansion as to which they can neither see nor know whether it exists at all".[23] But it is certainly not the ethical obsession of the Buddha which is responsible for his indefiniteness on metaphysical problems. The Buddha had a firm faith in meditation. His conviction of barrenness of intellectual flopping of wings in the vacuum prevented him from becoming a metaphysician.

L.P. Singh writes, "the dormant divinity when awakened with the ideation and incantation of *mantra* opens the gate of *Bhūmi* (consciousness). This divine power is known in Buddhist Tantra as *Herukā, Vajra-Tārā, Vajra-yoginī, Vajra-caṇḍikā. Herukā* is known in Hindu Tantra as *Kulakuṇḍalinī*. There are three chief forms of Buddhist Tantra,[24] *i.e.* Vajrayāna, Kālacakrayāna and Sahajayāna. According to *Tattva-ratnāvalī* (collected in the *Advaya-Vajra-Saṁgraha*) *Mahāyāna* has been divided into *Pāramitta-naya* and *Mantrayāna*. We find that Buddhism was divided into *Mahāyāna* and *Hīnayāna* on the acceptance of Tantrism. Those who are satisfied with the theoretical aspect and lack courage and determination are declared *Hīnayāna* which means 'a set of inferior ideology.' Mahā- yāna is decidedly the superior and sublime form of Buddhism."[25]

Guhyasamāja Tantra, which is considered as the Bible of Buddhist Tantra introduced the concept of *Śakti* for attainment of *Nirvāṇa*. *Guhyasamāja* is considered as the proper and the correct path for obtaining liberation through the esoteric process, while for formulating the principles and philosophy for the attainment of liberation, it has also dealt with the concept of *Siḍḍhis*, by means of which one can attain lot of occult powers. In the eighteenth chapter *Guhyasamāja Tantra* tries to elucidate and analyze the concept of *Siḍḍhis*. There are two kinds of *Siḍḍhis*, namely *Sāmānya* (ordinary) and *Uttama* (excellent), the *Siḍḍhis* like *Antaradhyāna* (miraculous disappearance) belong to *Sāmānya*. *Guhyasamāja Tantra* lays more importance to the second kind[26] of *Siḍḍhis*, which is known as *Uttama Siḍḍhis* because attainment of Buddhahood is possible only through the practice of *Uttama Siḍḍhis*.[27] *Uttama Siḍḍhis* can be attained by practicing *Ṣaḍaṅga-yoga*.

The *Sādhaka* who has realized *Śūnya*, which is transcendental reality for him the world appears as illusion. Such *Sādhaka* goes beyond the dualism of subject and object, sin or virtue. He becomes one with the *Parāśakti*, which creates, maintains and destroys the world. *Parāśakti* is to whom no part of the universe remains unseen, there is no kind who does not obey her, there is no scripture made by other, which is not known to her. *Parāśakti*:[28]

यस्यादृष्टो नैव भूमण्डलांशो यस्यादासो विद्यते न क्षितीशः।
यस्याज्ञातं नैव शास्त्रं किमन्यैः यस्याकारः सा परा शक्तिरेव।।

While enumerating the origin the *Guhyasamāja Tantra* seventeenth chapter of the treatise gives a very interesting account. Buddha declares that he never preached the mystic doctrine embodied in the *Guhyasamāja*, in his past lives, when he incarnated as Buddha Dīpaṁkara or as Kāśyapa Buddha, because people were not sufficiently equipped to understand the esoteric meaning and significance of the doctrine. The followers of Guhyasamāja School were able to obtain inscription spontaneously. Boddhisattva in the past could not expect to obtain Buddhahood by persistent exertion. But now one who would follow and practice *Guhyasamāja Tantra* would certainly attain Buddhahood and would find respectful place amongst the *Tathāgatas* as a Buddha in this very life.[29]

Tāntric treatises have been written in *Sandhyābhaṣā* and their technical terms, concepts and phraseology are difficult to understand. These terms and concepts are of great esoteric significance for the *Sādhaka*. However, *Guhyasamāja* is an exception because it has devoted the entire eighteenth chapter in which the doctrines and the phraseology have been elaborately discussed and explained terms like *Guha, Samāja, Yoga, Tattva, Rahasya, Parama, Boddhicitta, Vidyā-puruṣa, Vajradhṛk, Jinajik, Ratnadhṛk, Arolik, Prajñādhṛk, Kula, Moha, Dveṣa, Rāga, Vajra, Rati, Sampad, Yamāntakṛt, Prajñāntakṛt, Padmāntakṛt, Vighnāntakṛt, Samanta-caryā, Mantracaryā, Japa, Mudraṇa, Dharmodaya, Sambara, Sattvārtha, Maṇḍala, Nyāsa, Puṣpa, Caitya, Jñānacakra, Pada, Codana, Preraṇa, Āmantraṇā, Bandhana, Abhiṣeka, Vadyāvrata, Pañcāmṛta, Pañcavīrya, Sāmānya-Siḍḍhi, Uttama-Siḍḍhi, Upāya, Upeya,* etc., are some of those which are clearly defined in the eighteenth chapter.

The fifth chapter of the *Guhyasamāja Tantra* deals with the doctrines that emancipation through Tāntric practice as enumerated in the *Tantra* is possible of liberation for all men howsoever vicious, immoral or criminal may be, even, the worst kind of persons could get liberation through the practice of *Tantra*. When the Buddha declared the above views and gave this sermon, there was a great upheaval, among the Boddhisattvas and they registered their protest in this form: "Why Oh Lord ! The master of the *Tathāgatas* ! Are you taking recourse to these sinful utterances in a respectable assembly full of the *Tathāgatas*."[30]

Buddha was greatly surprised and pained with the reaction of Boddhisattvas and said: "Oh Kulaputras! Do not speak thus. The conduct I have preached is known as the Boddhi conduct which is immutable (*Dharmatā*), and pure, and is considered as such by the Buddhas who have realized the true essence (*Sārjñāninam*), and which springs from the interpretation of essential truth (Sāradharmārthasambhūta)".[31] After listening the sermons of the Buddha, the Boddhisattavas present in the Assembly became senseless and confused. The Tathāgatas who could understand the esoteric and the philosophical imports of the sermon of the Buddha were unaffected and made an appeal to the Buddha to revive the Boddhisattvas, who could not understand the inner and the real meaning of the truth due to their ignorance. The Buddha did special kind of meditation, which resulted in emanating spiritual light out of his body. All the Boddhisattvas came to life and sitting in the respective places and recited several *gāthās* in praise of the Buddha.

This manifestation of occult power has many dimensions. It could be argued that the Buddha took recourse to occult power, because it had been regarded as most effective tools in vanquishing the arguments of the opponents. It could be argued from other point of view that the protest of the Boddhisattvas was so strong that it would have been impossible to convince them without miracle. It would have been impossible to convince the Boddhisattvas the veracity and the authenticity of *Tantra* without the help of miracle because the ignorance and misgivings of Boddhisattvas was very strong. The result of miracle was colossal. The Boddhisattva did realize the esoteric significance and importance of the sermons of the Buddhas on Boddhi conduct during their unconscious state.

There is another story of the protest in the ninth chapter of the *Guhyasamāja Tantra*, where Buddha propounded that the truth of the five *Kulas* can be realized even having recourse to theft, adultery, defamation, falsehood etc. The Boddhisattvas were shocked and surprised to receive this kind of sermon from the Buddha. This time Buddha did not take the help of occult power to convince the Boddhisattvas, rather he tried to philosophise that the theft, adultery, defamation and falsehood are not the intrinsic nature of the reality. They are adventitious and they do not have the co-existence with the transcendental truth. The Buddha says, "For instance, Oh Kulaputras! It is well-known that smoke originates from the combination of three factors: namely, the churning of rod (*Kāṇḍa*), the churning pot (*Mathaniya*), and the efforts made by the hands of a person (*puruṣahastavyāyāma*). From that smoke fire is generated. That fire does not reside either in the churning rod or in the churning pot or in the effort made by the hands of a person. Thus, Oh Kulaputras! The conduct of the Tathāgatas should be understood, i.e., constant coming and going."[32]

After understanding the philosophical import and esoteric significance of teachings of the Buddha, Boddhisattvas in their utter surprise and devotion recited the following stanza :

महाभ्दुतेषु धर्मेषु आकाशसदृशेषु च।
निर्विकल्पेषु शुद्धेषु संघतिस्तु प्रगीयते।।[33]

The above teachings of the Buddha have great metaphysical import and ethical significance. The transcendental reality does not get affected by adventitious ideas and feelings. The act of theft, adultery etc., do not effect the transcendental nature of truth. According to Vedānta also *Ātman* remains unaffected by the good and the bad deeds of *Jīva*, because the transcendental nature of *Ātman* does not undergo any change and transformation. Thus, every *Jīva* is a dormant Śiva (cosmic being), microcosm is hybernated macrocosm. It is through the practice of *Yoga* and *Tantra*, alone one could realize the transcendental nature of reality. It is why there is no metaphysical problem for Ratanakar becoming a Bālmīki. Shantideva in his *Engaging in the Boddhisattva Deeds* (*Boddhisattvacaryāvatāra*), writes that according to the teachings of the Buddha even bees and donkeys can attain *Nirvāṇa* if they follow and practice the path taught by the Buddha. Human being has a special privilege to attain Buddhahood, if he or she can follow the doctrine and practice the *Dhamma*.

There is some misconception about the introduction of element of *Śakti* in Vajrayāna. It is not true that *Śakti* has been introduced for the first time by *Guhyasamāja Tantra; Śakti* has been inevitable principles of esoteric practice for obtaining emancipation since the very origin of the *Tantra*. *Guhyasamāja Tantra* has only introduced the new idea of five Dhyāni Buddhas presiding over the five *Skandhas* or factors of which the universe is composed along with *Śakti*. These five *Skandhas* are : *Rūpa* (form), *Vedanā* (feelings), *Saṁjñā* (name), *Saṁskāra* (impression) and *Vijñāna* (consciousness). *Sādhanamālā*[34] describes the names, colours and symbols of the different Dhyāni Buddhas. The names are: Vairocana, Ratna Sambhava, Amitābha, Amoghasiddhi and Akṣobhya. Their colours are: white, yellow, red, green and blue; and they are depicted in different *Mudrās*, namely: *Bodhyaṅgi* (teaching), *Varada* (grace), *Dhyāna* (meditation), *Abhaya* (protective) and *Bhūmisparśa* (earth-touching).

The female (*Śakti*) counterparts of the five Dhyāni Buddhas are: *Locana, Vajradhātvīśvarī, Pāndārā, Māmakī* and *Tārā*. These five consorts of *Dhyāni* Buddhas belong to the five families of *dveṣa, moha, rāga, cintāmaṇi* and *samaya*. The names of the five Bodhi-sattvas of the Dhyāni Buddhas are: Vajrapāṇi, Samantabhadra, Padmapāṇi, Ratnapāṇi and Viśvapāṇi.[35]

Padmavajra, one of the great exponent of Vajrayāna highlights the importance of Dhyāni Buddhas and he is of the opinion that by these five forms alone enlightened can be attained. The five forms are *Śāśvata* (*Vairocāra*), *Akṣobhya, Ratna, Āyuṣa,* (*Amitābha*) and *Kūlādya* (*Amoghasiḍḍhi*).[36] The attainment of Boddhi is a very difficult proposition, but according to Padmavajra if one is initiated in the esoteric practice of *Śrī Samāja* he may obtain divine perfection by coming in contact with *Mahāmudrā*. In *Tantra*, the role of *Guru* is very important. Without the initiation (*Abhiṣeka*) from a *Guru* one cannot attain spiritual perfection.[37] M. M. Gopinath Kaviraj has dealt in detail in his paper entitled "*Guru Tattvā and Sad Guru-Rahasya.*"[38] According to him the first duty of *Guru* is to help his disciple from the cessation of suffering. So long the self could not differentiate himself from the matter till then one could not be liberated from the cycle of suffering. One who imparts such knowledge, which would liberate from the nescience or one who helps the disciple in cutting asunder the trammels of *Māyā*, is real *Guru*. This kind of knowledge is known as *Prajñā*. The phenomenal world is of different dimensions and hence the *Vivekajñāna* alone can help the sentient being in differentiating what is real and what is adventitious. The knowledge, which is of supreme nature and which helps in establishing oneself in his own being and existence, is real knowledge; this is known as *Kaivalya* or liberation, some people call it *Nirvāṇa*.[39]

The Mālanivijaya says,

"...... स यियासुः शिवेच्छ्या। भुक्तिमुक्तिप्रसिद्ध्यर्य नीयते स्त्रदुयं प्रति।।"

According to M.M. Gopinath Kaviraj unless one takes refuse in *Guru* one cannot attain the state of equanimity between the enjoyment and liberation and, one cannot obtain the state of perfection. In *Probodhapañcadaśikā* —

"तस्या भोक्त्र्याः स्वतन्त्राया भौग्यैकीकार एष यः।
स एव भोगः सा मुक्तिः स एव परमं पदम्।।"[40]

Padmavajra is of the opinion that *Tantra* was introduced by the Buddha himself and the teachings of *Tantra* has been first recorded in *Śrī Samāja* which is the only another name of *Guhyasamāja*. He says that *Śrī Samāja* is the quintessence of Tāntric Buddhism. There is no better treatise of Buddhist Tantra in the three worlds.[41] Further Padmavajra says that the teachings of Vajrayāna which is most secret of all secrets and, is without *Śvabhāva* (real nature) and is pure and incomparable.[42] He emphasizes the importance of *Prajñā* and *Upāya*, which has been kept secret from the gaze of the common people. According to him, the attainment of Buddhahood is not possible without the help of *Śakti*.[43] He throws some light on the importance of the practice of *Mahāmudrā* conjoined with *Upāya*. People have great misunderstanding about the concept of *Śakti* or *Mahāmudrā*. It is true that in *Tantra* the importance of *Śakti* is unquestionable, but *Śakti* does not mean the female only, everybody is endured with both male and the female energy. Padmavajra propagates to enjoy *Mahāmudrā*, which resides in body of every sentient being. The knowledge of *Mahāmudrā* which is most divine and auspicious is of an esoteric nature, which can be attained by one's ownself.[44]

According to Vajrayāna *Prajñā* and *Upāya* reside within the body of sentient being. *Upāya* resides in the high plexus (*Uṣaṇīṣa Kamala*) and the *Prajñā* dwells in the lowest plexus (*Mūlādhāra*), the sacrococcygeal plexuses. The central objective of the Tantra *Sādhanā* is to awaken the *Prajñā* (*Herukā*), from the lowest plexuses and making her proceed in an upward movement till she becomes united with *Upāya* in *Uṣaṇīṣa Kamala*. In Vajrayāna man represents *Upāya* and woman represents *Prajñā*. The esoteric commingling of the two is the giver of supreme bliss (*Mahāsukha)*, it leads from spiritual discipline and yogic control, it leaves to the spiritual oneness, which is the state of the *Boddhicitta*. Vajrayāna accepts and leads to the equipollence of *Prajñā* and *Upāya.*

Vajrayāna is a physico-spiritual process. It seeks to weave yoga into every detail of life. It is an inner yoga of progression from the human to the divine. It is an esoteric process of mystic transformation and spiritual sublimation. Padmavajra has given great importance to the practice of *Mahāmudrā* (great women). According to him no emancipation is possible without the practice of *Mahāmudrā*. If one is initiated into *Mahāmudrā* practice, success is inevitable even though he indulges in practices which are against all laws, social or religious.[45]

In other form of spiritual *Sādhanā*, a man is not permitted to enjoy mundane existence. He is required to lead ascetic life. According to the common belief, a man who is living a normal life cannot attain liberation. Vajrayāna heralds a new era of spirituality, which is the meeting ground of enjoyment (*bhoga*) and *Yoga*. According to Vajrayāna the world is the manifestation of Buddha nature. With the help of incantation of proper *Mantra* and cosmic ideation, the physical activity becomes the means for release, *Bhoga* (enjoyment) turns into *Yoga*. Vajrayāna is suited to men of all kinds, it is esoteric process to impart the *Sādhanā* not merely for salvation but also for enjoyment, not merely for beatitude (*niśreyasa*) but also for progress (*Abhyudaya*).

Tantra Sādhanā is a spiritual synthesis. Tantra Sādhanā is based on the basic principles that *Boddhicitta* is to be realized through the human body. Sentient being is an epitome of the cosmos. There is no real distinction between sentient being and *Boddhicitta*, and every sentient being is a dormant divinity. The cosmos is its manifestation in space and time. According to Vajrayāna, sentient being awakens his own dormant divinity with the conviction and belief that reality (*Boddhicitta*), i.e. experienced within is the reality that pervades the whole universe.

The *Jñānasiḍḍhi*, the treatise on Vajrayāna deals in detail about the practice of Buddhist esotericism. According to Jñānasiḍḍhi liberation or salvation can be attained only through knowledge. The term knowledge connotes the knowledge of *Dhyani Buddhas*. According to the first chapter entitled *'Tattvanirdeśa'* the treatise says that Vajrayāna is the quintessence of all Tantrās and those who are ignorant about Vajrayāna become the victim of snares of false subjectivity. Those who are aware of this kind of knowledge, which has been propagated in *Jñānasiḍḍhi*, he can attain perfect knowledge (*Boddhi*), even if he indulges in immorality and crimes. This treatise also speaks of the paramount importance of *Guru* (spiritual preceptor). While enumerating the concept of knowledge, the *Jñānasiḍḍhi* says that the knowledge of Tathāgatas which connotes three terms Vajrayāna, Samantabhadra and Mahāmudrā, this knowledge is further sub-divided into five *Adarśajñāna*, *Samatajñāna*, *Pralyavekaśnājñāna*, *Kriyānuṣṭhānajñāna* and *Suviśu-ddhajñāna*. Each of these five kinds of *Jñāna* represent one of the five Dhāyani Buddhas. One who is in position of these five kinds of knowledge becomes *Śūnya* in essence. *Sādhanamālā* says, "The persons who have attained these five kinds of *Jñāna*, there is no restriction of food nor any class of women forbidden. Women of the lowest classes such as the Caṇḍālas or the Dombis are especially recommended for the purposes of *Mahāmudrā* perfection, though daughters of higher castes such as Brahmins are also recommended with the remark that the worshipper must take care that his mind is not in any way troubled, always bearing in mind that there is no better truth than that which is experienced by himself."[46]

There is some misunderstanding and confusion regarding the subject matters of *Sādhanamālā*. For a common man, it becomes difficult to understand the so called conflicting rules imposed on the *Sādhakas* by the *Sādhanamālā*. *Sādhanamālā* says at one place that a Sādhaka must observe the strict moral discipline and abstain from taking non-vegetarian and other objectionable food such as onion, oil, salt etc. He must observe celibacy.[47] In the next place it is stated in the *Sādhanamālā* that offerings should consist of meat, wine and other objectionable items.[48] Again it is stated that *Sādhanā* should be performed after purifying the body by taking bath and by following the rules of celibacy and yet in another place there is a contradiction in the statement. It is stated that no restriction is required for taking any kind of food,[49] again it is stated that *Sādhaka* attains salvation by incanting the *Mantras* only and no help of *Maṇḍala* worship or purifying oneself by fasting is required.[50]

The reason for this apparent contradiction and confusion are due to lack of proper understanding of the inner meanings of the different terms and concepts. According to some the different rules of *Vinaya* has been propagated for the different kinds of sentient beings. Indrabhūti says that there are three kinds of disciples, *i.e.* *Mṛdu*, *Madhya* and *Adhimantra*. According to different kinds of psychic development the different kinds of *Vinaya* rules have been prescribed. Dawsan, has classified Vajrayāna into six stages such as :

1. Kriyātantrayāna
2. Caryā (Upāya) Tantrayāna.
3. Yogatantrayāna.
4. Mahāyogatantrayāna
5. Anuttarayogatantrayāna
6. Atiyogatantrayāna.

According to another tradition *Tantras* are classified namely (1) *Kriyātantra*, (2) *Caryātantra*, (3) *Yogatantra*, and (4) *Anuttara-yogatantra*. *Sādhanamālā* also recognizes these four kinds of *Tantra*. According to the Vajrayāna, the beginners are initiated into *Kriyātantra*, where strict moral discipline like observance of celibacy is enjoined. The practice of *Yogatantra* is permitted to those who are considered to be equipped with moral-power to come in contact with *Śaktis*. The *Anuttaryoga* is considered highest *Yoga Tantra* and for *Sādhakas*, who are initiated into it, they are considered as immune from all disciplines. The *Anuttaryogins* are called *Siddhas*, as they are supposed to be in possession of occult powers and miracles.

Vajrayāna is monotheistic. The generic idea of Vajrayāna is *Śūnyatā* and *Karuṇā* that constitute *Boddhicitta*. The unification of *Śūnyatā* and *Karuṇā* is known as *Advaya*.

Śūnyatā is the creation and recreation of the universe. According to Vajrayāna *Siḍḍhi* can be attained by the divine grace of *Śūnyatā*. *Sādhanamālā*, while enumerating and analyzing the concept of *Śūnyatā* writes that it consists in thinking and realizing all *Dharmas* (elements) as transitory and non-self, they are mistaken by the mind like the objects seen in the dream, endowed with beginning and end, and natural purity, non-existence, unborn and emptiness like *Tathata*.[51] The concept of *Karuṇā* occupies important place in the *Sādhanamālā*. *Karuṇā* has been defined as the resolve on the part of Boddhisattva to lead and help all beings getting enlightenment including beings born from the eggs, uterus, or endowed with form or formless, conscious and unconscious being who abide neither in consciousness.[52] *Karuṇā* is further explained and elucidated as strong resolve to decimate right knowledge among the people who due to motivation (*tṛṣṇā*) are ignorant and cannot realize the continuous transmigration caused by the motivation. In order that they may lead life in accordance with the law of *Patitasamudpat* (dependent origination).[53]

However, Vajrayāna has been greatly misunderstood due to the lack of proper understanding of the concepts of Dhyānī Buddhas. Even B. Bhattacharya speaks of his lack of proper understanding of Buddhist esotericism. He writes, "It has been seen how primitive Buddhism, a taught by Buddha, passed through many changes and underwent degeneration owing to a variety of circumstances which cropped up in later times. This degenerated form of Buddhism is what is called Vajrayāna, or Tāntric Buddhism. We have already mentioned that Buddhism was a challenge to and a repudiation of earlier Brahmanism. It was now the part of Tāntric Buddhism to challenge the authority of Buddha and repudiate the original Buddhism."[54] Vajrayāna is neither degenerated form of Buddhism, nor it is a challenge to the authority of Buddha. It would be wrong to assume that with the introduction of the doctrine of five Dhyānī Buddhas, the Buddha lost his importance in the religion founded by him. Teachings of Buddha are pregnant with profound metaphysical and mystic imports, and because of this profundity and depth of the teachings different Ācāryas has interpreted, his teachings differently at the different period of history, out of which grew different schools and religious sects of Buddhism. The different schools and religious sects do not challenge the authority of Buddha rather they establish the fact that the Buddha was one of the greatest thinkers and religious teacher that world has witnessed.

Again, there is misunderstanding regarding the concept of *Nirvāṇa* as *Śūnya*, *Vijñāna*, and *Mahāsukha*. The comparison between the conditions of Boddhi mind in the state of *Nirvāṇa* with the embrace of a woman has also been greatly misunderstood. The bliss that is experienced in the state of *Nirvāṇa* has been compared with *Ātmarati*. This speaks of the experience of *Rati* (copulation) which is the highest degree of intensity of enjoyment in the physical world. It does mean that Tantra permits the embrace of women or the copulation with women to every *sādhaka*. We would discuss this matter in detail later on while making comparison of Vajrayāna with Vāmācāra Sādhanā. B. Bhattacharya further writes, "The Theory of *Karuṇā* was a direct challenge to this form of *Nirvāṇa*. But the *Tantrics*, who were leading lives of great sin and immorality, found in the theory of *Karuṇā*, or self-sacrifice, an excuse for their heinous doings. The Boddhisattva, they stated, is daily making untold sacrifices for suffering humanity, and, therefore, there is nothing that he should not do,[55] meaning thereby that the theory of *Karuṇā* gives him a blank charter for committing all kinds of heinous offences and violating all laws, human or divine."[56] The theory that Boddhisattvas were allowed to indulge in all kinds of immoral acts, because of their sacrifices for a suffering humanity would go against the concepts of Boddhisattvas. Boddhisattvas is one, who has acquired condition for attaining final and supreme enlightenment, because of his persistence and long practice of *Dhamma* and living a spiritual life as enjoined by *Patimokha*. But he refused to attain the state of *Nirvāṇa* until every sentient being attains *Nirvāṇa*.

It is stated that one who strives after *Nirvāṇa* should enjoy *Prajñāpāramitā* (perfect truth). This *Prajñā* resides in every woman, but it does not mean that Vajrayāna recommends the enjoyment of women, good, bad, diseased and depraved. Again, it would be wrong to assume that no distinction should be made between women of higher caste or lower caste closely related and be allowed to escape.[57] Some of the profound philosophical tenets of Vajrayāna have been enumerated by Anaṅgavajra in his work entitled *Prajñopāyaviniścayasiddhi*.[58] Anaṅgavajra greatest contribution is the concept of *Prajñopāya* compassion which is called *Upāya*, because it leads towards salvation. *Prajñā* is the realization of *Śūnyatā*, after having acquired distinction between the knowledge and the object of knowledge. The unification of *Prajñā* and *Upāya* is like the commingling of water and milk. In the state of unification distinction is obliterated and attains the state of supreme oneness, which is called *Prajñopāya*. The *Prajñopāya* is the creative matrix of the cosmos and everything has emanated from this principle of Supreme creativity. It is called *Mahāsukha* also because this creative matrix is the source of eternal happiness.

According to Anaṅgavajra *Prajñā* is absolute and compassion is also absolute. They both unify together in cognition. B. Bhattacharya writes, "When this commingling takes place, there is neither the knower, nor the knowledge, nor the object of knowledge; and that is exactly what is called the highest knowledge. There is neither any doer nor enjoyer, because it is free from the knowledge of either the doer or the enjoyer. It is called the knowledge of the great truth. In this there is no receiver, no giver, no object to be given, no object to be taken. Those who have realized this great truth acquire innumerable attainments, even while doing ordinary things such as seeing, hearing, talking, laughing and eating, when their attention is otherwise diverted. This truth is also known as non-duality, the Boddhi-mind, thunderbolt or Vajrasattava, the enlightened one or the enlightenment. This is also known as *Prajñāpāramitā*, the embodiment of all *Pāramitās*, or *Samatā* or equality, of the best object of meditation for all classes of the Buddha."[59]

The concept of *Prajñāpāramitā* has been analysed and enumerated properly by B. Bhattacharya. If the *Prajñāpāramitā* is embodiment of all *Pāramitās* (perfection) and the highest object of meditation and veneration for all classes of Buddhas, then how *Prajñāpāramitā* would be equated with women for enjoyment. *Prajñāpāramitā* is a symbol or metaphor for the enlightenment. Mādhyamikā philosophy is the systematization of the *Prajñāpāramitā* treatises. The transcendental nature of reality is known by uncovering the opacity of idea. The Vajrayāna Sādhanā performs this functioning after the intense meditation and the incantation of the *Mantra,* when the mind becomes pure and transparent and all kinds of distinctions are obliterated; this is called the state of *Prajñāpāramitā*. *Prajñāpāramitā* is the highest knowledge. T.R.V. Murti while analysing the concept of *Prajñāpāramitā* writes, Metaphysics or true philosophy (*Prajñā*) is non-dual knowledge—Intuition of the Real. The possibility of intellectual intuition is not only accepted but is taken to be the very heart of reality. It is the Truth. In intuition, knowledge and reality coincide; essence and existence are identical. . . . . . Non-duality, for the Mādhyamikā, is not attained, as in Hegel, by synthesis of particular points of view, but by their negation."[60]

A theory is negated when we are aware of its falsity. The falsity means here that what appears true and simple turns out as a full of contradictions. The philosophical basis of Vajrayāna is to some great extent *Vijñāna-vāda*. According to *Vijñāna-vāda* illusion starts with wrong objectification of what is really a state of consciousness. An idea is wrongly accepted as an external object. The given object is falsely constructed while consciousness is indispensably rare. The phenomenal world is like a dream. All individuals are composed of chain of transitory consciousness, which passes through the cycle of birth and rebirth. Emancipation from the birth and rebirth is the realization of *Prajñāpāramitā*. The practice of *Sādhanā* brings about the realization of non-self (*nairātma*), which cut asunder the trammels of ignorance. While enumerating the importance of meditation of *Prajñopāya*, Ānandavajra speaks meditation which is neither *Śūnya* nor its opposite, nor the negation of the both. In this concept of meditation and endeavour has been made to reject both *Śūnya* and *Aśūnya*. Ānandavajra analysis of concepts of *Saṁsāra* and *Nirvāṇa* speaks of the transcendental philosophy, which Vajrayāna propounded and propagated. *Saṁsāra* is defined as the condition of mind which is overwhelmed with the darkness arising out of numerous false construction is as fleeting as the lightning in a storm, and is besmeared with the dirt of attachment, etc., not easily removable.

अनल्पसंकल्पत्तमोऽभिभूतं प्रभंजनोन्मत्ततताडिञ्चलं च।
रागादिदुर्वारमलावलिप्तं चितं हि संसारमुवाच वज्री।।[61]

He defines *Nirvāṇa* as the opposite condition of the mind. This definition reminds us of the well known differentiation made by Nāgārjuna in his *Mādhyamikā Kārikā*.[62] While analysing the concept of *Nirvāṇa*, he says that *Nirvāṇa* is another condition of mind, which is bright with purity, is free from all false mental construction and defilement of attachment etc., which does not know and cannot be known, and is eternal.

प्रभास्वरं कल्पनया विमुक्तं प्रहीणरागादिमलप्रलेपम्।
ग्राह्यं न च ग्राहकमग्रसतेत्तवं तदेव निर्वाणवरं जगाद।।[63]

While discussing the *Tāntric* practice known as *Tattvācārya* Anaṅgavajra says that even the some of the greatest Hindu gods like Śiva, Indra, Kubera and Murāri were conversant with this kind of *Tantra-Sādhanā*. The practice consist in following the different rules enjoined by *Mantrayāna* such as the *samayas*, partaking the *Prādīpa* (ordures) and constant company who are different forms of *Prajñāpāramitā*. He further says that the perfection can be attained through enjoyment provided the mind is directed towards the Boddhi. The cultivation of right perception of inner nature of the phenomenal world as empty and if one tries to help other he would attain *Nirvāṇa* in one's life.

We find great similarity between Vajrayāna School of Buddhist Tantra and *Śākta Tantra* of Hinduism. According to the *Śākta Tantra Śiva* and *Śakti* have been anthropomorphically described as husband and wife. *Śakti* is the creation and recreation of the universe. She is the *magma mater*. She is more important than *Śiva*. *Śiva* is a corpse without *Śakti*.[64] W. Norman Brown writes: "The feminine principle, or *Śakti* (power), personified as the Goddess Devī, is the first and supreme principle of the universe. It includes both the spiritual and material principles and hence may be understood to comprise both Soul (*Puruṣa*) and Nature (*Prakṛti*) of the Sāṁkhya system. As such it is equivalent to the neuter Brahman of the Advaita thought."[65] *Śakti* is the creative aspect of the Reality. The absolute in *Tantra* is represented by *Bindu* (the personified form of Devī and Śiva). The feminine principle in conjunction with the masculine principle creates the cosmos. However, the masculine principle or Śiva-tattva is always secondary in the creative manifestation of the universe. The material universe has evolved from the great feminine principle, of spouse of Śiva, which is called Mahāmāyā.[66] However, *Śakti* cannot be identified with *Nirguṇa Brahman* of the *Advaita Vedānta*. In our opinion Parama Śiva is the same as Nirguṇa Brahman of the Advaita school but they differ in the spiritual and metaphysical import.[67]

Both Vajrayāna and *Śākta Tantra* believe in the mystic and metaphysical power of sounds and waves. Everything is vibrational. Every letter of the *Mātṛkā Varṇa* is imbued with the divine power of *Prajñāpāramitā* or *Śakti*. *Mantras*, the mystic syllables framed from these letters, according to esoteric formulae become potent techniques to cut asunder the trammels of *Avidyā*. Both in Vajrayāna and *Śākta Tantra*, *Mantra* plays a very important part in liberating the *Sādhaka* from the bondage or nescience. Vajrayāna and *Śākta Tantra* are scientific and esoteric approach to spirituality. Esoteric practice plays an important role in both these systems. Yoga means esoteric unification of *Prajñā* and *Upāya* or *Śiva* and *Śakti*. In *Śākta Tantra*, *Śakti* is called *Kuṇḍalinī*, in Vajrayāna *Prajñāpāramitā* or Mahāmudrā is called *Herukā*. *Śiva* and *Upāya* are *Bindu*, *Mūlādhāra* is the dwelling place of *Herukā* or *Kuṇḍalinī*, *Sahasrāra* or *Uṣṇīṣa-Kamala* is the abode of *Śiva* or *Upāya*. Both according to Vajrayāna and *Śākta Tantra* cosmos has been conceived as the body of *Mahāmudrā* or Devī, which has been evolved in six stages. The six stages have been described as six *Cakras* (*Padmas*). In the *Sahasrāra Cakra* or *Uṣṇiṣakamala* (pineal gland) which is the thousand petalled lotus, both the feminine and masculine principles co-exist before the creation of cosmos. The esoteric identification with *Śakti* or *Prajñā* can be obtained through the grace of *Prajñāpāramitā* or by incantation of *Mantra*. Both according to Vajrayāna and *Śākta Tantra* the whole universe has been created by *Mahāmāyā* (*Śakti*), *Mahāmudrā* is the creative matrix (*Sṛṣtirupā*). Every sentient being is a transcendental being, but due to nescience sentient being forgets his real nature and being, one forgets one's identity with transcendental reality. This is the split within, which creates the other. Transcendental reality is one whole, cosmic and universal. But it becomes divided and split into finite and limited consciousness. This takes place, because one identifies oneself with non-self. To achieve the unification of the split consciousness into the one whole is the aim of Tantra Sādhanā. L. P. Singh writes, "Psychic unification cannot be attained by any objective methods. One has to look within. Through the subjective approach alone can one gain the lost unity. The different mental tendencies (*Vṛttis*) are the splitting force. One will have to overcome the weaknesses of different tendencies. One will have to sublimate (*nirodha*) all the mental tendencies and temperaments."[68]

The Vajrayāna and *Śākta Tantra* are esoteric processes for transforming finite and the fragmented consciousness into the infinite and cosmic consciousness. The *Herukā* or *Kuṇḍalinī* is the *Parāśakti*. The esoteric awakening of this dormant divinity through the incantation of the *Mantra* and with the practice of *Maṇḍala* or *Yantra* is the central theme of both the schools. Most of the occult powers are acquired in the state of mystic dualism. It is most difficult state of a *Sādhaka*. Vajrayāna and *Śākta Tantra* are like walking on a razor's edge. It is full of esoteric allurements to which there is every possibility of *Sādhaka* becoming a victim, and get degenerated. The *Sādhaka*, therefore, takes refuse in *Guru* who could alone help the disciple to overcome the allurements and egoism. However, the practices of *Prajñopāya* and *Śakti* worship are surest and most scientific way of achieving monistic oneness with the transcendental reality. It is definite esoteric techniques though dangerous. The objective of Vajrayāna and *Śākta* Sādhanā is to enable one to overcome infatuation with the worldly enjoyments, and so that sentient being could realise that there is higher or a greater even an intenser enjoyment and bliss in spiritual realization.

Vajrayāna and *Śākta Tantra* strive for the ceaseless struggle to restore equilibrium. Every instinct or tendency has both the dark and the bright side. It can work on both sides. *Mahāmudrā* or *Śakti*, as a liberating force represents the bright side of the reality. The *Mahāmudrā* or *Śakti* as a binding principle (*Avidyā*) is the cause of suffering. Anaṅgavajra, while enumerating the process of *Abhiṣeka* of the disciple into *Prajñopāya,* he says that the *Guru* is to be approached by the disciple in the company of *Mahāmudrā,* who should appear charming and must be profusely decked in ornaments. The *Guru* imparts the disciple lesson on *Sambara, i.e.* restrained imposed on Boddhisattva. The practice of *Mahāmudrā* has been greatly scandalized. The disciple after getting initiation from the *Guru* consider himself as nothing but a chain of transitory consciousness. He cultivates compassion for suffering humanity. He invokes the *Śūnya,* the ultimate reality which is constituted of *Śūnya, Vijñāna,* and *Mahāsukha*. With the practice of esoteric *Sādhanā* and incantation of *Bīja-mantra, Śūnya* transforms itself in the form of divinity, which is identified as Boddhi-mind. With the commingling of the Boddhi mind with *Mahāmudrā* the *Sādhaka* acquires great occult power and he is able to do the work for which the *Mahāmudrā* has been invoked. Both the Vajrayāna and *Śākta* systems of esoteric practices speak of the many deities and the aims, and the objects of such esoteric practices are to show how many multifarious duties the deities live to perform and in how many forms they have to perform by transforming themselves into different astral bodies.

M.M. Gopinath Kaviraj while enumerating the importance of Tāntric Buddhist Sādhanā he argues that there is great similarity between the Buddhist and Hindu Tāntric practices. He says the one non-dual knowledge is called *Brāhman, Paramātmā* and *Bhagavāna*. The same reality is known from the knowledge point of view as *Brāhman,* from Yoga point of view *Paramātmā,* from devotional point of view *Bhagavāna. Yoga* is science of action — योग कर्मसु कौशलम्. Hence, knowledge, action and devotion are integrated into one, *Nirguṇa-Brahman, Niḥśakti* and *Nirākāra* are one. The *Śaguṇa Paramātamā, śakti* is in the form of *Jñāna. Saguṇa Brahmana* and *Śakti* are of different forms. The differences are due to differences in attributes, but all three constitute one reality. This non-dual knowledge has been described in the treatise of Vajrayāna entitled अद्वयवज्रसिद्धि as:

यस्य स्वभावो नोत्पत्तिविनाशो नैव दृश्यते।
तच्ज्ञानमद्वयं नाम सर्वसंकल्पवर्जितम्।।

According to M.M. Gopinath Kaviraj, what is the place of *Bhakti* in the *Bhagavata,* the *Karuṇā* has the same place in the *Āgamic* literature of Buddhist. The objective of the unification of *Prajñā* transcends the effects of defilements. The *Karuṇā* alone cannot help one to obtain *Nirvāṇa.*

प्रज्ञया न भवे स्थानं कृपया न शमे स्थितिः।

First, there is a practice of *Paramitā-naya* followed by *Mantra-naya*, both these *naya* (path) have been expounded by Buddha himself. The prupose of both are the same.[69]

There is a great similarity between Vajrayāna and Vāmācārya. Both are aggressive spiritualism. Sex (*kāma*), anger (*krodha*), temptation (*lobha*), attachment (*moha*), egoism (*mada*), jealousy (*mātsarya*), hatred (*ghṛṇā*), shame (*lajjā*), fear (*bhaya*) are the dominant instincts in sentient beings which keep him veiled from his real nature. Both Vajrayāna and Vāmācārya Sādhaka goes to cremation ground in the dead of night and perform *Sādhanā*. After seeing the end of mortal frame in the form of ashes and skeleton, a sense of renunciation develops in him, and he gradually becomes detached from the mundane existence. The sentient being who goes to cremation ground in the dead of night will certainly overcome the instinct of fear. In the *Upaniṣad*, it has been said that self is not attainable by the weakling.[70] *Tantra* does not believe in suppression and repression of human instinct. It is esoteric techniques of sublimation and transformation, what appears to be an obscene and repulsive esoteric practice to a layman is a healthy and positive science of sublimation. With the help of incantation of *Mantra* the sentient being tries to establish a mystic communion with his own individual existence (incantative rhythm) to cosmic consciousness. In other words it is a mystic process of unification of *Kuṇḍalinī Śakti* or *Herukā* with *Śiva* or *Upāya*. The *Śiva* or *Upāya* is represented by the red *Bindu* (sperm) and *Śakti* or *Prajñā* by the white *Bindu* (Ovum). *Śiva* and *Śakti* or *Prajñā* and *Upāya* constitute the *miśra Bindu*. Tantra does not allow free sex, rather it is imperative for every Tantra Sādhaka to lead a life of high morals. However, both Vajrayāna and Vāmācārya are very difficult and risky *Sādhanā*. Only a man of higher spiritual attainment can practice this *Sādhanā*. Without proper moral discipline and a *Guru* of high order, one should not dare practice otherwise there is every possibility of a fall and degeneration. Sometimes *Sādhaka* gets enamoured of the occult power and forgets his destination. Vajrayāna and Vāmācārya Sādhanā is only for those who have dedicated their whole lives for spiritual salvation and for the upliftment of the mankind. In both these *Sādhanā* mind gets immediately concentrated partly due to the esoteric condition created by the circumstances and partly because of the *Mantra* and use of *Maṇḍala* or *Yantra*.

According to *Pātañjalayoga Sūtra* the *Sādhaka* attains victory over the five fundamental factors (*bhūtas*) by getting control over the Crude (*sthūla*), Subtle (*sūkṣma*), Purport (*anvaya*), Real Nature (*svarūpa*) and Real Significance (*arthatattva*) of the Created Beings (*bhūta*).[71] It leads to be acquisition of occult powers (the eight *Siḍḍhis*) and *Kāya Siḍḍhis*.[72]

Kāya Siḍḍhi is of great spiritual significance. The physical body of the Sādhaka becomes divinized. Each and every cell of the body becomes supramentalized. It starts secreting subtler and divine waves. The physical appearance becomes lustrous (*lāvaṇya*) and glorious. The body of such a *yogi* becomes pure, powerful and supramental.[73]

Tantra has been greatly scandalized due to the use of *Pañcamakāra*. But *Tantra* is based on scientific principles. It is a positive method of overcoming the strong desires for sensuous enjoyment. For a person having strong desires for physical enjoyment *Tantra* prescribes the crude *Pañcamakāra Sādhanā* as it does not encourage suppression and repression of unfulfilled desires. Normally, man is dominated by animal desires of hunger, sleep, fear and sex (*Āhāra, Nidrā, Bhaya* and *Maithuna*). The dominance of such crude desires differ from man to man. When these desires are dominant in a man he struggles for their fulfilment. Resistance on the part of such a person is an uphill task. Spiritual *Sādhanā* and higher values do not attract a parched up soul. Only persons who are elevated can abstain from material enjoyment and lead a spiritual life. But *Tantra* does not abhor material enjoyment. Suppression and repression of instincts lead to immorality. A man may suppress or repress his instincts for a short duration in the beginning but with the passage of time, a volcanic eruption is bound to occur. This was the cause of degeneration in the Buddhist monastery. Immorality and sin in the garb of yellow robe is not a sign of healthy society.

Pañcamakāra Sādhanā comprises *Madya* (wine), *Māṁsa* (meat), *Matsya* (fish), *Mudrā* (grain) and *Maithuna* (copulation).[74] This *Sādhanā* is enumerated in all *Tantras* of both Hindu and Buddhist provenance. "Wine, meat, fish and parched rice as well as sexual union, this pentad of *Pañcamakāra* applies in the union of *Śiva* and *Śakti*."[75]

Pañcamakāra Sādhanā is directed to gain control over the physical desires. The use of the crude *Pañcamakāra*, according to prescribed esoteric disciplines, lead to detachment and inner purification. A man who is addicted to drinking will reduce the quantity of liquor as part of spiritual discipline. This will give him inner strength for moral control over his baser instincts. Wine is used for the release of the senses from their engrossment in their outer objects. The surface consciousness of the mind which is exposed to the shocks and attachment is temporarily suspended and the deeper, expansive, and subliminal spheres of consciousness are opened up. It enables the *Sādhaka* to gain control over the inner recesses, and work for the sublimation and purification of being. In Tantra Sādhanā, wine is used for the purification of mind (*citta*).[76] But it is not to be drunk in the manner suggestive of animal drinking. It leads to degradation.[77] The Supreme Lord is invoked, worshipped and the dedication is sanctified by the prescribed esoteric *mantra*. The use of *mantra* includes incantation and repetition, and invocation of the presiding deity. The *Sādhaka* identifies his whole being and consciousness with the deities and *mantra* in the course of *Śava Sādhanā* before the use of wine. One who does not know the science of *Tantra Sādhanā* has no right to perform this *Sādhanā*. To hell he goes who dares to infringe these conditions and seeks to enjoy wine and women.[78] He is a sinner and libertine. Drinking of wine that is not sanctified is as reprehensible as rape.

One who is addicted to drinking has no sense of proportion. For him there is no meditation, no *tapas*, no worship, no *dharma*, no sense of moral activity, no prudence, no *Guru*, no thought of his self; he cannot be a votary of *Tantra Sādhanā*.[79] Such a person drinks liquor, eat meat, and indulges in sex not for true worship and dedication but for his own animal enjoyment. He may be learned in the *Śāstras* but indeed he is condemnable.

The subtler meaning of wine is not liquor. The mystic interpretation of the word *madya* (wine) means the hormones secreted from the pineal gland. Hormones are secreted from every endocrine gland. The hormone secreted from the pineal gland is partly controlled by the moon (*Soma*), and the nectar (hormone) secreted from this gland is known as *Somadhārā* or *Somarasa*. It revitalizes the different glands and gives divine bliss. Man does not have any experience of this bliss till the *Kuṇḍalinī* is awakened and made conscious, rises upward and drinks the pineal nectar.

"From the *Mūlādhāra Cakra*, the *Kuṇḍalinī Śakti* goes up again and again to the *Brahmarandhra* (pineal gland); the divine bliss issues out of this mystic unification of the *Kuṇḍalinī* and the Moon of Pure Consciousness. The nectar which flows from the lotus in the supreme ether above is the real wine. What is drunk otherwise is only liquor."[80] According to the *Āgama Śāstra*, "wine is the *Somadhārā* or lunar ambrosia which drops from the *Sahasrāra*."[81]

Māṁsa (meat) *Sādhanā* does not mean the eating of meat. The animal that is killed involves a moral problem of good and bad. The real meaning of *Māṁsa Sādhanā* is to overcome the dualism by *yoga*. It means to free Consciousness from the bondage of fetters with the sword of Divine Knowledge. The Consciousness so freed is merged with the Supreme Godhead. This is the esoteric meaning of *Māṁsa Sādhanā*.[82] The other meaning of *Māṁsa* is tongue or speech. The word *Mā* means tongue. *Māṁsa Sādhanā* means control over speech.[83] It also means dedication of all action to the *Lord Mam*.[84]

Matsya (fish) *Sādhanā* means control of breath through a psycho-physical discipline like *Prāṇāyāma*. It symbolizes the fishes moving in the Gaṅgā and the Yamunā, *i.e.* the two currents of breath, expiration and inspiration, constantly moving in *Iḍā* and *Piṅgalā*. Eating of fish means the controlling of breath. The other meaning of *Matsya Sādhanā* is the controlling of the senses. The senses are brought under the control of mind and yoked to Self. This is the true eating of fish.[85] The other eating is merely hurting the creatures.

Mudrā does not mean parched rice in the mystic sense of the term. It means detachment from the evil that keeps the soul in bondage. Association with the immoral leads to bondage, with the divine to liberation. To cut off all connection with evil is *Mudrā Sādhanā*.[86]

The last of *Pañcamakāra Sādhanā Maithuna* has been greatly scandalized and grossly misunderstood. *Tantra* is based on divine principles. It does not ignore the biological and psychological aspects of human personality. *Maithuna Sādhanā* (copulation with woman) is allowed in *Tantra*. The idea behind this is to enable the *Sādhaka* to control and sublimate the sex instinct. A man can do this only gradually, by practicing restraint. However, the subtler and esoteric meaning of *Maithuna Sādhanā* is the copulation of *Śiva* and *Śakti*. The woman to be waited upon is none other than the inner divine power, which is lying asleep in the ordinary animal-man and is awake in the *Kaula*. This *Kuṇḍalinī Śakti* is to be awakened, served and attended to. "The divine nectar of Spiritual Bliss that ensues on the meeting of this Divine Pair, the Supreme *Śakti* (*Kuṇḍalinī*) and the Supreme Self (*Śiva*), the Lord that waits above, that is real *Maithuna*, the final *Ma*. Anything else is only copulation."[87] According to *Tantrasāra* and *Yāmala* the union of *Śiva* and *Śakti* is the true yoga and the joy, which arises out of it, is known as Supreme Bliss.[88]

Arthur Avalon writes: "When, therefore, the Vīra eats, drinks or has sexual intercourse he does so not with the thought of himself as a separate individual satisfying his own peculiar limited wants; an animal filching as it were from nature the enjoyment he has, but thinking of himself in such enjoyment as *Śiva*, saying "Śivo'haṁ", "Bhairavo'haṁ". Right sexual union may, if associated with meditation and ritual, be the means of spiritual advance, though persons who take a vulgar and animal view of this function will not readily understand it."[89]

Vajrayāna is psycho-spiritual process to transform the sentient being into a divine being. It is scientific, positive, esoteric and mystic *Sādhanā* of inner progression. It makes a man pure and powerful, it gives vision and strength. The practice of *Mahāmudrā* (the great woman) depends on the ideation and motivation, wife is kissed with one feeling, a daughter is kissed with another motivation.[90] Vajrayāna does not sanction immoral satisfaction of carnal desires. The desire is an enemy, but it can be made an ally. Vajrayāna does not believe in the suffering of body and mind. The physical body of man is the only media through which one can attain Buddhahood. The physical body is an expression of the *Boddhicitta*. The manifest world has been created by *Mahāsukha*. In the copulation of man and the woman the same bliss is experienced in lesser intensity, if it is done with spiritual motivation and under strict esoteric disciple, the physical is ennobled and divinized.

The Vajrayāna has imbibed all the best philosophical concepts and doctrines and incorporated all that is the best in Buddhism and because of this fact, it became very popular. Vajrayāna is one of the greatest contribution made by Buddhism towards the world civilization because of its adherence to the philosophy of spiritual perfection and esoteric technique of transforming a sentient being into Buddhahood.

REFERENCES

1. *Sādhanāmālā*, Benoytosh Bhattacharya, vol. II, p. xxii.
2. *Introduction to Buddhist Esoterism,* by Benoytosh Bhattacharya, 2nd ed., Varanasi, 1964, p. 35.
3. धर्मं शरणं गच्छामि समग्रं महायानम् । *Sādhanamālā*, p. 225.
4. *Sarvadarśanasaṅgraha*, p. 23.

5. *Advayavajrasaṁgraha*, p. 19, II, 21-22.
6. *Prajñāpāramitā jñānam advayaṁ sā tathāgataḥ, Sādhyā tādarthyayogena tācchabdyaṁ granthamāryayaḥ*: This is from the Prajñā-pāramitā *Piṇḍārtha Nirdeśa* of Diṅnāga, quoted in Haribhadra's *Abhisamayālaṅkārāloka twice*. (pp. 28; 153). According to Obermiller, *Prajñāpāramitā-Saṅgraha* is another name for this – *Doctrine of Prajñāpāramitā*, pp. 5; 7. See also *Buston* vol. I, P.S. Tucci has published the entire work with an English translation in the *JRAS*, 1947, pp. 53-75.
7. *The Central Philosophy of Buddhism, A Study of Mādhyamikā System*, T. R. V. Murti, Pub. 1955, p. 213.
8. तस्यद्धारातिधिं वक्ष्ये योगाचारानुसारतः। *Sādhanamālā*, vol. I, p. 210
   मन्त्रतन्त्रादिसिद्धिज्ञो योगाचाररक्षः क्वचित्।। *Ibid.,Vol. II*, p. 481.
9. एषोऽहमनुत्तरसम्यक्सम्बोधिमार्गश्रयामि यदुत वज्रयानम्व;
   स प्राप्नोत्यचिरादबोधिं वज्रयानप्रवर्त्तनीम्। *Ibid.*, p. 421
10. Quoted from *Yogaratnamālā in the Bauddha Gān O Dahā*, p. 8. Also from *Vajraśekhara in Advayavajrasaṁgraha*, p. 23, II. 23-4.
11. Samasrami's Edition, p. 21.
    या (ता 2) वदवलोकितश्वरस्य बोधिसत्वस्य दृढ़प्रतित्ता न परिपूरिता भवन्ति सर्वसत्त्वाः सर्वदुःखेभ्यः परिमोक्षिताः यावदनुत्तरायाः (याः?) सम्यक्सम्बोधौ न प्रतिष्ठापिता भवन्ति।
12. *Tattvasaṅgraha* (G.O.S. No. XXX), p. 75.
    त्स्याश्चाविद्याया योगाभ्यासादसमर्थतरतमक्षणोत्पादक्रमेण व्यपगमात्परिशुद्ध- ज्ञानसन्तानोदयादपवर्गप्रप्तिः।
13. *Sādhanamālā*, vol. II, Benoytosh Bhattacharya, p. xxvi.
14. *Bendall: Catalogue of Buddhist Sanskrti*, MSS, p. 70.
15. *A Tibetan Accounted of Nagarjuna*, an article by S.C. Sarkar in the *Sino-Indian Journal*, December, 1948.
16. *Tantra: Its Mystic and Scientific Basis*, L.P. Singh, p. 30.
17. *Sacred Books of the East*, vol. XX, p. 78.
18. They are : *Chando* (will), *Viriyam* (efforts), *Cittan* (thought), and *Vimaṁsa* (investigation). See R.C. Childers, *Dictionary of the Pali Language*, p. 157.
19. *The Cultural Heritage of India*, vol. IV, p. 260.
20. Lama Angarika Govind in an article on Mantra in the *Stepping Stones*, vol. II, no. I, published from Kalimpong.
21. *Ibid.*, p. 21, Śl.40 :
    तथा तथा पवर्त्तेत यथा न क्षुभ्याते मनः।
    संक्षुब्धे चित्तरक्तन्नै तु सिद्धिर्नैव कदाचन।।
22. *Studies in the Tantras*, Dr. P.C. Bagchi.
23. *Indian Philosophy* (Seventh Impression), vol. I, p. 467, London, 1956.
24. According to some expert on Buddhism, there are four schools of Buddhist Tantra for four different types of disciplines, namely: (1) Cārya Tantra, (2) Kriyā Tantra, (3) Yogātantra, and (4) Anuttarayoga Tantra. See *The Cultural Heritage of India*, vol. IV, p. 265.
25. *Tantra: Its Mystical and Scientific Basis*, p. 32.
26. अन्तर्द्धानाद्यः सिद्धाः सामान्या इति कीर्तिताः।
    सिद्धिरूत्तममित्याहुर्बुद्धा बुद्धत्वसाधनम्।।
    Guhyasamāja Tantra or *Tattagatataguhyaka*, Gaekwad's Oriental Series, Baroda, 1931, p. 162.
27. सेवाषड्गयोगेन कृत्वा साधनमुत्तम्।
    साधयेदन्यथा नैव जायते सिद्धिरूत्तमा।। *Ibid*, p. 163.
28. *Nityotsava of Umānandanātha*, Published as no. XXIII of the Gaekwad's Oriental Series, p. 1.

29. भूतपूर्वं भगवन्तः सर्वतथागता अनभिलाप्यानभिलाष्यबुद्धज्ञेत्रसुमेरूपरमाणुरजः समाः कल्पाः क्षीणा यावत् भगवतो दीपङ्करस्य तथागतस्यार्हतः सम्यक्सम्बुद्धस्यातिक्रान्तस्य काश्यपस्याभि महामुनेरमिसम्बुद्धस्य न भाषितम्। तत् कस्मात् हेतोः। अभव्या भागवन्तः सत्त्वा अस्य महागुह्यपदार्थस्य तेन कालेन तेन समयेन मया न भाषितम्। ...... तदिहैव जन्मनि गुह्यसमाजाभिरतो बोधिसत्त्वः सर्वतथागताना बुद्ध इति संख्या गच्छति।
Guhyasamāja Tantra or *Tattagatataguhyaka*, p.144.
30. किमयं भगवान् सर्वतथागतस्वामी सर्वतथागतपर्षन्मण्डललमध्ये दुर्भाषितवचनोदाहारं भाषते। *Ibid.*, p. 21.
31. अलं कुलपुत्रा मा एवं वोचत ।
दूयं सा धर्मता शुद्धा बुद्धानां सारज्ञानिनाम्।
सारधर्मार्थसम्भूता एषा बोधिचरिपदम्।। *Ibid.*, p. 21.
32. तद्यथा अपि नाम कुलपुत्राः काण्डं च मथनीयं च पुरुषहस्तव्यायामं च प्रतीत्य धूमः प्रादुर्भवति। अग्रिमभिवर्त्तयति स चाग्रिर्न काण्डस्थितो न मथनीयस्थितो न पुरुषहस्तव्यायामस्थितः। एवमेव कुलपुत्राः सर्वतथागतवज्रसमया अनुगन्तव्याः। गमनागमनाद्यैरिति। *Ibid.*, p. 38.
33. *Ibid.*, p. 38.
34. *Jino vairocanokhyāto ratnasambhava eva ca,*
Amitābha-amoghasiddhir-akṣobhyośca prakirtitaḥ,
Varṇa amisum sitaḥ pito rakto harita-mecakan,
Bodhyaṅgi varado dhyānammudrā abhayabhusparśani.
35. For details see B. Bhattacharya, *Indian Buddhist Iconography.*
36. पञ्चाकाराभिः सम्बोधिरेषु प्रोक्तास्तथागतैः।
शाश्वनाक्षोम्भरत्रायुर्कुलाद्यैः समवस्थितम्।। *Sādhanamālā*, vol. II, p. xlix.
37. अनेन जन्मना सिद्धिं यः कश्चिदश्विवाच्छति।
तेन गुह्यव्रतं धार्यं सर्वद्वन्द्वनिषूदनम्।।
अमिषिक्ते समाजाख्ये तन्त्रे सर्वसुखोदये।
महामुद्राभिषेकेन दिव्यसिद्धिप्रदायिका।।
ततः स्वच्छन्दमास्याय आदियोगैकतत्परः।
अभ्यासयोगरत्रन्तु गुरूवक्राद्विनिःसृतः।। *Ibid.*
One copy exists in the Oriental Institute MSS. Library and another is with MM H.P. Shastri of Calcutta, p. 195.
38. *Bhāratīya Saṁskṛti Aur Sādhanā*, (Hindi), vol. I, p. 253.
39. *Ibid.*, p. 243.
40. *Ibid.*, p. 243.
41. श्रीसमाजात् परं नास्ति रत्नभूतं त्रिधातुके। *op. cit.*, p. xiii, index.
42. अहो गुप्तातिगुप्तस्य वज्रयानस्य देशना।
निःखभावस्य शुद्धस्य विद्यते यस्य नोपमा।।
43. अतस्तत् कथ्यते गुप्तं प्रज्ञोपायविभावनम्।
स्मरणं चित्तवज्रस्य गुप्तात् गुप्ततरं परम्।।
ये न जानन्ति तं शुड़ं खदेहेऽपि व्यवस्थितम्।
निर्वृतिं तं पदं दिव्यं तेषां सम्यक् ब्रवीभ्यहम्।।
44. महामुद्रां निषेवेत खदहोपायसंयुताम्।
खसंवेद्या हि सा विद्या महामुद्रा परा शुद्धा।।

45. येन येन बध्यन्ते जन्तवो रौद्रकर्मणा।
सोपायेन तु तेनैव मुच्यन्ते भवबन्धनात्।।
46. *Sādhanamālā*, vol. II, p. liii.
47. *Op.cit.*, p. 251.
चिकालस्नायी मद्यमांसवसापलाण्डुतैललवणविवर्जितस्त्रिकालं जपेत्।
48. *Op.cit.*, p. 885. मांसजम्बुडिकामद्यपुष्पधूपविलेपनं, etc.
49. *Op.cit.*, p. 336. न्यासमित्थं विधानेन प्रकुर्यात् ब्रह्मचर्चतः।
50. *Op.cit.*, p. 388. अत्र स्थाननियमो नास्ति नापि भोजने नियमः। अत्र मन्त्रजाएस्तु क्रियमाणः यथा न कश्चित् प्रत्येति तथा कर्तव्यः।
51. *Sādhanamālā*, p. iii : अनित्या ज्ञणिका निरात्मानः चित्त-विठयिताः स्वन्पेन्द्रजालसदृशाः प्रतिभासमात्रा आदिशान्ताः प्रकृतिपरिशुद्धा अभावा अजाता अनुत्पन्ना: तथताभूतकोटिशून्या सर्वधर्माः। etc.
52. *Ibid.*, p. 26 : यावन्तः सत्त्वाः सत्त्वसंग्रहेण संगृहीताः अण्डजा वा जरायुचा वा संखेदजा वा औपपादुका वा रूपिणो वा अरूपिणो वा संज्ञिनो वा असंज्ञिनो वा नैवसंज्ञानासंज्ञिणो वा etc. ते सर्वे मया अनुपधिशेषनिर्वाणधानौ प्रतिष्ठापयितव्या।
53. *Ibid.*, p. 111: तृष्णावशात् अमी सत्त्वा अविद्यान्धीकता अर्कमविपाकदर्शिनः तेभ्यो गम्भीरं प्रतौत्यममुत्पादकर्मक्रियावताराय धर्मं देशयिष्यामीति करुणाया अप्यधिवचनम्।
54. *Buddhist Esoterism*, p. 32.
55. Kern, *Manual of Indian Buddhism*, p. 64
56. *Op.cit.*, p. 33.
57. *Prajñopāyaviniścayasiddhi*, in Two Vajrayāna Works, G. O. S., no. XLIV, p. 23, verse 31.
58. *Published in the Gaekwad Oriental Series*, under the title *Two Vajrayāna Works.*
59. *Buddhist Esoterism*, p. 40.
60. *The Central Philosophy of Buddhism*, p. 214.
61. *Buddhist Esoterism*, p. 41.
62. निर्माणस्य च या कोटिः कोटिः संसरणस्य च।
न तयोरन्तरं किंचित् सुसूक्ष्ममपि विद्यते।। Chap. XXV, *Kārikā* 20.
63. *Buddhist Esoterism*, p. 41.
64. *Kubjikā Tantra*, ch. I; *Tāntric Texts*, vol. IX, p. 44, Luzac & Co., 46, Great Russell Street, London, 1972.
65. *Saundaryalaharī*, p. 6.
66. *Ibid*,. p. 85.
67. *Tantra: Its Mystic and Scientific Basis*, p. 115.
68. *Ibid.*, p. 117.
69. *Bhāratīya Saṁskṛti aur Sādhanā*, p. 426.
70. नायं आत्मा बलहीनेन लभ्य,
नायं आत्मा बलहीनेन लभ्य,
न च प्रदात्त्पसो वाप्यलिङ्गत्
एतैरूपायैर्यतते यस्तु विद्धां-
स्तस्यैष आत्मा विशते ब्रह्मधाम ।।4।। मुण्डकोपनिषद्, खण्ड, 2.
71. स्थूलस्वरूपसूक्ष्मान्वयार्थतत्त्वसंयमाद्भूतजयः। *Patañjali Yoga-Sūtra*, vol. iii. p. 45.
72. ततोऽणिमादिप्रादुर्भावः कायसम्पत्तद्धर्माभिद्यातश्च।।
Following are the eight Siḍḍhis:
(1) *Aṇima*—the esoteric power to become small in size, or to become microscopic objects in full detail. (2) *Mahimā*—to expand in size or in space the intuitive power of viewing the far reaches of

the universe. (3) *Laghimā*—to offset the force of gravity or make one's body lighter than air. (4) *Garimā*—the mystic power to increase one's weight, apparently increasing gravitation. (5) *Prāpti* the power of transporting oneself anywhere, instantly, or of gaining anything by the mere act of reaching out and having it appear. (6) *Prakamya*—the mystic power which fulfils all desires including that of becoming visible or invisible. (7) *Īśatva*—the divine power to create or nullify by thought, making things and beings appear or disappear. (8) *Vasita*—the power to control the different manifestations of the world, so they will act as the Yogi desires.

73. स्पलावण्यबलवज्र संहननत्वानि कार्यसम्पत्। *Ibid*, v.iii.47.

74. *Mahānirvāṇa Tantra*, p. 89.

75. मद्यं मांसं तथा मीनं मुद्रा मैथुनमेव च
मकार-पञ्चकं सेव्यं शिव-शक्तिं समागमे। *Meru Tantra*

76. मदिरा ब्रह्मागा: प्रोक्ता: चित्तशोधनसाधना:।
तासामेकां समाहृत्य पूजाकर्म समाचरेत्।। 41 ।। *Kulārṇava Tantra*, p. 191.

77. पशुपानं विधौ पीत्वा वीरोपि नरकं व्रजेत् ।। 63 ।। *Ibid.*, p. 196

78. असंस्कृतं पिब्रेद्द्रव्यं बलात्कारेण मैथुनम्।।
स्वंप्रिपेण हतं मांसं रौरवंनरकं ब्रजेत ।। 66 ।। *Ibid.*, p. 197.

79. मदप्रछादितात्मा च न किञ्चदपि वेत्ति च।
न ध्यानं न तपो नार्चां न धर्मं च सत्क्रियाम् ।। 102 ।।
न देवं न गुरूनात्मविचारो न स कौलिक:।
केवलं विषयासक्त: पतत्येव न संशय: ।। 103 ।। *Ibid.*

80. आमूलाधारमाब्रह्मरन्ध्रं गत्वा पुन: पुन:।
चिच्चन्द्रकुण्डलीशक्तिसामरस्य: सुखोदय: ।। 106 ।।
व्योमपङ्कजनिस्यन्दसुधापानरतो नर:।
सुधापानमिदं प्रोक्तमितरे मदपायिन: ।। 108 ।। *Ibid.*, p. 198.

81. *Śakti and Śākta*, p. 606.

82. पुण्यापुण्यपशुं हत्वा ज्ञानखड्गेन योगवित्।
परे लयं नयेच्चितं पलाशी स निगद्यते ।। 106 ।। *Ibid.*

83. *Cosmic Society—An Anthology*, p. 142.

84. *Ibid., Kulārṇava Tantra*, p. 53.

85. मनसा चेन्द्रियगणं संयम्यात्माने योजयेत्।
मत्स्याशी स भवेद्देवि शेषा: स्यु: प्राणिहिंसका: ।। 110 ।।
Kulārṇava Tantra, p. 53; *Cosmic Society—An Anthology*, p. 142.

86 सत्संगेन भवेन्मुक्ति: सत्संगेषु च बन्धनम्।
असत्संगमुद्रणं यत् तन्मुद्रा परिकीर्तिता। *Tantra and Sādhanā; Ibid.*, p. 143.

87. पराशक्त्यात्ममिथुनसंयोगानन्दनिर्भर:।
य आस्ते मैथुनं तत् स्यादपरेस्त्रीनिषेवका:।। 112 ।। *Kulārṇava Tantra*, p. 198

88. *Śakti and Śākta*, p. 607.

89. *Ibid.*, pp. 628-29.

90. भावेन चुम्बिता कान्ता, भावेन दुहितानाम्। *Śakti and Śākta*, p. 643.

4 Sahajayāna

Sahajayāna is logical and esoteric development of Vajrayāna. Sahajayāna esoteric belongs to devotional school of Buddhist Tāntric Tradition. Without devotion one will not be able to tread the spiritual path. With the grace of *Guru* alone one can attain Buddhahood. Swami Ramakrishna Paramahansa attained salvation through the practice of *Tantra*. His whole life was transformed with the initiation into *Tantra Sādhanā* by Bhairvi Brahmāṇī. He says, "The Brahmāṇī put me through all the exercises mentioned in the sixty-four principal *Tantra* books. Most of these were extremely difficult *Sādhanās*. Some of them so dangerous that they cause the devotee to lose his footing and sink into moral degradation. But the infinite grace of the Mother carried me through unscathed."[1] Swami Ramakrishna was one of the greatest devotional figure and Tāntric Sādhakas of India at the turn of the nineteenth century. In our view he was a Tāntric Vaiṣṇavite till he received initiation into Dhyāna-Yoga from Totapuri.[2]

Lakṣmīkarā Devī (729 A.D.), sister of Indrabhūti, the King of Uddīyāna, is one of the great exponent of Sahajayāna. Sahajayāna was a philosophical and esoteric movement to incapitulate the basic tenets of the Vajrayāna and to give them a new interpretation, which had attracted the then seekers of enlightenment. This new movement which emerged as new school of thought and practice emphasized the devotional aspects of Vajrayāna. In this new school of thought exercised great influence on the literary movements of that times. The profound thoughts got literary expression in the songs of eighty-four Siddhācārya. Lakṣmīkarā was the sister of Indrabhūti. She advocated a new kind of doctrine in her work entitled 'Advayasiddhi'. This work exercised great influence on this new school of thought which is known as Sahajayāna. B. Bhattacarya writes, "In the Advayasiddhi a most remarkable and bold innovation has been introduced by the authoress. Hitherto the Vajrayānists advocated the worship of the five Dhyānī Buddhas and their innumerable emanations, but what Lakṣmīkarā advocated was quite out of the way and strange, even though since her time this new teaching has gradually won for it many adherents who are styled Sahajayānists, and who are still to be met with among the Nāḍhā Nāḍhīs of Bengal and especially among the Bāula."[3]

Lakṣmīkarā tried to revolutionized the teachings and tenets of Vajrayāna by introducing the new concept of devotion both in theory and practice. She tried to rid of Vajrayāna from some of its dead dogmas and lifeless rituals. She says, "There is no need of undergoing suffering, no fasting, and no rites, nor bathing nor purification and other rules of society. Nor do you need to bow down before the images of gods which are prepared of wood, stone or mud. But with concentration offer worship only to your body where all the gods reside."[4] We are aware that transcendental truth is neutral. The practice of norms and values are stepping stone. It is not the goal. When sentient being attains *Nirvāṇa,* he goes beyond the categories of good and bad, virtue and sin. In the state of choiceless awareness sentient being lives a life of naturalness (*Sahaja*). Lakṣmīkarā while elucidating her thought enshrined in her work *Advayasiddhi,* she thinks that after the realization of truth the sentient being goes beyond the dualism of subject and object, good (*kuśala*) and bad (*akuśala*) deeds. According to her the woman should be treated with all respect and humility as she is an embodiment of *Prajñā*.[5]

M.M. Haraprasad Shastri has done a great work on the song of Siddhācāryas by publishing in four volumes entitled *Baudha Gāna O Doha.*

1. चर्याचर्यविनिश्चय। 2. दोहाकोष–सरोजवज्रकृत। 3. दोहाकोष– कृष्णपादाचार्यकृत। (सहजाम्नाय–पञ्जिका) और 4. डाकार्णव।

It would not be out of place to mention here the contributions of Matasayenderanātha and Gorakhanātha; both these great thinkers have tried to interpret and expound the philosophy and practice of *Śrī Vidyā Tantra* in a very simplistic language, which could be easily understood by the common people. Though the subject matter of the *Nāthism* is complex but the credit goes to Matasayenderanātha and Gorakhanātha to make it communicative. The chief characteristics of language are communication and signification from the linguistic point of view. The teachings of Siḍḍhācāryas are of great importance. Indrabhūti is one of the eighty-four Siddhācārya[6] of Sahajayāna.

As against the doctrine of five Dhyāni Buddhas and innumerable emanations. Lakṣmīkarā expounded a devotional and straight path of Herukā (*Kunḍaliṇī*), Sahaja means straight. The perfection is possible only by the help of Vajra-Tārā (another Buddhist name of the *Kuṇḍaliṇī*) whose path is Avadhutikā. The path of Avadhutikā is straight and not zig-zag like that of Lalanā and Rasanā. In Hindu Tantra *Kunḍaliṇī* Sādhanā is also known as Ṛju Mārga (straight path). And those who attain perfection with the help of Herukā are known as Siddhas.

The Siddha literature has been composed in lyrical and *Muktaka-kāvya* forms. The whole literature is primarily poetical. The Siddha literature is a manifestation of profound sensibility and ethical thought. It speaks of great vertical depth and vision, it follows to some extent the rules of *Saṅgīta Ratnākara. Encyclopedia of Indian Literature* writes, "Siddha Literature (*Apabhraṁśa*) covers the vast range of the Vajrayānī Tantrikā literary tradition that arose out of the Mahāyāna Buddhism. In the tradition of the Tantrikās there were eighty-four Siddhas. It is remarkable that they were profound scholars in Sanskrit and Apabhraṁśa language, literature, poetics and prosody. They were mystics too, and their language was suggestive and symbolic. The period of the Siddha literature is said to be between AD 800 and 1200 – a period when the Tantrikā practice was in full force in India."[7]

Sahajayāna has made great impact on the Nāthism and Sufism. M.M. Haraprasad Shastri, Probodh Chandra Bagchi and Rahul Sanskritayan[8] have made great contribution by publishing the Siddha literatures and making it available to the world of scholarship. Suniti Kumar Chatterji, Sahiudala, Sukumar Sen have also done some valuable works. The word Siddha connotes the acquisition of occult power through the practice of *Mantra*. The man who acquires this kind of occult power through the incantation of *Mantra* is known as Siddha 'मन्त्र सिद्धि विशिष्टः'[9]।

The whole literature of Sahajayāna has been composed in *Sandhyā Bhāṣā* (Twilight language). The language of Siddhacārya is esoteric (*Guhya*) which reveals the real meaning only to the initiates. Though the symbols of this language are sexual and have amatory connotations but their hidden meaning is related to profound mysticism. Most symbols are based on the names of the females of the low caste. In *Hevajra Tantra*, *Prajñā* is addressed as *Yuvati* (young woman), *Janani* (mother), *Bhaganī* (sister), *Rajaki* (washer woman), *Nartaki* (dancing girl), *Dombī* (doma-girl). *Prajñā* is called *Janani* because she is the cause of creation. She is called *Nartaki* because the manifest universe is but a cosmic dance of *Prajñā* and every object is in a dancing posture (*nṛtaratā*). She is called *Dombī* because she is beyond the touch of human mind and senses. In the *Atharva-Veda* Brahman is called *Vrātya* (un-touchable). She is called *Dombī* because she cannot be grasped by the senses.

Lakṣmīkarā, while explaining and elucidating the concept of *Prajñā* is of the opinion that when the *Boddhicitta* is realized a man goes beyond the question of vice and virtue. She says:

गम्यागम्यविकल्पन्तु भक्ष्याभक्ष्यन्तथैव च।
पेयापेयं तथा मन्त्रो कुर्यान्नैव समाहितः।।
सर्ववर्णसमुद्भता जुगुज्ञा नैव योषितः।
सैव भगवती प्रज्ञा सम्वृत्या रूपमात्रिता।।

The philosophical basis of Sahajayāna is that the transcendental reality can be realized without undergoing any kind of physical or mental sufferings. M.M. Gopinath Kaviraj says that Sahajayāna is based on the philosophy and the practices of *Āgama*. According to him the symbols such as *Hakāra* and *Thakāra* represent moon and sun and the unification the *Hakāra* and *Thakāra* brings about the unification of the moon and sun. The same could be said about the differences between *Iḍa* and *Piṅglā nāḍī*. According to *Haṭhayoga* the multiplicity is the cause of origin of the world. So long the equanimity remains there is no origin of the world. This is known as

Advaita. When the equanimity is disturbed and multiplicity is created, phenomenal world comes into existence. This is the state of dualism, *i.e.* subject and object. This is the root of creation.[10]

The different *cakras* (nerve plexus) have been conceived to be the abodes of different mystical gods and goddesses, who grant different types of mystic power (*Siḍḍhi*), and are known as a different places of pilgrimages. The top-most *cakra* is known as *Mahāsukha Cakra*. The sole objective of Tantra Sādhanā is to cross these different *Cakras* and reach the *Mahāsukha Cakra*, the fountainhead of Infinite Bliss and Beatitude.

A psychological analysis will show that these *cakras* or nerve plexuses control certain human tendencies. When a *Sādhaka* crosses a certain *cakras*, he acquires mastery over the human tendencies controlled by this particular *Cakra*. This gives the *Sādhaka* tremendous mental strength which in common parlance is known as occult power. That is why these different stations are known as sacred places of pilgrimages like Uddīyāna, Jālandhara, Pūrṇagiri and Kāmarūpa.

The word Uddīyāna here stands for the mystic kingdom of pilgrimage and not for the historical place of which Indrabhūti styled himself as king. Uddīyāna here means the *Mahāsukha Cakra* which Indrabhūti conquered with the help of *Herukā* and thus became Siddha (the perfect being).

The quintessence of Sahajayāna is to attain the supreme unification of one self with *Boddhicitta*. This state of infinite unity is both an enjoyment and salvation. Sahajayāna rejects the philosophy of nihilism and pessimism. The realization of divine presence of *Prajñā* puts an end to all physical, mental and spiritual suffering and inspires the sentient being to live up to the ideal and glory of Buddha. Sahajayāna treats world as neither an illusion nor reality. It puts emphasis on the realization of *Mahāsukha* without ignoring the material aspects of life.

Sarahapada, who is one of the great exponent of Sahajayāna is considered as the first poet of Hindi literature. However, it is a controversial point because some scholars and historians think that *Sarahapada* is a great ancient literary figure and poet of Baṅglā or Uriyā literature. Rahul Sanskritayan thinks that *Sarahapada* is the first poet of Hindi literature, because we find the elements of *Apabhramśa* and the beginning of Hindi language. From the following examples it seems that the language and the composition of *Sarahapada's* poems is nearer to Hindi.

Sarahapada:

(अ) घोर अँधारे चन्दमणि जिमी उच्जोअ करेइ।
परम महासुह ऐखु कण, दुरिअ अशेष हरेई।।

(आ) पण्डिअ सअल सन्त वक्खाणइ, देहहि रूद्ध बसन्त न जाणइ।
अमणागमण ण तेन विखवण्डिअ, तोवि णिलज्ज भणइ हउँ पण्डिअ।।

The impact of Sahajayāna was so great on the Baṅgalā, Uriyā, Asamiyā, Maithilī and Hindi literature, because of its philosophical profundity and its appeal to the higher sensibility. The whole literature, which has emanated from Sahajayāna is full of grace and lyricism. It is known as Sahajayāna because it tried to make the life of spiritual pursuits simpler and natural. Naturalism and simplicity are the hallmark of Sahajayāna. The Siddhācārya have followed the practice of *Yoga* and *Tantra* in a very serious and committed way without getting themselves involved in any kind of physical and mental suffering with the awakening of *Kuṇḍaliṇī*.[11]

The *cakra*, which are the Substratum of *Śakti* resides in the different parts of human body, so long *Śakti* remains entangled, it remains disciplined slave. The moment the *Kuṇḍaliṇī* is awakened and starts piercing different *cakras* the man becomes conscious of his divine origin and power. The Siddhācārya enumerates the concept of esoteric practice in the following verse:

"परमशून्यस्थानादुपरि गत्वा योगी न जायते न म्रियते न गच्छति नागच्छति। स च योगी तिष्ठति युगे युगे ज्योतिः समेत्य।।"[12]

According to some there are two kinds of yoga, *i.e.* Saṁnyāsayoga and Kaivalayoga. Those who follow Saṁnyāsayoga attain the supreme sublimity by crossing solar system, but one who follows the path of Sahajayāna after piercing the Suṣumṇānāḍī enters into Sahasracākra where sun and moon are unified and out of their unification emanates divine nectar. *Sādhaka* after drinking this divine nectar attains the state of *Samādhi* (*Turīya*). The oneness with infinite unity is called qualified and non-qualified state of Buddhahood. Different names have been ascribed for different kinds of Yoga Sāddhanā such as *Mantranaya*, *Layayoga*, *Haṭhayoga*, *Bihaṅgamayoga*, *Mahāyoga*, and *Rajayoga* etc. Really speaking yoga is a mystic practice to awaken one's own dormant divinity and attain enlightenment after conquering all the mental tendencies and dispositions. Sentient being is wrapped in *Avidyā* unless he eliminates the positive effect of *Avidyā* he cannot get rid from the defilements. One can retrace one's way against the positive force of Avidyā only with the help of some negative force. *Kuṇḍalinī* is the negative force of individuation. *Kuṇḍalinī* is *Parāśakti*.[13] It is the spiritual force behind all mental and physical activity. M.M. Gopinath Kaviraj says: "The name of the *Kuṇḍalinī* is *Ādhāra Śakti*. It is the substratum of all realities and remains the primordial basis of all beings. When it awakens it becomes one with consciousness by becoming unsubjectivated (*nirādhāra*) and the moment the *Kuṇḍalinī* becomes objectless the whole universe becomes objectless. When the *Kuṇḍalinī* becomes conscious the whole world takes the form of consciousness. The awakening of the *Kuṇḍalinī* and the realization of "*Sarvaṁ khalvidaṁ Brahman*" (All is Brahma) of *Śruti*, and the *Sādhanā* of spiritual experience of all-pervasiveness of consciousness are one.[14] The *Kuṇḍalinī* remains in a sleeping state. When it is awakened through yogic practice *Sādhaka* attains the intuitive power to visualize the divine effulgence. According to Sahajayāna this state of *Mahāsukha* is both transcendental and immanent. Transcendental aspect of *Mahāsukha* is *Śūnyatā* and immanent part of it is *Karuṇā*. It would be wrong to think that the transcendental aspect (*Śūnyatā*) is real and immanent part (*Karuṇā*) unreal. Both Śūnyatā and *Kuruṇā* constitute the infinite unity. This eternal co-existence (*Samarasatā*) of two is known as *Mahābindu*. The division of the two is the origin of creation.

The *Parā-Bindu* has sub-centres in all created beings. These sub-centres are also the *Parā-Bindu*. In *Tantra*, the cosmic sub-centre is called the *Sahasrāra Cakra*. It is the seat of Parama Śiva. The *Parā-Bindu* is the starting point of cosmic creation. The starting point of the cosmic being is known as *Kāmabīja*. This is the point of origin of the fundamental element. In Tāntric esotericism it is said that Parama Śiva resides on the back of *Śambhu Liṅga*. The *Kuṇḍalinī Śakti* lives on the back of *Svayambhu Liṅga*. The *Kuṇḍalinī* being the force of fundamental negativity, its starting point is negative *Kāmabīja* of created being. *Mūlādhāra Cakra*, being the controlling station of the crudest matter (solid factor), is the starting point of negative *Kāmabīja*. *Mūlādhāra* is the lowest nerve plexus. Herein resides the *Kuṇḍalinī*, the Serpent Power. Tantra Sādhanā is mainly devoted to the awakening of the *Kuṇḍalinī*. Its whole purpose is to bring about the unification of *Kuṇḍalinī Śakti* with Parama Śiva, whose abode is *Sahasrāra*. Only with the mystic unification of *Śiva* and *Śakti* the non-qualified liberation (*Mokṣa*) can be attained.

When the *Kuṇḍalinī* is awakened and made conscious, it forces its passage through the different *Padmas* and excites them to action. With the rising of the *Kuṇḍalinī*, the *Boddhicitta* opens up all occult powers and mystic visions come to the *Sādhaka*. When it reaches the Uṣṇīṣa-Kamala the *Sādhaka* becomes one with the infinite unity and he becomes free from all defilements. It cuts asunder the trammels of nescience and *Boddhicitta* becomes free from the bondage of selfhood. The *Kuṇḍalinī* is neither a biological nor a psychic principle. It is a esoteric concept but she can be seen intuitively. She has the brilliance of million of suns.

The identification of *Mahāsukha* with *Nirvāṇa* (enlightenment) brought about great change and transformation in the conception of transcendental reality. Thus, Sahajayāna heralded a new era of *Mahāsukha*. S.B. Dasgupta writes, "The Mahāyāna conception of the production of *Boddhicitta* (*bodhi-citto-tpāda*) is transformed in Sahajayāna into the production of a state of intense bliss through the sexo-yogic practice; and as after the production, the *Boddhicitta* rises upwards through ten stages (technically known as the *Boddhisattva-bhūmis*) so also Sahajayāna practice involves the yogic process of breath-control and other psycho-physical practices through which the disturbed semen should be checked in the *Maṇipūra* (situated near the navel) known generally as the *Nirmāṇa-cakra*, and then it must march upwards through the *Dharma-cakra* situated in the heart and the *Sambhoga-cakra* situated in the throat and then reach the *Uṣṇīṣakamala* (*i.e.* the lotus in the head) where it will produce the *Mahāsukha* of the nature of *Nirvāṇa*. The word *Boddhicitta* sometimes in Vajrayāna and almost always in Sahajayāna is synonymous with the word semen."[15]

According to Sahajayāna there are two *Nidis Lalanā* and *Rasanā,* which pass from the *Mūlādhāra Padma* to *Uṣṇīṣa-Kamala* from left and right. *Lalanā* and *Rasanā* represent *Prajñā* and *Upāya*. There is a third *Nāḍi,* which is called *Avadhūtikā*. *Avadhūtikā* represents *Boddhicitta*. The *Lalanā* and *Rasanā* cross each other at the different *Padmas*. These *Padamas* or *Cakras* represent the different stages of esoteric advancement. The *Hevejā Tantra* says, "At the base of the genitals where all three channels come together, *Lalanā* descending from the left, *Rasanā* descending from the right and *Avadhūti* ascending at the centre, there resides the *Boddhicitta* in its relative condition (=*Śukra*) and quiescent. At the summit of the head (*brahma-randhra*) there resides the *bodhicitta* in its absolute condition (=*mahāsukha*) also quiescent and known as Moon."[16]

According to Vajrayāna *Mahāsukha* is the quintessence of transcendental reality. This infinite unity is realized when we experience the *Boddhicitta* as the *Mahāsukha*. The central objective of Vajrayāna is to attain this state of *Mahāsukha*. In our ordinary life the experience of the highest happiness is in the state of copulation. *Tantra* is not a sexo-yogic *Sādhanā* but it is a psychological and esoteric process of transforming the mundane experience into supra-mundane or spiritual experience of *Mahāsukha*. The human body is the only medium through which one can realize and experience the transcendental nature of reality, which is *Mahāsukha*. Infinite bliss is the quintessence of Brāhmaṇa, the ultimate being according to Vedānta philosophy. Brāhmaṇa has been conceived as *Sat-cit-Ānanda*. From this infinite bliss the world has been emanated and it is sustained in this state of bliss and again it returns back to a state of bliss.

The human body is the epitome of macrocosm. Through the practice of esotericism the breath becomes quiescent. It awakens the *Boddhicitta,* which is the unification of *Prajñā* and *Upāya,* sun and the moon. The *Bīja-mantra* of the *Parāśakti,* which is addressed as *Caṇḍālī* is 'अ'. The *Caṇḍālī* does not mean the women belonging to the untouchables caste. The *Parāśakti* has been called *Caṇḍālī,* because it is beyond the reach of our mind and sense and hence it is untouchable. She has been given another name as *Dombī,* because of the same reason. With the esoteric practice of *Maṇḍalas, Mudrās* and *Dhyāna* the *Parāśakti* or the *Boddhicitta* is realized which transcends all kinds of dualism of subject and object. This state of *Mahāsukha* and the supreme sublimity has been beautifully expressed in the following verses (*Doha*) of *Sarahapada:*

> When the mind goes to rest,
> The bonds of the body are destroyed,

And when the one flavour of the Innate pours forth,
There is neither outcast nor Brahmin.
Here is the sacred Jamunā and here the River Gaṅga,
Here are Prayāga and Benares, here are Sun and Moon.
Here I have visited in my wanderings shrines and such places of pilgrimage.
For I have not seen another shrine blissful like my own body.[17]

The *Boddhicitta* is sometimes represented as *Śukra* and sometimes it is represented as the unification of *Prajñā* and *Upāya*. In esoteric language it is called *Rakta* and *Śukra*. *Hevajrā-Tantra* itself is consistent in its allusions to this theory. The basis is provided by the three bodies (*kāya*) of a Buddhas, increased by addition of the fourth, known as the 'Self-Existent Body' (*svabhāvikakāya*), the 'Innate Body' (*Sahajakāya*) or the 'Body of Great Bliss' (*mahāsukhakāya*). In Sahajayāna the *Nirvāṇakāya*, *Sambhogakāya* and the *Dharmakāya* identify with different *Padmas*. The Sahajakāya is identified with *Uṣṇīṣa-Kamala*. It is also known as *Mahāsukha Cakra*, because of its transcendental nature of bliss.

Buddhist Tantra has emphasized the importance of yogic practice without which attainment of enlightenment is an impossibility. As the fire in the log would never be manifested without friction, so the Buddhahood would never be realized without esoteric practice. *Tantra* has always emphasized the practice of Yoga, which is of course very complex and risky. There is every chance of physical or mental degeneration and aberrations. If it is not properly practiced under the proper guidance of proper *Guru* it could be very harmful. It is for this reason that *Tantra* has enjoined for every *Sādhaka* to be very cautious in the selection of *Guru*. The purpose of Vajrayāna Sādhanā is to arrest the downward movement of *Boddhicitta* and to take it towards upward and unify it with *Uṣmahāsukha* (*Uṣṇīṣa-kamala*). The rising of *Boddhicitta* through the piercing of different *cakaras* is like the Mahayāna conception of march of *Boddhicitta* through the different stages of *Pāramitās*. When the *Boddhicitta* awakens and reaches the navel *cakras*, Goddess Caṇḍālī is awakened. This awakening of the divine force is resulted into the flow of nectar which rejuvenates the mind and the body of the sentient being. The goddess Caṇḍālī variously known as *Dombī*, *Yoginī*, *Sahaja-sundarī*, *Nairātmā* (or *Nairāmaṇī*) is described in different *Tantras*, *Dohās* and songs. In the process of rising from the lowest *Cakra* to the highest, she transforms herself variously, causing new realizations to the Sādhaka. From all that is said about her nature it seems that she is of the nature of a strong internal perception—something like a force of nature of intense bliss produced through the esoteric yogic practice. The exposition of the nature of the *Śakti* is the basic subject matter of *Dohās* and songs of Siddhācārya. The observation of S.B. Dasgupta about the comparison between the philosophical schools of Mahayāna and Tāntric Buddhism following the common middle path is misleading. S.B. Dasgupta writes, "Another important point, noticeable in this connection, is the regulation of the *Boddhicitta* through the middle path. We have seen that the philosophical schools within Mahāyāna were, or at least professed to be, all followers of the middle path in as much as all of them declared that the final state is neither a state of *bhāva* nor a state of *Nirvāṇa*,— but it transcends or synthesizes both. This Mahāyānic principle has been adopted by the Tāntric Buddhists in their practical Yoga in regulating the *Boddhicitta* through the middle path (i.e., the middle nerve Avadhūtikā) avoiding the two extremes which are represented by the two nerves in the right and the left."[18]

The concept of Avadhūtikā is quite different from the concept of middle path of Mahāyāna Buddhism. The avoidance of two extremes is quite different from the concept of *Lalanā* and *Rasanā*. According to *Tantra* unless one acquires the mystic power, one would not be called a real Yogi. These powers could be acquired by different means but nature of such power are momentary and unreal, but when one attains the infinite unity and result of which one is established in his own true being and existence. One obtains the mystic power which is true and real. After pursuing the path of yoga for quite long time one could succeed in cutting asunder the cycle of tendencies and motivations and after that the yogi attains Mahāsiddhi at will. According to Siddhācārya, this is the hallmark of differentiation between the liberated and the self-bondage. Though who have become *Jīvanmukta* (liberated) he must have acquired supernatural powers and virtues and this is the identification of liberated soul. According to **"योगशिखोपनिषद्"** Siddhi is the only criteria through which you can differentiate the man who is liberated and one who is in bondage.[19]

M.M. Gopinath says, "The Pañcakośa-Viveka of Vedānta, *Cakaraveda* of Tantra, *Aṣṭāṅga Yoga* of Patañjali and *Anūpurva-Vihāra* of Bauddha are essentially one system.[20] According to Sahajayāna there are eight kinds of Siddhis. They are: (1) *Khaḍga*, (2) *Añjana*, (3) *Pādalepa*, (4) *Antardhyāna*, (5) *Rasa-Rasāyāṇa*, (6) *Khecara*, (7) *Bhūcara*, (8) *Pātāla*.[21] These Siddhis are of great importance. The first Siddhi refers to the supernatural power with which one can conquer his enemy with the help of sword. Second is the occult power, which enables the *Sādhaka* to have some kind of supernatural vision with which one can see something which is buried under the earth or hidden from the normal eyes. Third refers to the mysterious power of moving around without being perceived by anybody. The fourth refers to the supernatural power which makes man disappear before everybody present. The fifth is an occult power with which one can transform the normal metal into gold. The sixth is a power, which provides the *Sādhaka* to move in firmament. The seventh is supernatural power to visit anywhere in the world and the last eight is an occult power to enter into another regions. These superhuman power which is known as occult power is part and parcel of Tantra Sādhanā. The Pātañjala Yoga has also discussed in detail about these supernatural power in Bibhūtipāda.

The concept of Ṣaṭkarma or six rites occupy an important place in Tāntric literature. The six rites are: *Śānti*, *Vaśī-Karaṇa*, *Stambhana*, *Vidveṣaṇa*, *Uccāṭana* and

Māraṇa. The first rite is related with the attainment of tranquillity and equanimity of mind. The *Vaśī-karaṇa* means the power to overcome man and woman and get them work as per the *Sādhaka* command. *Stambhana* means the power to stop others for performing any action. Even one can stop the burning power of fire. Vidveṣaṇa is another important power with which one can show the seed to differences among the friends, relatives, lovers etc. *Uccāṭana* stands for a power that enables one to make his enemy leave the place with disgrace. The last one *Māraṇa* is probably the most dangerous power with which one can kill his enemy with the incantation of *Mantra*. Because of the eight *Siddhis* and six rites (*Ṣatakarma*) the path of Tantra has been very risky and dangerous. Even *Upaniṣad* speaks about this kind of spirituality like walking on the razor's edge.[22] However, in the Sahajayāna the *Sādhaka* does not pursue the path of esotericism for the attainment of any kind of these supernatural powers. Though the powers come to *Sādhaka* in a natural way but *Sādhaka* due to his commitment to higher values and goal he does not get disturbed or enamoured by their *Siddhis*.

There has been a long tradition of *Siddha-Carya*, *Līlāvajra* (471 A. D.) was a direct disciple of Lakṣmīkarā. He wrote a number of treatises on *Siddha* literature, which are preserved in Tibetan translation in Tangyur Collection. These are some of the treatises which have been written in *Līlāvajra*:

1. *Śrī Sahajaguhyasamājasādhanā.*
2. *Śrī Sahajasiḍḍhi.*
3. *Āryanāmasaṅgītiṭīkā.*
4. *Yamāntakamantramūlārtha Vajraprabheda.*
5. *Ḍākinīvajrapañjara–pañcaḍākinīsādhanā.*
6. *Kṛṣṇayamāritantrasya Pañjikā.*
7. *Mahātīlakakrama.*
8. *Guhyasamājatantranidāna gurūpadeśa bhāṣya.*
9. *Vajrasattvasādhananibandhana.*

Another name which occupies an important place in M.M. Haraprasad Shastri's *Baudha Gana Doha* is that of *Darikapada* (753 A.D.) the disciple of *Līlāvajra*.[23] According to M.M. Haraprasad Shastri, Darika belonged to Bengal and he composed many songs and *Doha* in old Bengali literature. Due to the obeisance to *Luipa* in many of Darikas songs or *Doha*. M.M. Shastri thinks that Darika was direct disciple of *Lui*. He has written some valuable treatises on Vajrayāna and Kālacakra, some of his books have been translated in Tibetan. The following are the list of his books.

1. *Śrī Kālacakratantrasya Sekaprakriyāvṛtti.*

2. *Tathāgatadṛṣṭi.*
3. *Cakrasaṁvarasādhānātattvasaṅgraha.*
4. *Cakrasaṁvaramaṇḍalavidhi tattvāvatāra.*
5. *Cakrasaṁvarastotra sarvārthasiḍḍhi viśuḍḍha cūḍāmaṇi.*
6. *Yogānusāriṇī nāma Vajrayoginī ṭīkā.*
7. *Vajrayoginī pūjāvidhi.*
8. *Kāmakalā tāraṇa sādhanā*
9. *Śrī Oḍḍiyānavinirgata Mahāguhyatattvopadeśa.*
10. *Prajñāpāramitā hṛdayasādhanā.*

Another important female Siddhācārya, who is held in a high esteem is Sahajayognicinttā (765 A.D.) the disciple of Darikapada. Her work in Sanskrit entitled '*Vyaktābhāvānugata-tattva-siddhi*' is considered as a work of high value and importance. From her work it is evident that she was a great thinker and she tried to provide philosophical basis for Sahajayāna. According to her Buddhism is a philosophy of mind (*Cittadarśana*). According to her the universe is manifestation of *Citta* (mind). *Prajñā* and *Upāya* are also creation of mind, when *Prajñā* and *Upāya* are united it gives rise to *Mahāsukha*, which infact is the external forms of manifestation of this *Mahāsukha*. Another Siḍḍhācārya, Dombi-Herukā (77 A.D.) the disciple of Sahajayāna is famous through the publication of *Bauddha Gana and Doha*. He wrote treatises on Vajrayāna and Sahajayāna. However, his book of songs entitled *The Dombi-Gitika* occupies important place in Siddha literature. Following song which has been taken from *Dombi-Gitika* speak of the mystic depth and literary grace and poetic lyricism.

गङ्गा जऊना माझेँरे वहई नाई।
तँहि वुडिलि मातङ्गी पोहआ लीले पार करेइ।
वाहुत डोम्बी वाहलो डोम्बी वाटल भइल उकारा।
सद्गुरू पाअ पए जाइव पुनु जिनऊरा।।[24]

His other works, which have been translated into Tibetan, are of great importance from both philosophical and esoteric point of view. His Sanskrit work entitled *Sahajasiddhi* is also of great importance. He has initiated the doctrine of *Mahāsukha* and he has enumerated the four successive stages of happiness. They are: *Ānanda*, *Paramānanda*, *Viramānanda*, and *Sahajānanda*. Dombi Herukā also introduced the concept of goddess Nairtma which is incorporated in *Sādhanamālā*.[25] It appears from the opening lines of this *Sādhanā* that he followed the practices and the tenets of *Hevaja Tantra*:

डोम्बोहेरूकपादैर्देवीचक्रस्य भावना कथिता।
सञ्चिन्त्य सकलं तत्वं हेवज्रात् योगिनीतन्त्रात्।।

There is a great controversy about the founder of Sahajayāna. According to one tradition *Luipā* is acknowledged as the founder of Sahajayāna. According to another tradition *Sarahapāda* is the first Siddhācārya. Rahul Sanskritayana is of the opinion that *Sarahapāda* is Ādi-Siddha and he has tried to give some proofs also in support of his contention. According to yet another tradition Gorakhanātha is considered as the exponent of Sahajayāna. However, after evaluating the claims and counter claims for acknowledging the Ādi-Siddha we come to the conclusion that Sarahapāda was the Ādi-Siddha. Even Tarānātha while enumerating the tradition of teachers he thinks that *Sarahapāda* was the first who introduced and practiced *Sādhanā* of *Mahāmudrā* and attained its resultant Siddhi. *Sarahapāda* speaks of Yogani in his song and *Doha*. The talks of four kinds of a Yogani and esoteric path which leads to the attainment of Yogani Siddhi. Sarahapāda has been known as *Sarojvajr*, a Padam, Padamavajra and Rahulbhadra. According to some belief Saraha was born in Eastern India from a Brahmin father and Dakani mother. According to Tibetan oral tradition, he was born in Orissa. Tarānātha says, "that he was a great master of Veda and Vedānta from his very childhood. He studied Buddhist Tripiṭakas in Madhya Pradesh and he took initiation in Buddhism and he became Ācārya at Nālandā University. From all accounts *Sarahapāda* was a great teacher and Siddhācārya. He was one of the great thinkers and exponents of Sahajayāna. However, after analysing and evaluating the historical account and the teachings of Siddhācāryas, we come to the conclusion that Sahajayāna was a great religious and philosophical movement to rid the Buddhism from the superstitious believe and practices and make it simple, which could be beneficial and acceptable to the common mass.

The concept of Siddha has many connotations. *Encyclopedia of Indian Literature* says, "Siddha Literature (Tamil), there are many different connotations in which the term 'Siddha' is used; one, the mystic saints who have attained God-realization; two, those who have mastered the eight 'Siddhis' (attainments) like '*aṇimā*' (the ability to reduce oneself to an atom), '*mahimā*' (To enlarge oneself to the size of a mountain), '*laghimā*' (to make oneself as light as the air), '*garimā*' (to harden oneself like gold), '*prāpti*' (to exercise command on everyone), '*prakaśyam*' (to enter into another body), '*iśitvam*' (to accomplish anything at will) and '*vaśitvam*' (to mesmerize anyone at will); three, those who have attained yogic powers by controlling their breath and concentrating the mind on the six crucial centres of the body, enabling them to raise the *Kuṇḍalinī*; four, those Tāntrics who are set on the path of conquering death. Anyone of these is known as a 'Siddha' the whole Siddha tradition originated in the North with the Nava Siddha (*Sadoga, Satta, Ādi, Anādi, Mataṅga*, etc.)."[26]

Siddha tradition is very famous throughout India. Siddhas are known as saints and poets. They have made great contributions in almost all literary traditions of India. In Tamil Nadu the Siddha tradition originates with Thirumoola of the fifth century. He is considered as saint, mystic and a thinker. His work *Thirumandiram* is considered as the source of Śaivasiddhānta. *Encyclopedia of Indian Literature* writes, "We come across names like Bogar, who was a Chinese Taoist (a contemporary of Thirumoolar, so it is traditionally reported), Macha Muni (Machendranātha) and Gorakhar (Gorakhanātha), the two names figuring as among the nine original Nava Nātha Siddhas; Kaka Bhusundar (there is a Kaka Bhusunda of north-east India, the author of *Bhusuṇḍī Rāmāyaṇa*), Thirumaligai Devar (Malika Deva), Vālmīki, Nandī Eswwarar, etc. There are also Siddhas who are reported to have come from Egypt and China and composed poems in a colloquial Tamil tongue which are sung in folk tunes, and then, of course, the places are listed, according to tradition, where they are reported to have attained *Samādhi*.[27]

Siddhas have come from all walks of life. The main stream of philosophic and the literary tradition has accepted Siddhācāryas as a mystic poets and saints. They have been the voice of sanity and wisdom as they did not believe in any kind of institutionalized religions and practices. To them religion is not denominational rather it is an art of living with the fullness of creativity and bliss.

There is a great similarity between *Sahajayāna* and *Vaiṣṇava Tantra*. The *Pañcarātra* is known as Tāntric Vaiṣṇavism. *Pañcarātra Āgama* is the basis of Tāntric Vaiṣṇavism. The system is known as Pañcarātra, because it expounds five kinds of knowledge.[28] Like *Sahajayāna Vaiṣṇava Tantra* also accepts *Śakti* as the immanent principle. She is the creative matrix. Like *Prajñā* and *Upāya*, *Śiva* and *Śakti* are inseparable. They are like *Dharma* (substance) and *Dharmi* (attributes). Like Sahajayāna Tāntric Vaiṣṇavism also believe that with the worship of *Śakti*, man will not only attain liberation from the snares of life but will have control over celestial beings. These celestial beings become tool of his hand.[29]

Śrī Vidyā cult belongs to *Vaiṣṇava Tantra*. *Śrī* is the consort of Viṣṇu, *Śricakra* is the abode of Viṣṇu. *Śrī* is the womb of the universe. Due to the eternal co-existence and association of this immanent force (*Ādi Śakti*) divinity is perfect and absolute. *Śrī Vidyā* (divine science) and *Bhakti Mārga* (path of devotion) constitute Tāntric Vaiṣṇavism. Like Sahajayāna, in the Tāntric Vaiṣṇavism, we find the predominance of devotion. Both Sahajayāna and Tāntric Vaiṣṇavism are the paths that lead to the state of spiritual enjoyment and beatitude. Both in the state of Sahajayāna and Tāntric Vaiṣṇavism man becomes divinely intoxicated. The awakening of the *Kuṇḍalinī* creates a tremendous spiritual vibration. The *Sādhaka* starts enjoying the inner happiness of the infinite unity. The shedding of tears, the limping of the body, continuous laughing and dancing are some of the outward manifestations of the inner happiness. They are known as *Aṣṭabhāva*. These outward manifestations have been the hallmark of both the followers of Sahajayāna and Tāntric Vaiṣṇavism.

This inner experience of happiness is known as the state of God intoxicated. This has been wrongly misunderstood both in the Hindu and the Buddhist tradition that these outward manifestations are due to the consumption of alcohol. According to *Rudrayāmala* and *Brahāmayāmala* Vaśiṣṭha approached the Buddha to help him in obtaining perfection (Siddhi). According to *Rudrayāmala*, when Vaśiṣṭha approached Buddha he saw that the Buddha was surrounded by a large number of women drinking wine and engaged in obscene rites. Vaśiṣṭha requested the Buddha to help him in resolving his doubts and misunderstandings. As per the *Yāmala Tantra* he obtained enlightenment by incanting the *mantra* and the free use of five *Makāras*.[30]

According to *Rudrayāmala* Vaśiṣṭha went to China and he was initiated into Tāntricism which is known as Cinā-cāra. Being a follower of Vedic tradition Vaśiṣṭha was shocked and surprised at the strange rites of Cinā-cāra. However, he was asked to follow the path of Cinā-cāra for the attainment of liberation by Buddha, who was in a state of drunkenness.[31] We have already discussed in detail about the real meaning and significance of *Pañcamakāra Sādhanā* in the previous chapter. Whenever, a man succeeds in awakening his *Kuṇḍalinī* and making it united with *Śiva* at the *Saharāracakra* after piercing different *cakras*, he experiences the inner bliss (*Mahāsukha*) and after the drinking the pineal nectar man becomes God intoxicated. So, Buddha was not in the drunken state but he was in the state of supreme bliss and beatitude. Because of the use of *Pañcamakāra* and profound ignorance of its meaning and significance both Hindu and Buddhist Tantra have been greatly scandalized.

Both the Sahajayāna and Tāntric Vaiṣṇavism are the finest and the sublime form of spirituality. With the practice of Sahajayāna and Tāntric Vaiṣṇavism man's whole being is transformed into cosmic existence. He sees himself in everything. The feeling of one in all and all in one is the mystic realization of both Sahajayāna and Tāntric Vaiṣṇavism. In our view *Saundaryalaharī* is the canonical literature of Tāntric Vaiṣṇavism and not of the Samaya school of Śaktism, because it is a devotional hymn of praise (*stotra*). *Śrī Cakra* belongs to Tāntric Vaiṣṇavism. *Saundaryalaharī* is a Tāntric text. It dwells upon *Śrī Vidyā Sādhanā*. The unification of *Śiva* and *Śakti* is the sole objective of Tantra Sādhanā. *Śrī Cakra* is the abode of *Śiva*. *Śakti* also resides in *Śrī Cakra* along with *Śiva*. One can have the experience of *Śiva-Śakti* in *Śrī Cakra* with the help of *Bhakti Sādhanā*. Devotion and *mantra* constitute the *Śrī Vidyā* cult of Tāntric Vaiṣṇavism.

The Sahajiya cult of Bengali is a historical evidence of the development and growth of Tāntric Vaiṣṇavism as a distinct cult. The Vaiṣṇava Sahajiya as a distinct sect was originated and developed in Bengal before Caitanya. The elements of Tāntric Vaiṣṇavism are found in abundance in the life and teachings of Caṇḍidāsa who lived in fourteenth century. The mystic sect of Bāul has also its origin in Tāntric Vaiṣṇavism. The elements of mysticism and esotericism are the *kernels* of Bāul songs. The mysticism of Bāul sects speak of its Tāntric character.

Sahajayāna is the straight path of Herukā (*Kuṇḍalinī*), which brings the infinite bliss. The perfection is possible only with the help of Vajra Tārā (another Buddhist name) of the *Kuṇḍalinī* whose path is Avadhūtikā. The path of *Avadhūtikā* is straight and not zig-zag like that of *Lalanā* and *Rasanā*. In Hindu Tantra also *Kuṇḍalinī Sādhanā* is known as a *Ṛju Mārga* (straight path). Those who attain perfection with the help of Herukā are known as Siddhas.

Different *cakras* have been conceived to be the abodes of different mystical gods and goddesses, who grant different types of mystic power (Siddhi), and are known as different places of pilgrimages. The topmost *cakra* is known as *Mahāsukha Cākra* or *Uṣṇīṣakamala*. The central objective of Tantra Sādhanā is to cross these different *cakras* and reach the *Mahāsukha Cakra* or *Uṣṇīṣakamala*, the fountainhead of infinite bliss and beatitude.

The psychological and biological analysis will show that these *Cakras* control certain human tendency (*Vṛtti*). Whẹn a *Sādhaka* crosses certain *cakra*, he acquires mastery over the human tendencies controlled by this particular *cakra*. This gives the *Sādhaka* tremendous mental strength which in common parlance is known as occult power. That is why these different stations are known as sacred places of pilgrimage like Uddīyāna, Jālandhara, Pūrṇagiri and Kāmarūpa. The state of spiritual sublimity which remains ever unpolluted by the humming of the longings and desires is known as Sahaja. It is a stage of desirelessness and motionlessness. This state of Sahaja is created only when the sentient being buries his individual ego consciousness and merges into the *Mahāsukha*. When this state is attained the objective multiplicity are merged into the infinite unity and everything else dwindles into non-existence. The sentient being comes to the realization of Buddhahood, which is totality of all beings and existence. This is known as Sahajayāna.

REFERENCES

1. D. S. Sharma, *Hinduism Through the Ages* (1st ed.), Bhartiya Vidya Bhavan, Bombay, 1956. p. 131.
2. Tantra: *Its Mystic and Scientific Basis*, p. 119.
3. *Sādhanamālā*, vol. II, p. lv.
4. न कष्टकल्पनां कुर्यात् नोपवासी न च क्रियाम्।
   त्रानं शैचं न चैवात्र ग्रामधर्मविवर्जनम्।।
   न चापि वन्दयेछेवान् काष्ठपाषाणमृण्मयान्।
   पूजामस्यैव कायस्य कुर्यान्नित्यं समाहितः।
5. गम्यागम्यविकल्यन्तु भक्ष्याभक्ष्यन्तथैव च।
   पेयापेयं तथा मन्त्री कुर्यान्नैव समाहितः।
   सर्ववर्णसमुद्भूता जुगुणा नैव योषितः।
   सैव भगवती प्रज्ञा सम्वृत्या रूपमात्रिता।।
6. 1. Lāhiā, 2. Līlāpā, 3. Virūpā, 4. Bombipā, 5. Sābara (Sābaripā), 6. Saraha (Rāhulabhadra), 7. Kaṅkāli, 8. Mīna, 9. Gorkṣā, 10. Caurangi, 11. Vīṇā, 12. Śānti, 13. Tānti, 14. Carmari, 15. Khaḍga, 16. Nāgārajuna, 17. Kāṅhupā. 18. Kānarī (Āryadeva), 19. Thagana, 20. Nāda-pāda, 21. Śālipā (Śṛlipā-pāda), 22. Tiḷo-pā (Tailikapā), 23. Chatra, 24. Bhaḍra, 25. Dvikhaṇḍi, 26. Ajogi, 27. Kada-pāda, 28. Dhovī, 29. Kaṅkaṇa, 30. Kamabala, 31. Tenki, 32. Bhāde, 33. Tandhī, 34. Kukkuri, 35.

Cujbi (Kusūli), 36. Dharma, 37. Mahi, 38. Acintya, 39. Babhani, 40. Nalina, 41. Bhūsuku, 42. Indrabhūti, 43. Megha-pāda, 44. Kutharī, 45. Karmāra, 46. Jālandhari, 47. Rāhula, 48. Garbharī, 49. Dhakari, 50. Medinī, 51. Paṅkaja, 52. Ghaṇṭā, 53. Yogi, 54. Celuka, 55. Vaguri (Guncari), 56. Luñcaka, 57. Nirguṇa, 58. Jayānanda, 59. Carṣati, 60. Campaka, 61. Viṣana, 62. Bhali (Teli Taite), 63. Kimari, 64. Carpati, 65. Maṇibhadra, 66. Mekhalā, 67. Mankhalā, 68. Kalakala, 69. Kanthaḍi, 70. Daṇḍi, 71. Udhaḷḷ, 72. Kapāla, 73. Kila, 74. Puṣkara, 75. Sarvabhaksā, 76. Nāgabodhi, 77. Dārika, 78. Puttali, 79. Panaha, 80. Kakilā, 81. Anaṅga, 82. Lakṣmīṅkarā, 83. Sāmudra, 84. Bhalipā.

7. *Encyclopedia of Indian Literature*, vol. V, Sahitya Akademi, New Delhi, p. 4091.
8. मंगलबिहारी शरण सिन्हा, सिद्धो की सन्धा भाषा (पटना: बिहार हिन्दी ग्रन्थ अकादमी, 1973) पृ. 328.
9. (अ) राधाकान्त देव, शब्दकल्पद्रुम (पञ्चमो भाग:) व्याख्याकार-वरदा प्रसाद वसुना-हरिचरण वसुना (वाराणसी: चौखम्बा संस्कृत सीरीज), 1967, पृ. 1967 (आ) हलायुध भट्ट, हलायुध कोश, सं. जयशंकर जोशी (लखनऊ: हिन्दी समिति, 1967), पृ. 711.
10. *Bhāratīya Saṁskṛti aur Sādhanā*, vol. II, p. 256.
11. *Ibid.*, p. 282.
12. *Ibid.*, p. 284.
13. परैव सूक्ष्मा कुण्डलिनी शक्तिः। *Tantrāloka, II*, p. 77.
14. *Bhāratīya Saṁskṛti aur Sādhanā*, pp. 303-4.
15. *An Introduction to Tāntric Buddhism*, p. 144.
16. *Heveja Tantra*, part I, p. 36.
17. Saraha's *Dohakośa*, pp. 230-31.
18. *An Introduction to Tāntric Buddhism*, p. 173.
19. सिद्धिभिर्लक्षयेत् सिद्धं जीवन्मुक्तं तथैव च।
    अलौकिकगुणस्तस्य कदाचिद् दृश्यते ध्रुवम्।
    सिद्धिभि: परिहीनं तु नरं बद्धं तु लक्ष्येतु।।
    योगशिखोपनिषद् (प्रथम् अध्याय)
20. *Bhāratīya Saṁskṛti aur Sādhanā*, vol. II, p. 290.
21. P. 350— खड्गाञ्जनपादलेपान्तर्धानरसरमायनखेचरमूचरपातालसिद्धिप्रमुखा: सिद्धी: साध्येत्।
22. उत्तिष्ठत जाग्रत प्राप्य वरान्निबोधत।
    क्षुरस्य धारा निशिता दुरत्यया दुर्गं पथस्तत्कवयो वदन्ति।।14।। कठोपनिषद् 1.14.
23. *Catalogue due Fonds Tibetain*, 11, p. 212.
24. *Bauddha Gān and Doha*, p. 25.
25. *Sādhanamālā*, vol. II, p. 443.
26. *Encyclopedia of Indian Literature*, vol. V. p. 4092
27. *Ibid.*, p. 4093.
28. रात्रञ्च ज्ञानवचनं ज्ञानं पञ्चविधं स्मृतम्।
    तनेदं पञ्चरात्रञ्च प्रवदन्ति मनीषिण:।। *Nāradapañcarātra*, 1.1.44.
29. *Ahirbudhnya-Saṁhitā of the Pāñcarātrāgama*, vol. I, p. 259.
30. मद्यं मांसं तथा मत्स्यं मुद्रा मैथुनमेव च।।
    पुन: पुन: साधयिता पूर्वयौगी बभूव स:।।
31. अथासौ नं समालोका मदिरामदतिङ्कल:।
    प्राऊ बुद: प्रसन्नात्मा किमर्थं त्वमिहागत:।।

National Museum, New Delhi

1. Dhyānī Buddha, Pāla 12th Century A.D. Bihar

National Museum, New Delhi

2. Buddha in Earth Touch Mudrā, Pāla, 11th Century A.D. Eastern India

National Museum, New Delhi

3. Dhyāna Buddha, Vajrasattva Pāla, Bengal 11th Century A.D.

National Museum, New Delhi

4. Ādi Buddha (Bronze), Nepal, 16th Century A.D.

Courtesy Tibet House, New Delhi

5. Kālacakra (Union of Humanity with Divinity)
Top-Guhya Samāja, Vajradhara and Herukā Cakra Saṁvara

National Museum, New Delhi

6. Sarva Buddha Ḍākinī, (Bronze), Nepal, 18th Century A.D.

National Museum, New Delhi

7. Saṁvara with His Shakti (Painting), Nepal, 17th Century A.D.

National Museum, New Delhi

8. Hevajra (Bronze) Tibet, Early 17th Century A.D.

Courtesy Tibet House, New Delhi

9. *Central Figure :* Padmasaṁbhava
Seen clockwise from top centre : Zalandhara, Rahul, Medhinipā, Ghantapā Nirgunepā, Sangkazepā, Kotalipā, Zokipā, Dhokaripā, Dharmapā

National Museum, New Delhi

10. Buddhist Tantric Diety, 16th Century A.D. Nepal

Courtesy Tibet House, New Delhi

11. *Central Figure :* Śākya Muni
Seen clockwise from top centre : Manibadra, Mekhalapā, Odhilipā, Kandhāli Sakaripā, Kirabalā, Kapalipā, Dahulapā, Kalakalapā, Karnakāla

National Museum, New Delhi

12. Manjuśrī, 17th Century, Nepal

National Museum, New Delhi

13. Tārā, Pala 11th Century A.D. Bihar

National Museum, New Delhi

14. Vajra Tārā, Pāla 11th Century A.D.

National Museum, New Delhi

15. Avaloketeśvara, Pala, 8th Century A.D. Eastern India

National Museum, New Delhi

16. Buddhist Tantric Diety, 16th Century, Nepal

National Museum, New Delhi

17. Saṁvara and his Śakti (Painting) 17th Century, Nepal

National Museum, New Delhi

18. Manjuśrī, Utpala Dynasty, 11th Century A.D. Kashmir

5 Kālacakra Tantra

According to Buddhist mythology, the Buddha appeared one year after he attained *Nirvāṇa* under the *Boddhi*-tree at Bodhgayā. The Buddha appeared at vulture peak at Rājagṛha in the dress of a monk and he gave sermon, which is known as Perfection of Wisdom. As per the tradition and belief the Buddha simultaneously appeared at *Dhanyākaṭaka* in South India he propounded the most sublime and profound Tāntric treatise and practice, which is known as *Kālacakra Tantra*.

However, according to the other tradition and the sacred history *Kālacakra Tantra* was propounded by the Buddha one year before his *Mahāparinirvāṇa*. George. N. Roerich has identified *Dhanyākaṭaka* as Amravati in Guntur District of Tamilnadu [1]

According to the same tradition and belief the *Tantra* was expounded on the request of king Suchandra.[2]

Suchandra is considered an incarnation of Boddhisattva Vajrapāṇī and he is associated with preachings of many other. Tāntric teachings. According to Hindu tradition Sambhala has been mentioned in some Pauraṇic texts, according to which Sambhala is the birthplace of the Kalki—the incarnation of Viṣṇu. However, to my mind Sambhala does not belong to history. It is part of Buddhist mythology.

Kālacakra is the development of Vajrayāna. This school of Tāntric Buddhism has been greatly misunderstood by many. As per the Tāntric tradition the secrets of the tāntric practice have always been transmitted from preceptor to disciple. Tāntric texts and their esoteric practices have never been the subject of academic discussion. Though some valuable commentaries like *Vimal-prabhā* and *Śekoddesatikā* are available but in want of the secret knowledge of the tāntric practice, it would be very difficult to critically examine and evaluate *Kālacakra Tantra* from academic point of view. However, we are trying to provide to the academic community to present *Kālacakra Tantra* both from academic and esoteric perspectives.

Kāla (time) has been understood in different religions and philosophical traditions differently. *Kāla* is conceived as supreme force by some religious and philosophical traditions.

Gopinath Kaviraj considers *Kāla* as the supreme form of all elements. He says.

> "*Kāla* is in the form of supreme Godhood". When the *Śakti* manifested in

> the form of phenomenal world *Śakti* remains immanent as इदमहं because *Jñāna* (knowledge) and the *Kriyā* (activity) being one of the causal form of activity and the world as manifestation of its knowledge form, it remains one with the *Ātman*. This form of supreme reality as God or *Kālaśakti* is known as *Kālatattva*."[3]

Kālacakra is esoteric system of meditational practice. The central objective of *Kālacakra Tantra* is to attain mystic unification of *Śūnyatā* and *Karuṇā*. The introduction of *Kālacakra Tantra*[4] is attributed to *Māñjūśrī* and its commentary, *Vimal Prabhā* was written in one thousand two hundred *Granthas* by one Puṇḍarīka.[5]

According to Dr. Bhattacharya[6] the *Kālacakrayāna* embodies in its teachings and practices all the best of Vajrayāna, Nathism and Sahajayāna. Dr. Gopinath Kaviraj[7] is of the opinion that the *Kālacakra*, which implies the unity of *Prajñā* and *Upāya*, technically known as Vajrayoga, represents in fact the state of Supreme oneness.

According to some *Kālacakra* means cycle of time and the *Kālacakra Tantra* presents three such cycles external, internal and alternative. The external and the internal cycles deal with the normal time while the alternative cycle stands for gaining liberation from the external and internal cycles. Alexander Berzin writes :

> "The structure of the external and internal cycles are analogous, similar to the parallel between macrocosm and microcosm discussed in Western philosophy. This means that the same laws that govern a universe also pertain to atoms, the body and our experience of life. The practices of the alternative cycles also follows this structure so as to allow us to engage with and surmount these forces in an efficient manner. Such mimicking is, in fact, one of the distinguishing features of the *Anuttarayoga Tantra* technique."[8]

Normal time exercises a great impact on our cycles of birth and death. Each lives unfold the Karmic potential from our previous life. These cycles are known in *Kālacakra* system as winds of *Karma*. Karmic potentialities give rise to spectrum of impulses and motivation, which control our lives. Time has neither beginning nor, however, the spectrum of change would always be associated with the passage of time. The alternate cycles of time brings about desirable spiritual change as transformation in one's life due to the esoteric practice of *Tantra*. Alexander Berzin writes :

> "The process begins with the *Kālacakra* initiation. Properly empowered, we engage in generation and then complete stage meditational practice

> in the form of the *Buddha*-figure called *Kālacakra*. Through these two stages, we access and utilize the subtlest level of our mind to see reality. Remaining continually focussed on reality with it eliminates forever confusion and its instincts, thus bringing liberation from the external and internal cycles of time. This is possible because our basis of Tantra, our individual clear light mind, underlies each moment of experience and, like time, it has no end. Once our subtlest mind is freed from the deepest cause giving rise to the impulses of energy that perpetuate cycles of time and bondage to them, it gives rise, instead, to the bodies of a Buddha, in the form of *Kālacakra*."[9]

Kāla has been regarded in India as Supreme force by different religious and philosophical traditions. In the passage of time there has been harmonious blending between the Hindu and the Buddhist systems of religious practices and thoughts. Hence, it is no wonder that innumerable Hindu deities have been incorporated in the *Maṇḍalas* of *Śrī Kālacakra*. *Śrī Kālacakra* has been conceived as Lord Supreme. Biswanath Banerjee writes :

> "The *Kālacakra* system and the concept of *Kālacakra* as the Supreme Lord are two bright examples of the process of cultural fusion as going on in India. The Lord *Kālacakra* has been depicted (I.21) in the *Maṇḍala* as the central figure with Hindu gods as the guardians of directions (*digrakṣa-pālāḥ*). In the *Maṇḍala* in the east is *Indra*, *Agni* in the south-east, *Yama* in the south, demon (*danu*) in the south-west, *Varuṇa* in the west, *Vāyu* in the north-west, *Hara* in the north-east, above is Brahmā and down Viṣṇu along with their attendants, and in the middle is *Kālacakra*, the absolute."[10]

Kālachakra Tantra is the culmination of *Vajrayāna* system of esoteric practices and thoughts. Hence *Śrī Kālacakra*, the supreme godhood is philosophically and esoterically is of the same nature as the conception of *Vajara-sattva* as found in different Vajrayāna texts. *Kālacakra* is the unity of *Prajñā* and *Upāya*. The Bodhicitta the ultimate reality, which symbolizes the Supreme Bliss (*Mahāsukha*), the deity is without origination and destruction and is embodiment of Supreme knowledge. He is considered as the Supreme Lord and creator of all the Buddhas and Ādibuddhas.

Both in Hindu and Buddhist Tantra *bīja-mantras* are of great esoteric importance and significance. The *Vimalaprabhā* throws some light on the esoteric importance of *Bīja-mantras* while explaining the term *Kālacakra*, *ka* stands for causality, *la* means absorption or dissolution, *ca* signifies the unstable mind and *kra* denotes cycle of change and transformation.[11] *Kālacakra* is a state of unification of *Prajñā* and *Upāya*,

Śūnyatā and *Karuṇā*. As we are aware that every man and woman are hibernated cosmic being and hence *Tantra* considers body as the epitome of the macrocosm. The belief in the identity of the microcosm and macrocosm is the corner stone of Tantra Sādhanā. The objective of *Kālacakra* is to transcends the cycle of birth and death and attain Buddhahood. To transcend the cycle of birth and death we will have to go beyond the influence of time. It is in the flow of the *Prāṇavāyu* time reveals itself and if a *Sādhaka* gets control over the *Prāṇavāyu* through esoteric practice, such as meditation and Vipāsanā, he can have the control over the time (*Kāla*) and thereby he can attain the state of infinite bliss (*Mahāsukha*). *Tantra* prescribes *Ṣaḍaṅga-yoga* to have the absolute control over time and attain the state of *Mahāsukha*.

Tantra explains the whole creation as the organic functions of the body. *Tantra* considers body as the only medium through which *Nirvāṇa* can be realised. Some of the Tāntric texts like *Śrī Kālacakratantra-Rāja* identifies the universe with the body and it locates the seas, rivers, mountains and the planets in the different parts of the body. *Tantra* believes that there is an isomorphic relation between human body and the universe, between microcosm and the macrocosm.

Further, it is said that all the letters and syllables of *Kālacakra* imply certain mystic meaning; *Ka* is the *bīja-mantra* of effect Brahma (*Kārya Brāhmaṇa*). Thus *Kālacakra* stands for the merger of unit consciousness into the original cause-potency, which is *Śūnyatā*, *i.e.* the pure consciousness, the supreme subjectivity. Like the *Vajra-yāna*, *Kālacakrayāna* aims at the attainment of spiritual salvation, for the individual as well as the mankind. Thus, it is a cult of collective welfare like Hindu Tantra, which can be summarized in one sentence: *Ātma mokṣartaṁ jagathitayaca*.

Philosophically speaking the first step in the process of esoteric practice is to identify the innately misconceived the *I*, as inherently existence. According to the schools of Sāṅkhya and Vedānta, the bondage is the erroneous identification of *I* with non-self. According to Buddhism there is no inherent existence except *Bodhicitta* everything is in a state of flux. The Dalai Lama writes :

> "If you do not have a fairly clear sense of an inherently existent I, you will mistake the refutation as negating the I itself rather than a specific reification of the I. Śāntideva's *Engaging in the Bodhisattva Deeds (byand chub sems dpa'i spyod pa la 'jug pa, Bodhisattva-Caryāvatara,* IX. 140) says:
>
> *Without contacting the superimposed existent,*
> *Its non-existence cannot be apprehended.*
>
> If an image of the object of negation does not appear well to the mind, the meaning of the selflessness that negates its cannot be ascertained."[12]

As we are aware that any endeavour at a philosophical exposition belongs to the sphere of diversity and it is only relative. One may talk of historical development of Buddhist thought, however, one would remain aware that the practical end, which one would like to define and understand, is necessarily lands one into the metaphysical polemic. Buddhism itself have undergone great change and transformation, its schools and sub-schools are bewildering. The indescribability of the ultimate reality is the basic concern of Buddhism and Hinduism. Professor Radhakrishnan writes,

> "If the Buddha declined to define the nature of the Absolute or if he contented himself with negative definitions, it is only indicated that absolute being is above all determinations.[13] Why, they, did Buddha not admit in expressed terms the reality of the absolute. Buddha refused to describe the absolute, for that would be to take a step out of the world of relativity, the legitimacy of which he was the first to contest. The absolute is not a matter of empirical observation. The world of experience does not reveal the absolute anywhere within its limits.[14]

The Buddha was aware of the antinomical character of the reason. The Buddha did examine and evaluate various theories of reality prevalent at that time and rejected all of them. The Buddha transcends the consciousness of conflict in reason and resolves by rising above the plane of reason. This is dialectic. The Buddha says, "To hold that the world is eternal or to hold that is not, or to agree to any other of the propositions you adduce, Vaccha, is the jungle of theorizing, the wilderness of theorising, the tangle of theorising, the bondage and the shackles of theorising, attended by ill, distress, perturbation and fever; it conduces not to detachment, passionlessness, tranquillity, peace, knowledge and wisdom of *Nirvana*. This is the danger I perceive in these views which makes me discard them all."[15] The *Brahmajāla Sutta* of *Digha Nikāya* considers all speculations as dogmatism (*diṭṭhi-vāda*), because it is aware of the interminable nature of the conflict which could be resolved only by rising to the higher plane of criticism. Criticism is in itself a freedom as it liberates human mind from all kinds of passions and entanglements. D.L. Snell Grove writes, "Now, the basic philosophical position of *Tantras* is *Mādhyamikā*. It asserts the fundamental unity of *Nirvāṇa* and *Saṁsāra*, of mystical and sensual experience, and it regards all means as relative to the needs of the practitioner. It is in fact, *Tantras* that are realized to some extent the serious consequences referred to above, but only to some extent, for the process is checked by the conservative tendencies represented by the *Yogācāra*, and the whole movement remains essentially Buddhist after all, as subsequent developments show."[16] The central objective of the *Kālacakra Tantra* is to get a clear sense of the reified status of the *I* as inherently existent. Each one of us are greatly rooted in strong belief in reified *I*, that we identify with it and as such we have the feeling that it is not true than nothing is true. Chandrakirti rightly asserts that there is no self other than the aggregates because apart from the aggregates, its conception does not exist. Dalai Lama says, "With such conviction, the decision reached is that the *I* cannot be found under such analysis; this shows, not that the *I* does not exist, but that it does not inherently exist as it was identified as seeming to it in the first essential. This infindability is emptiness itself, and realization of it is realization of emptiness, selflessness."[17]

Kālacakra Tantra refers to immutable bliss and various empty forms. Time stands for absolute bliss (*Mahāsukha*) and wheel refers to different empty forms. *Kālacakra* recognizes two kinds of emptiness aspected and unaspected. The unaspected emptiness denotes concordant ultimate for a wisdom of consciousness that realizes emptiness. Aspected emptiness stands for empty forms. The object of negation of aspected emptiness is material phenomena composed of particles. Thus, the aspected emptiness denotes the various forms, or physical objects, that are beyond materiality.

While making destination between *Kālacakra Tantra* and *Guhyasamāja Tantra,* Dalai Lama is of the opinion that *windyoga* is mentioned in *Kālacakra Tantra* and *Guhyasamāja Tantra* but *Kālacakra Tantra* does not give importance to *Windyoga* because empty forms are not achieved by way of wind.[18] I think there is some misunderstanding about *Windyoga*. The *Windyoga* is not Sāddhanā, it is Sāddhanāṅga both according to Hindu and Buddhist-esoteric tradition. *Kālacakra* stands for the unification of immutable bliss (*Mahāsukha*) and empty form (*Śūnyatā*) the objective of the esoteric practices of *Kālacakra* is to attain Buddhahood and hence it is imperative on the part of practitioners to maintain delicate balance between external, internal and alternative *Kālacakras*. The external *Kālacakra* denotes the phenomenon world which constitutes homes, mountains, constellation of stars etc. The internal *Kālacakra* refers to the *Sādhaka's body, i.e.* winds, drops of essential fluid, nervous system and nature of channels. The most important is the alternative *Kālacakra* refers esoteric techniques of purifying the external and internal *Kālacakra*. The *Condensed Kālacakra Tantra* deals in detail the three *Kālacakra*—external, internal and alternative subject matters. The ten letters of *bīja-mantra* of *Kālacakra, haṁ kṣhaḥ ma la va ra ya* are only esoteric way to understand the importance and significance of external, internal and alternative *Kālacakra*. Dalai Lama writes, "The *mantra* is called the powerful one having ten aspects (*ṛṇaṁ bcu dheng Iden*). In *haṁ kṣhaḥ ma la va ra ya,* there are the seven letters – *h, kṣḥ, m, b, u, r* and *y* – as well as the *visārga* (in *kṣhaḥ* which appears as a holy moon) the *anusvāra* (in *haṁ*) and the vowel *a* which is the 'life' (of the consonants), thereby making ten. Also there is an eleventh symbol, the *nāda* (a wiggly line rising from the *dat* on top)."[19] These *Bīja-mantra* seem to be a nonsensical syllables for the layman but for the initiates they are powerful esoteric tools to awaken the dormant divinity which is the only way through which one can attain Buddhahood.

According to Mahāyāna treatise the *Aṣṭasahasrikā-Prajñā-Pāramitā* the *Prajñā-*

Pāramitā-Dharaṇī was evolved and from this again evolved *Prajñā Pāramitā-Mantra*. From the *Prajñā-Pāramitā Mantra Bīja-mantra* was entered. The in centralism of *bīja-mantra praṁ*, *Śūnyatā* gets transformed into goddess *Prajñā-pāramitā*. The *bīja-mantra* refers to some particular god and goddess. The *bīja-mantra 'a'* represents Vairocana, *'ya'* Akṣobha, *'ra'* Ratnasambhava, *'ba'* Amitābha and *'la'* Amoghasiddhi. The *bīja-mantra 'Huiṁ'* represents Vajra-Sattva. The vowel *'a'* being the most powerful acoustic vibration and the first and the independent *Dhvani* (sound) represents *Śūnyatā* or *Prajñā*.

According to *Kālacakra Tantra* our body is said to exist not only on the physical level but also on subtle level about which we are profoundly ignorant. The ordinary physical body which is composed of physical elements, undergoes change, decay and death but there exists a subtle body, which is called *Vajra* body in Buddhist tradition and *Kāraṇa Śarīra* in Hindu tradition. The *Vajra Body* or the *Kāraṇa Śarīra* does not undergo any decay and death, as it is indestructible. Our physical body is constituted of nervous system the *Vajra body* is constituted of innumerable *nāḍīs* (channels) which keep flowing the *prāṇa* (the vital energy) and *bindus* (drops) which are the source of our true being and pure bliss. The purpose of Tāntric meditation is to become aware and alive of this *Vajra body* and to attain and experience the divine effulgence.

Dalai Lama, Tosong-ka-pa and Jaffrey Hopkins write, "With respect to the 'Vajra Vechicle', the Stainless Light (*Vimalaprabhā*). A commentary on the *Kālacakra Tantra* by Rik-den-pad-ma-kar-po (Rigs-Ida-pad-ma-dkar-po) and Emanation Body of Avalokiteśvara) says, "*Vajra*, means the indivisible and the great unbreakable. That is the Mahāyāna; this Mahāyāna is the *Vajra* vehicle. It is a combination as one taste of the *Mantra* mode having the nature of the cause. The meaning of '*Vajra* Vehicle' is given through taking '*Vajra*' as an indivisibility of the effect the *Mantra* mode—and the cause—the Perfections mood. Here, 'cause and effect' refer to totally supreme emptiness and supreme immutable bliss. The Brief Explication of Initiations (*Śkhoddeśa*) (included in the *Kālacakra* cycle) says:

> That bearing the form of emptiness is the cause,
> That bearing immutable compassion is the effect.
> Emptiness and compassion indivisible
> Are called the mind of enlightenment."[20]

The Vajrayāna has referenced to Highest *Yoga Tantra* and it does not belong to lower *Tantra*. One can realize the supreme bliss in the system of *Kālacakra* when one attains the meditative stabilization. The other three lower *Tantras* do not concern the cause vehicle. The cause vehicle is as means through which one experiences spiritual progress and effect vehicle is one, which is progressing. In short an effect vehicle is through which one is progressing and cause vehicle is that by which are progressed. The word effect stands for a bond, body, resources and deeds, which are a Buddha's palace, body, fortune and activity. Shraddha-karavarma's *Introduction to the meaning of the Highest Yoga Tantras* says, "It is called 'Effect' because one enacts the ways of thoroughly pure body, resources, abode and deeds".

The basis of purification is the Buddha nature. The Buddha nature is viewed in two ways. First is considered as positive phenomenal, which is clear light nature of the mind and the other is the emptiness of inherent existence of the mind, a negative phenomenal. Dharmakīrti has made a comment on these two aspects. In the commentary on (Diṅnāga's) "Compendium (of teachings) on Valid Cognition" (*ṣhad ma ṛṇaṁ'grel, Pramanana-varittika*).[21]

According to *Kālacakra Tantra Nirvāṇa* is state beyond the reach of mind and senses. Buddha has been compared with a physician and *Sādhaka* with a patient taking the medicine from Buddha's doctrine in order to be cured from the basic illness and to achieve a state of health necessary for living altruistic life. In Mahāyāna tradition the concept of Boddhisattva occupies an important position both from philosophical and esoteric point of views. Boddhisattva is to engender an altruistic motivation to become enlightened, which, through esoteric practice has become so spontaneous that it is as strong outside as it is within meditation. This is known as *Bodhi Citta*. It is a altruistic intention to become enlightened. It has got two aspects the first is a motivation for the services and blessedness of others and second for once own attainment of Buddhahood. It is in keeping with the highest form of *Anuttara Yoga*. The latter is seen as a means for attaining the first through the motivation. It is to attain once own enlightenment which must be accomplished first in order to bring about others welfare, service to others is prime in terms of motivation. The enlightenment of Buddha is considered as an example to perpetuate the tradition to live altruistic life. Buddha being enlightened person, he knew the predisposition and interest of the other being. Between the two bodies of Buddha, truth body and form body, *Dharmạkāya Nirmanakāya* Boddisattava prefers *Nirmanakāya* since it is through physical form that one can accomplish altruistic mission in life. Though the *Dharmakāya* and *Nirmanakāya* accompany each other and are achieved together the Bodhisattva emphasis is achieving *Nirmanakāya* in order to appear in myriad forms suitable to the interests and dispositions of *Sādhakas*.

Dalai Lama says, "Buddhahood, which such altruistically oriented knowledge and activity, is the final aim– in the sense that it is the path of no more learning, there being no further development of new levels of understanding or compassion. It is a beginning in the sense that for the first time one can serve others to one's full capacity, forever, unceasingly, as long as there are beings who need to be helped, and that is forever.

"This heroic effort to bring about others' welfare is conceived in terms of there being (1) a basis for such purification and transformation within US, (2) objects a purification, (3) a path that serves as a means of purification, and (4) a fruit of that purification."[22]

The clear light nature of the mind has got complete exposition in *Anuttarayoga*

Tantra such as, *Guhyasamāja Tantra* and *Kālacakra Tantra*. It has got a place of importance in *Maitreya* sublime continuum of the great vehicle. And it is considered as the basis of all the phenomena both of cyclic existence and of *Nirvāṇa*. Buddhism does speak of suffering as the first noble truth in order to provide a philosophical foundation for the radical transformation of the condition of the suffering to a state of *Nirvāṇa*. From the Buddhist point of view all phenomena except emptiness are called *Saṁvṛti-Satya*. *Saṁvṛti* is understood as that which covers. Truth here is specified as meaning that which exists. The way it appears and only ignorant person takes objects such as table or mind to exists the way they appear. These objects are truth for ignorance.

According to Buddhism only emptiness exists the way it appears indirect perception and this emptiness in only truth. This does not mean that other phenomena do not exist. Both emptiness and all other phenomena exist. Objects of knowledge-existent—being divided into two classes—*Saṁvṛtisatya* and *Paramārthic Satya*. However, ultimate consciousness is not final consciousness, a Buddhas' omniscient consciousness, but it is non-conceptual consciousness. The Dalai Lama writes, "Thus, both the clear light nature of the mind and the emptiness of inherent existence of the mind are the Buddha nature, the nature of the mind that allows for transformation into Buddhahood. The Buddha nature is, therefore, the basis of purification and transformation in that it is that from the company of which defilements are removed."[23]

According to B. Bhattacharya[24] the *Kālacakrayāna* embodies in its teaching and historical practices all the best of *Vajrayāna*, *Nāthism* and *Sahajayāna*. Dr. Gopinath Kaviraj[25] is of the opinion that the *Kālacakrayāna* which implies the unity of *Prajñā* and *Upāya*, technically known as *Vajrayoga*, represents in fact the state of Supreme Oneness.

Thus, *Śrī Kālacakra* represents the metaphysical concept of reality, which is one, eternal and transcendental. In *Śekoddesaṭīkā*[26] at salutation offering to the deity *Kālacakra*, he has been addressed as *'Prama-kṣara'*, *'Śūnyatā-Karuṇā-bhinnaṁ bodhi-cittaṁ yad akṣaram'*. We find here a strong insistence on the ideal of oneness of *Śūnyatā* and *Karuṇā*, which constitute *Kālacakra* or *Vajra-Sattva*. The word *Akṣara*[27] means that which undergoes no change. It conveys the sense of reality, which is indestructible. Nevertheless we must observe that the monotheistic concept of Godhead of *Kālacakrayāna* is analogous to what we find in the Tāntric school of non-dualistic thought of both Hindu and Buddhist Āgamic Systems.

Buddhist Tantra is normally divided into three schools *Vajrayāna*, *Sahajayāna* and *Kālacakra*. There is great similarity between the schools of Hindu Tantra mainly *Śākta Tantra*, *Vaiṣṇava Tantra* and *Śaiva Tantra*. The *Kālacakra Tantra*, which is the highest *Yoga Tantra* of Buddhism, has been greatly misunderstood. Waddell writes, "In the tenth century A.D. the Tāntric phase developed in Northern India, Kashmir and Nepal, into the monstrous and polydemonist doctrine, the *Kālacakra*, with its demoniacal Buddhas which incorporated the Mantrayāna practices, and called itself the Vajrayāna or the 'Thunderbolt-vehicle', and its followers were Vajrācārya 'followers of the Thunderbolt'."[28]

Further, he says, "the extreme development of Tāntric phase was reached with the *Kālacakra*, which, although unworthy of being considered as a philosophy, must be referred to here as a doctrinal basis. It is merely a coarse Tāntric development of the Ādi-Buddha theory combined with the puerile mysticism of the *Mantra-Yāna*, and it attempts to explain creation and the secret powers of nature, by the union of the terrible Kālī, not only with the Dhyānī Buddhas, but even with Ādi-Buddha himself. In this way Ādi-Buddha, by meditation evolves a procreative energy by which the awful Sambharā and other dreadful Ḍākinī fiend, all of the Kālī-type, obtain spouses as fearful as themselves, yet spouses who are regarded as reflexes of Ādi-Buddhas and the Dhyānī Buddhas. And demoniacal 'Buddhas', under the name of *Kālacakra*, *Herukā*, *Acala*, *Vajra-bhairava*, etc., are credited with powers not inferior to those of the celestial Buddhas themselves, and withal ferocious and blood thirsty; and only to be conciliated by constant worship of themselves and their female energies, with offerings and sacrifices, magic circles, special *mantra*-charms, etc."[29]

From the above enumeration of *Kālacakra* by Waddell, it seems he had no understanding of Buddhist Tantra. Demoniacal Buddha as understood by Waddell is not demoniacal or terrible Buddha. Buddha is essentially an embodiment of *Kuruṇā* (compassions) and *Śūnyatā* (emptiness). The word *Kālacakra* means the wheel of time. In Tibetan it is called " 'Dus-Kyi-' K'or-lo", which means the cycle of time. M.M. H.P. Shastri writes, "What is *Kālacakrayāna*? The word *Kāla* means time, death and destruction, *Kālacakra* is the wheel of destruction, and *Kālacakrayāna* means the vehicle for protection against the wheel of destruction."[30]

Kālacakra is an esoteric school of the highest form of Buddhist Tantra. Normally, the people, who do not have deeper understanding of Tāntricism, do get puzzled by Tāntric practice of *Deity-yoga*. These deities are not personal God of theistic religion. They are spiritual forms in which Buddhas manifested in order to help people to overcome their shortcomings and defilements. These mystic forms of Buddha represent enlightened state of spirituality and they symbolize compassion and wisdom. Avalokiteśvara symbolizes, compassion and Mañjūśrī represents wisdom. *Kālacakra* stands for the mystic abilities to face all situations, and power to resolve difficulties. The mystic practice structured around the *Deity-yoga* provides esoteric tools to overcome the shortcomings and march towards the path of enlightenment. It seems Waddell did not have the understanding of the practice of *Deity-yoga* and hence out of ignorance he described the *Kālacakra* deity as demoniacal Buddha. The text *Śrī Kālacakra Tantra* has expounded the esoteric and the spiritual significance of practice of *Kālacakra* Deity.[31] The study of *Śrī Kālacakra Tantra* does not confirm the statement the *Kālacakrayāna* is that school of Tāntric Buddhism which introduced the demoniacal Buddhas in its province,—at least it is not to the main characteristic through which the school should be recognized. In the beginning of the text we find that King Sucandra approached the Omniscient Lord Buddha with salutation and asked of him the yoga of the *Śrī Kālacakra* which is the way to salvation of all people of the Kali age.[32]

According to *Śri Kālacakra* text the *Kālacakra* is a mystic system of yoga, which, incorporates, the practice of *Maṇḍala* (mystic diagram) and initiation (*abhiṣeka*). As per this text the entire cosmos with all its elements and objects are situated, in our body and the different dimensions of time like day, night, fortnight, month, year etc., are situated in the different parts of human body.

The esoteric and the philosophical concept of Kālacakra has been discussed in detail by Abhinava Gupta in his celebrated work *Tantrāloka*. There is great similarity between *Tantrāloka* and *Śrī Kālacakra* regarding the spiritual signification and importance of *Kālacakra*. Abhinava Gupta in his *Tantrāloka* has expounded the doctrine of *Kāla* (time) and the spiritual process of keeping oneself above the influence of cycle of time. Abhinava Gupta while explaining the concept of time in all its dimensions has made reference to the importance of *prāṇa* and *apāna* which is organically related with our nervous system like the practice of *Kālacakra* as expounded in the text entitled *Śrī Kālacakra Tantra*.

The *Tantrāloka* also discusses the yogic practices of controlling *prāṇa* and *apāna* through which alone one could have the control over *Kāla* (time). The *Vimala Prabhā*, a commentary on *Kālacakra* has discussed in detail the esoteric and the philosophical importance of *Kālacakra Tantra*. According to this text *Vimala Prabhā*, *Śri Kālacakra* is accepted as *Śūnyatā* and *Karuṇā*. He is the symbol of *Prajñā* and *Upāya*. The deity *Śri Kālacakra* is beyond the origination and destruction. He is divine effulgence (*mahāsukha)*. He is the originator of all the Buddhas having three *kāyas, trikāladarśī*. He is the ultimate and primordial Buddha. The central objective of *Kālacakra Tantra* is to attend perfect enlightenment and to work for the enlightenment of all the sentient beings. S.B. Das Gupta writes, "That the conception of Kālacakra is substantially the same as the conception of *Vajra-sattva* and that Kālacakrayāna is not a distinct school of Tāntric Buddhism, but a particular name for the Vajrayāna school, will be clear also from the text Sekoddesa-ṭika,[33] which is a commentary on the Śekoddeseka section of the Kālacakra Tantra. There it is said that the ultimate, immutable and unchangeable one, remaining in the skylike *dharma-dhātu* (the element underlying all the *dharmas*) is called *Kāla*; it itself is the immutable knowledge. *Cakra* implies the unity of the three kinds of existence—the manifestations of *Kāla*. It (the *cakra*) is the body of Lord—point-like, containing the potency of the existence of the universe. *Kālacakra*, therefore, implies exactly the same as the unity of *Prajñā* and *Upāya*."[34]

However, S.B. Dasgupta has some misunderstanding about the esoteric and the philosophical basis of different schools of Buddhist Tantra. In his exposition of schools of Tāntric Buddhism, he writes that the Buddhist Tantras are generally divided into three schools *viz., i.e. Vajrayāna, Kālacakrayāna* and *Sahajayāna*. He further writes that we do not know on the authority of what texts this division of schools have been made. We personally feel that these divisions of schools of Tāntric Buddhism are not arbitrary or without any esoteric and philosophical basis. The *Vajrayāna, Sahajayāna* and *Kālacakrayāna* represent the different phases of spiritual enlightenment. They are metaphysical schools of Buddhist Tantra from which the central core of different sects of Buddhist Tantra was born. Different forms of Buddhist Tantra do not make any difference to a man so long as he is truly dedicated to the realization of the vast and incomprehensible *Kālacakra*. The mysticism of *Kālacakra* combines science and speculation, and knowledge and realization.

The different schools of Buddhist Tantra are divided according to the different deities practiced and esoteric procedure structured. As we are aware that the *Tantra* is full of symbols which are of great esoteric importance and significance. The every syllable of *Kālacakra* is pregnant with profound esoteric and philosophical significance. The *Bīja-mantra 'ka'* represents causality in which the final absorption is indicated by *Bīja-mantra 'la'*. Sekoddesa-tikā writes, "*Kāla*, therefore, means the state of absorption in the original cause-potency, this is the state of *Śūnyatā*; it is the pure consciousness or the principle of subjectivity. *Cakra* on the other hand means the principle of knowability, or the cycle of the world-process (*jñeyā-kāraṁ jagac-cakraṁ jñeyaṁ traidhātukaṃ ananta-bhāvalakṣanaṁ cakraṃ*), which is also the principle of *Upāya*. *Kālacakra*, therefore, means the absolutely unified principle of *Prajñā* and *Upāya*.[35] The syllable *'ka'* indicates unruffled causality in which there should be the final absorption as is indicated by the syllable *'la'*; *'ca'* indicates the unsteady mind, and *'kra'* means the series of event or the process.[36] According to Buddhist Tantra *Nirvāṇa* is always from a state that requires healings and to a healed state of release in Buddhism. The Buddha is compared with a physician and the practitioner viewed as a patient taking medicine from the Buddhist doctrine in order to be cured from a basic illness, *i.e.* from *Avidyā* (ignorance). It means the objective of Buddhism is to cure the sentient being from the illness of ignorance and defilement and to achieve state of spiritual health necessary for leaving an altruistic life.

The enlightenment of the Buddha is considered as a means to bring about others on the path of *Dharma* and rid the mind from defilement. The Buddha being enlightened one he is equipped with all possible mystic powers and esoteric techniques to be employed in curing the mind of the sentient being from illness according to the requirements and predisposition of each and every sentient being. From the two *kāyas*, the *Truth Body* and *Form Body* the *Tantras* preference is *Form Body* because it is through the physical form that one can help other in getting cured from the illness. In the *Tantra* different kinds of motivation has been described. According to some one would prefer the Boddhisattva's motivation like that of a king because, according to this view only after attaining full enlightenment one would be in a position to help others. There is other motivation, which is considered to be more profound. According to this motivation, one would like to be a boatman and prefer rather enjoy to arrive at the shore of enlightenment in the company of everyone else. There is another motivation described as like a shepherd. And they want to attend enlightenment in the company of others like a shepherd returning home at the rear of the flock. His holiness Dalai Lama writes, "What distinguishes someone as a Bodhisattva is to engender an altruistic intention to become enlightened, which, through training, has become so spontaneous that it is as strong outside as it is within meditation. This is called *Bodhicitta* literally "mind of enlightenment" but more like "mind towards enlightenment", "mind directed toward enlightenment." As Maitreya's ornament for clear Realization (*mngon ṛtogs ṛgyon, abhisamayālaṁkāra*) say:

> Mind generation is asserted as a wish for complete. Project enlightenment for the sake of others. This has been formulated into a definition of *Bodhicitta* or, as I translate it, "altruistic intention to become enlightened";

A main mental consciousness induced by an aspiration for [bringing about] others' welfare and accompanied by an aspiration to one's enlightenment.[37]

Buddhism is a philosophy of mind (*cit-darśana*). Philosophically speaking *Kālacakra* is the *Bodhicitta*. He is ultimate, immutable transcendental reality in form of motionless supreme bliss (*acintya-mahāsukha*). The philosophical basis of attaining enlightenment is to experience *Bodhicitta* both as emptiness and wisdom. There are two ways to bring about purification Buddha nature. One is the clear light nature of mind and other is emptiness of inherent existence of mind. Both these views are well-discussed and defined by Dharmakirti's commentary on Dignag's "Compendium [of teachings] on valid cognition."[38]

According to Dharmakirti the nature of mind is clear light. Defilements are adventitious. There is great similarity between the Buddhist concept of *Bodhicitta* and the *Vedantic* concept of *Ātman*. Both according to Buddhist and the *Vedantic* view defilements do not subsist in the very nature of the mind or *ātman* desire; hatred and ignorance do not reside in the very nature of mind, because the nature of mind is clear light and defilements can be removed without destroying the mind. According to *Vedānta* also the *māyā* does not reside in the very nature *ātman*. The realization of *ātman* is like the experience of *Bodhicitta*, which brings about enlightenment. The exposition of the philosophy of *Bodhicitta* as clear light nature of mind has been expounded in *Guhyasamāja Tantra* and the *Kālacakra Tantra*. In the above systems the clear light nature of mind has been described as fundamental innate mind. It is considered as fundamental and innate because it continues to exist forever, *i.e.* both while one's mind is afflicted and while one's mind is uninflected in the state of enlightenment. Thus, it is considered as the basis of both cyclic existence and *Nirvāṇa*. According to *Mādhayamikā*, which forms the philosophical basis of Buddhist Ṭantra the *Saṁsāra* and *Nirvāṇa* depend upon our perspective. From one perspective it is *Saṁsāra* from other perspective it is *Nirvāṇa*.

From this point of view all phenomena except *Śūnyatā* are called *Saṁvṛti-satya. Saṁvṛti* means that which obscures the transcendental nature of truth. The *Śūnaytā* speaks of the transcendental and ultimate truth. Dalai Lama writes, "Thus, both the clear light nature of the mind and the emptiness of inherent existence of the mind are the Buddha nature, the nature of the mind that allows for transformation into Buddhahood. The Buddha nature is, therefore, the basis of purification and transformation in that it is that from the company of which defilements are removed."[39]

Thus, philosophically speaking the empirical objects are not real. The radical illusion is not that of the individual self but of finite substances. Prof. G.C. Pande writes, "The distinction between the empirical and the absolute, *saṁvṛti* and *paramārtha*, was a part of the original doctrine and hence retained in some form in *Abhidharma*. The transient and gross objects of common experience, which could not be recognized when reduced to their constituents or which could not be identified without being demarcated from other objects were *saṁvṛti* but those which could not thus be deidentified, the basic self-recognizable causal elements, were regarded as *parmārtha, "yatra bhinnena tadbuddhir anyapohe dhiya ca tat / Ghaṭāṁ buvat saṁvṛtisat, paramārtha-sad anyathā"* such a distinction is obviously a product of *Abhidhārmic* metaphysics and has nothing to do with original Buddhism. In fact, the earlier *Abhidhārmic* Masters still preserved the ancient tradition when they held that *Paramārthasat* is what is the object of Supramundance knowledge (*Lokāttara jñāna*) as of its immediately following knowledge (*Pṛṣṭha-labdha-laukika-jñāna*), the rest is *saṁvṛti*.[40]

Buddhism has always emphasized the attainment of transcendental wisdom which could come only through intuition. The intuition could come only through the process of awakening the dormant divinity. Prof. G.C. Pande further writes, "It is difficult to identify such a doctrine with original Buddhism where the real is what the Buddha intuits and is infinite, eternal and absolute.[41] The empirical objects are not real, the illusion is not that of the individual self, but of the finite substances. The Mahāyāna formulated the principles of transcendental wisdom, absolute reality and phenomenal relativity out of the original doctrine propounded by the Buddha. It was the central objective of *Kālacakra Tantra* to restore Buddhism to its original mission of propagating and popularizing the path of *Dharma* by providing esoteric techniques to experience and realize transcendental wisdom.

Kālacakra is an ideo-realistic monism. *Bodhicitta* is a transcendental reality but its true being remains concealed by impurities and defilements. *Kālacakra* is a supreme godhead. He is the supreme subjectivity and hence, he cannot be the object of thought. He stands supreme. All the deities of Buddhist tāntric pantheon are merely of the nature of *Bodhicitta* dependent on *Kālacakra* to carry out their dispositions. He alone is the source from which the cosmos is vitalized throughout the course of creation, preservation and involution.

According to *Kālacakra* a practitioner enters into *maṇḍala* (mystic diagram) after getting proper initiation (*abhiṣeka*) and offers worship to the *Kālacakra* deity. He considers himself as individual part of the deity. He identifies his body with *Bīja-mantra* assigning each part of his body to the corresponding *Bīja-mantra*, according to acoustic arrangement of *mantra*. For the layman the *Bīja-mantras* may appear as nonsensical syllables but for the initiates they are full of esoteric significance. The incantation of these *Bīja-mantras* inculcates a cosmic ideation and transforms the individual consciousness into cosmic consciousness. These *Bīja-mantra* are embodiment of different acoustic roots of different cosmic vibrations.

Kālacakra is a compassionate appearance of a cosmic consciousness, which brings about the realization of emptiness of inherent existence. The nature of *Kālacakra* is, therefore, *Mahāsukha* (great bliss). The *Kālacakra* deity emits rays of five colour — blue, red, white, yellow and green.[42] His body is blue in colour. He has three necks—black in the centre, red to his right, and white to his left—and four faces. The black face in the centre, facing east, is fierce. Let us take around the corridor of the mind (*maṇḍala*) so that we can see other three faces clearly. Going to the left, we come near the southern door of the mind *maṇḍala*; from there we see that his right face is red and exhibiting desire. Proceeding on, we see that his back face is yellow and dwelling in meditative stabilization. Proceeding on, we see that his left face is white and very peaceful. All of the faces have three eyes. His body is adorned with various adornments— *vajra*-jewels, *vajra*-earrings, *vajra*-necklace, *vajra*- bracelets, *vajra*-belt, *vajra*-ankle bracelets, *vajra*-silk ribbons hanging from his crown, and *vajra* garlands. His lower robe is a tiger skin.

Viśvamātā is the consort of *Kālacakra*. She embraces him from the front[43], her right face is white, her left face is red, her central face is yellow, her back face is blue, each face has three eyes. She has four arms in each side. Her right hands hold a knife, iron hook, *ḍamaru (drum)* and rosary. Her left hand holds a skull, noose, white lotus with hundred petals and jewel. She wears a crown *Vajra-sattva*. She rises in mystic absorption with *Kālacakra*. *Kālacakra* and *Viśvamātā* are having three deities in one. *Kālacakra* is fused with *Akṣobhaya, Vajra-sattva* and Viśvamātā is absorbed with *Vajradhatrīśvarī* and *Prajñāpāramitā*. Akśobhaya is green with three faces — green, white and red — and six hands, holding in his three right hands a *Vajra*, knife and axes, and in his three left hands a *vajra*-bell, skull and head of Brāhma. He is embraced by *Prajñāpāramitā*. These symbols are of great esoteric importance. The Kalacakra is associated with ten *Śakties*. *Śakti* is personified as different consorts. According to these symbolisms, *siddhi* can be attained only through the divine grace of *Śakti*. *Śakti* is considered in *Kālacakra* as *Viśvamātā*. She is the route of transcendental knowledge, *i.e.* the route of all knowledge. The whole universe has been created by *Viśvamātā*. She is the creative matrix (*Sṛṣṭirūpā*). Every sentient being is a transcendental being but due to the defilements and impurities he forgets his real nature and being. *Bodhicitta* is not different from the sentient being. The sentient being forgets his own identity with *Bodhicitta* because of his identification of pure-intelligence with ego. This is known as non-self (*Anattā*) in Buddhism. *Bodhicitta* is one, whole, cosmic and universal. But it becomes divided and split into finite and limited consciousness. The different motivations are the splitting force. One will have to overcome the weaknesses of different motivations. *Kālacakra Tantra* is spiritual process for transforming the finite consciousness into *Bodhicitta*. The practice of *Kālacakra Tantra* removes the adventitious defilements and impurities from the expose of *Bodhicitta*. According to *Kālacakra* enlightenment is the state in which adventitious defilements are removed. The sentient being under the influence of conception of inherent existence does not want to be liberated from the cycle of existence. When one experiences that everything is impermanent one gets inspiration and spiritual motivation to overcome the conception of inherent existence. According to the needs and the making of different sentient beings the Buddha propounded different doctrines. His disciple had various dispositions, interests and abilities and hence he formulated different methods, which were suitable for each other. Those disciples who did not have the motivation and spiritual potentiality to strive for *Nirvāṇa,* he taught the methods which would ultimately lead to enlightenment. The quintessence of the Buddha's teachings is that Buddha nature is present in all sentient beings. It means, according to this doctrine it provides substantial course for the attainment of *Nirvāṇa* for all sentient beings. Shantideva's Engaging in the *Bodhisattva Deeds* (*Bodhisattvācaryāvatāra*) says that the truthful Buddha taught that even bees and donkeys can attain Buddhahood if they generate Buddha-nature. Therefore, since we now have attained a human body and have met with the doctrine, if we generate the power of courageous effort, why could we not attain Buddhahood.

According to Buddhist Doctrine all the sentient beings have potentiality and spiritual power to attain Buddhahood. The basic philosophical position of *Kāla Tantra* is based on *Mādhaymikā* doctrine of fundamental unity of *Nirvāṇa* and *Saṁsāra*. Essential nature is increate and independent of anything else. The *Nirvāṇa* is no different from *Saṁsāra. Saṁsāra* consists in form, in feeling and other faculties of sense. But all these elements are really *Nirvāṇa* and only for illusion they appear as *Saṁsāra*. But the *Saṁsāra* is really *Nirvāṇa* then all men are enlightened being. If all sentient beings are enlightened being then why ever sentient beings have not experienced of enlightenment. Philosophically speaking the sentient beings are obscured by adventitious defilements and that is why they did not have the realization that they are the Buddhas.

The objective of the *Kālacakra Tantra* is to remove the accidental defilements and with the removal of the adventitious impurities sentient being experienced Buddhahood at once spontaneously. The purpose of Tāntric practice is to rid sentient being from adventitious defilements, which arise from the wrong view of existence. D.L. Snellgrove writes, "The whole training consists in learning to conceive of existence in knowledge of its non-existence, and one will then automatically realize its true nature which is innate (*sahaja*) and a matter for self-experience (*svasamvedya*). But this can only be done by using existence itself as the means (*ūpāya*) for there is no other possible. One creates mentally (*bhavayati*) an idealized representation of the process of emanation of existence (*utpattikrama*), which is the *saṁsāra*, and by realizing the dream like nature of its apparent diversity; one realizes its unity in this process of realization (*sam pann akrama*), which is *Nirvāṇa*.[44] For the realization of supreme enlightenment, liberation from the cycle of existence is *sine-qua-non*. One must cultivate a mind cognizing emptiness, which would result in the reflection on all phenomena as a magician illusion. Inseparatability of esoteric practice and wisdom does not mean that the wisdom and methods are different entities. His Holiness Dalai Lama writes, "If, as in the *Kālacakra Tantra*, one posited method as the totally supreme form of emptiness and posited wisdom as the supreme immutable bliss, then this would not apply in general to all four *Tantras*. Therefore, what is the meaning of inseparable method and wisdom, or '*Vajra* vehicle', that applies to all four *Tantras?* The six perfections are included in method and wisdom, and in *Mantra*, method and wisdom are considered as the one entity of the *Vajrasattva* meditative stabilization."[45]

The practice of Kālacakra leads to the contingence of appearance of the deity and realization of its emptiness of inherent existence. *Kālacakra* represents the *Vajra-vehicle*. *Vajra* means indivisible and unbreakable. *Vajra*-vehicle stands for individual ability of the effect—the *mantra* mode and perfection mode. Here cause and effect stands for supreme emptiness and supreme bliss. The individuality of cause and the effect vehicle are of great esoteric importance. The one refers the means by which one progresses, the other refers the means by which one is progressing. According to Dalai Lama for the supreme immutable bliss can only arise when one has attained the branch of meditative stabilization [in the system of the *Kālacakrā*[46]] and thus the branches of mindfulness and those below must be the means of achieving it. The three lower tantras do not have all the factors that are included in these causal branches'.

> *Śekoddesaṭikā* the brief Explication of initiations says,
> "The bearing form of emptiness is the cause,
> That bearing immutable compassion is the effect.
> Emptiness and compassion indivisible
> Are called the mind of enlightenment."[47]

Kālacakrayāna is development of *Vajrayāna*. This school of Tāntric Buddhism was greatly misunderstood by many. The *Vimala Prabhā*'s commentary on *Kālacakara Tantra* occupies a unique position in Buddhist Tāntric tradition. Vimala Prabhā deals with Ayurveda, Rasaśāstra, Yogaśāstra, Vedas, Dharmaśāstras, non-Buddhist-

Tantras and other systems of Indian Philosophy.[48] According to the *Vimala Prabhā*, there are three kinds of *Kālacakra*, the outer *Kālacakra* (*Bāhya Kālacakra*), the spiritual *Kālacakra* (*Adhyātma*) and other *Kālacakra* (*Aparā*). The *Kālacakara* deals with *pratyāhara, dhyāna, prāṇāyāma, dhāraṇā, annuśamṛti* and *samādhi*. It is known as Ṣaṭaṅgayoga. The *Ṣaṭaṅgayoga* has been discussed in detail by other *anuttaryoga-tantra* like *Guhyasamāja-tantra*. However, *Kālacakara* differs from other *Tantras* on some point of esoteric importance. The topic, which has been discussed in the *Vimala Prabhā*, Vol. III, are the following :

1. Purification of the *rajomaṇḍala* by way of purifying the body-*maṇḍala* consisting in bones, elements etc.
2. Purification of the deities of body, mind and speech and six families of deities.
3. Six deity families corresponding to the six groups of consonants beginning with *ka*.
4. The thirty-six wisdom and method *Tantras* corresponding to the thirty-six letters beginning with *ka*.
5. Emission of the wisdom *tantras*, method *tantras, kriyā tantras, yoganuviddha tantras, mahāsaṁvaramaṇḍala* and six *cakravartins*.
6. The fourth initiation; accomplishment of the supreme unchanging gnosis of *Mahāmudrā*.
7. Emission of the gnosis-*maṇḍala*.
8. Practice of serving the *Bodhicitta*.
9. Accomplishment of *Mahāmudrā* which is endowed with all aspects of knowledge and knowables.
10. Investigation into all functions of body, speech and mind.
11. Teaching of eighty-four thousand aggregates of *Dharma*.
12. Dissolution of the Buddha-field.
13. Wandering in the space with the Bodhisattvas, the Mahāsattvas, equalling the particles of Sumeru.
14. Evolution of Buddha-field.
15. Blessing the Buddha-field of *Vajra*.
16. Teaching of *Dharma* according to the dispositions of various beings inclinations.
17. Accomplishment of bodily *siddhis* through quicksilver, alchemy and so forth.
18. Working for the purpose of all sentient beings through the supreme unchanging bliss.
19. Treatise on *Dharma*, mathematical terms.
20. Praise of *Pañcākṣara ṣaḍākṣara, mahāsūnya* and *Bindu-śūnya*.[49]

There is a great controversy regarding the origin of *Kālacakra*, Lokesh Chandra writes:[50]

> 'The *Kālacakra* is one of last Sanskrit work to have been written in Central Asia has whence it is said to have travelled into India."

We do not subscribe to this view. According to the oral tradition Kulika kings, were the followers and devotees of *Kālacakra Tantra*. As per this tradition Chilupā from Orissa travelled to *Shambhala* and became great master of *Kālacakra Tantra*. It is said that he returned to India in 966 A.D. and popularized and propagated the teachings of *Kālacakra Tantra*. But, according to the author of Blue Annals, the translator from *Goö, shhön-nu-bel* (*gos lo tsā ba bzhon nudpul*, 1392-1481) argues cogently that the *Kālacakra Tantra* has reappeared in India long before that time, since, among other reasons, Chilupā.[51]

> ...... had read (it) in the Vihāra of Rantnagiri (*Rinchen ri-bo*) which had been left undamaged by the Turuṣkhas, and was of the opinion that, in general, for the (attainment) of Enlightenment the Mahāyāna Guhyamantra (*gsan-snags*) was necessary, and that the text had to be studied with the help of the commentary by the *Bodhisattvas*. Accordingly he proceeded in search of the *Kālacakra* (so the *Kālacakra* must have been in existence at that time). Thus it has to be admitted that the system of *Kālacakra* seems to have reached Āryadeśa (India) at an early date and that (the system) became known to many people in the time of *Kālacakra-pada*, father and son.

Helmut Hoffman writes that Chilupā defeated Nadapada known as Nirupa, who was abode of Nalanda Monastery. *Tantra* was greatly practiced at Nālandā and Vikaramśilā, which were the great centres of Buddhism in those days. Hoffman is of the view that it seems the whole tradition of *Kālacakra* was popularized and decimated in India and Tibet.[52]

> It would seem that the whole tradition of Kālacakra derived from two places of learnings, i.e., Nalanda and Vikramsila, not only in India but also in Tibet.

It is stated that Nadapada initiated Atisha into the *Kālacakra Tantra*. Helmut Hoffman is of opinion that the *Kālacakra Tantra* came to be known in India from 966 A.D. with Chilupā's return and "became effective in India under King Mahipala of Bengal (C. 974-1026)."[53] The Samabhala is a mythical name and all the names of teachers who are associated with *Kālacakra* seems to be an original residents of India. From the available historical accounts, many scholars are in favour of eastern

India as the original home of *Kālacakra Tantra* from where it travelled to other parts of India, Tibet and Asia.

According to other Tāntric tradition Samantashri a student of *Nādapāda* practiced *Kālacakra Tantra* almost in six years in Kashmir. He persuaded his teacher to return to Tibet. *Bu-dön Rin-chen-drup cbu ston rin chen grub*, 1290-1364) and *Dol-b-ba śhay-rapgyel-tsen* (*dal pa pa shes rab rgyal mtsham*, 1292-1361) of the *Sā-gya* order who are called the two great expounders of the *Kālacakra* in the Lord of Snows,[54] received teachings from transmissions stemming from both the Translator Ra and the Translator Dro. *Kālacakra Tantra* become very popular in almost all the sects of Tibetan Buddhism, because of its distinctive features of transforming mind and body into *Bodhicitta*.

There has been some misunderstanding about Tāntric Buddhism. Even a scholar like Benoytosh Bhattacharya has given completely a wrong picture about Buddhist Tantra. He writes, "a clever organizer, as Buddha was, he did not fail to notice the importance of incorporating magical practices in his religion to make it popular from all points of view and attract more adherents thereby.[55] As per the Buddhist tradition *Kālacakra Tantra* was introduced by Śākyamuni Buddha himself.[56] *Kālacakra Tantra* refers to unification of immutable bliss and empty form. The esoteric meaning of the external, internal and alternative is contained in the ten letters of *Bīja-mantra* of *Kālacakara*. These *Bīja-mantras, haṁ kṣaḥ ma la va ra ya*. These *Bīja-mantras* are pregnant with profound esoteric significance. According to *Kālacakra* there are thirty-one categories of cyclic existence, which are condensed into eleven categories according to the levels of the deities.

There is great similarity between *Kālacakra Tantra* and *Śaiva-Tantra*. Both *Kālacakra Tantra* and *Śaiva-Tantra* belong to the metaphysical schools of Buddhist and Hindu *Tantra*. Both are aimed at the attainment of the state of spiritual illumination and the perfect enlightenment. It is a state of Tāntric Monism. The non-duality of *Kālacakra* and *Viśvamātā*, and *Śiva* and *Śakti* form the hallmark of these two Tāntric systems. Neither Viśvamātā is separated from *Kālacakra*, nor *Śakti* is separated from *Śiva*. Both the female deities are identical with *Kālacakra* and *Śiva*. The *prima facie* differences in the esoteric techniques and practices are in keeping with the basic principles necessary for working out a complete realization. According to the both systems a *Sādhaka* enters into mystic diagram, which is known in Hindu-Tantra as *Yantra* and in Buddhist Tantra as *Maṇḍala*. After taking purificatory bath *Sādhaka* worships deity. The *Sādhaka* considers himself an individual part of the Deity. The *Sādhaka* divinises himself with incantation of *Mantra*. He identifies his body with *Mantra* assigning each part of his body to the corresponding letters of the alphabet according to the esoteric arrangement of different *Mantras*.

A man cannot be liberated from the trammels of *Avidyā* through his own effort. The bondage of individuation is due to the self-limitations, which can be removed by the grace of Lord *Śiva* and Lord *Kālacakra* respectively. With the grace of *Śiva* or *Kālacakra* a sentient is being delivered from the false sense of dualism of subject and object.

Both *Kālacakra* and *Śiva* are beginningless, free from defects. Both are all knowing entities. Both remove from the infinitesimal soul, the web of bonds that obscures the true nature of the sentient being. Again there is a great similarity between *Kālacakra* and *Divyācāra*. Both are purely spiritual process. Both are profound and highest form of esotericism. According to *Divyācāra* the mystic unification of *Śiva* and *Śakti* is the true *Yoga*.[57] This is esoteric meaning of coition (*maithuna*) in *Tantra*. Both according to *Kālacakra* and *Divyācāra* body is considered as divine abode of deity. The incantation of different *Mantras* is associated with the esoteric techniques of invoking different deities. When the *Mantras* are incantated according to the strict esoteric discipline, it yields the desired results as insect becomes a bee by the force of meditation, so man God by dint of spiritual trance (*samādhi*).[58] The whole system of Hindu and Buddhist Tantra is based on this principle.

Kālacakra Tantra is a very difficult esoteric technique to attain Buddhahood. It is a risky form of mystic discipline. Everybody is not entitled to this practice of highest form of *Tantra Sādhanā*. According to *Kālacakra Tantra* a person who is prudent, pure, non-dualist, always engaged in doing good to all, abstaining from violence to all beings, with senses controlled and who takes refuse in *Dharma*, Buddha and *Saṁgha* is competent for *Kālacakra Sādhanā*. *Kulārṇava Tantra* presents a long list of qualifications necessary for a *Tantra Sādhaka*.[59] The person who is heretic, boastful, impotent, wicked, dry, untrue, cruel, foolish, unreliable, plagiarist, passionate, garrulous, libidinous, egoist, coward, crooked, dull, weak, afflicted, ugly, inactive, thief, is not entitled to Tantra Sādhanā.[60] The person chosen for *Tāntric Sādhanā* shall be one who is endowed with auspicious features. He must possess good qualities and culture, wise, devoted to *Dhamma*, gifted with faith and devotion.

Kālacakra Tantra is an esoteric process for sublimation of mind and consciousness. *Kālacakra Tantra Sādhanā* purifies the different cells and nerve-plexuses. All the cells start emanation of divine waves and vibrations. It imparts a subtle form of meditation. It leads to realization of Buddhahood. *Kālacakra Tāntric* path to Buddhahood is as sharp as the edge of razor. According to Hindu tradition also path to salvation is very dangerous and risky. The *Kaṭha Upaniṣad* says: "Arise, awake and learn by approaching the excellent ones. This wise ones describe that the path to be as impassable as a razor's edge, which, when sharpened, is difficult to tread on."[61] The Infinite in man is like the oil in the riverbed, or fire in the two pieces of wood.[62]

To get oil from sesamum seeds, we have to crush them, churn the curds before we can have butter. Dig the ground for water and rub the stick hard for fire. This is Tantra Sādhanā. Till man attains Buddhahood, he has to tread the risk and dangerous path. Tantra Sādhanā goes into detail and it weaves yoga into day-to-day life. It gives meaning and mystic interpretation to men's activities by making them all means for effectuation and transformation of inner consciousness of progression from sentient being to Buddhahood.

According to *Tantra* the practice of *yoga*, is just like playing with the high voltage electricity and a little carelessness may either bring death or untold sufferings. Because of this danger and risk *Tantra* has led down a detailed qualifications and conditions for the practices of *Tantra-Sādhanā*. *Tantra-Sādhanā* rightly practice sublimates the sentient beings, but wrongly practice, it takes vengeance and destroy the sentient beings. The *Kālacakra Tantra* is the greatest of all esoteric practices, because it aims at the spiritual perfection, psyche development of sentient being, and as such no one can deny that *Kālacakra Tantra* is the greatest contribution made by Buddhist tradition towards world civilization. *Tantra-Sādhanā* demonstrates, that the highest degree of the moral and spiritual power is necessary to follow the path of Buddhahood. *Kālacakra Tantra* in fact, was never meant for all. *Tantra* was opened to practice, only for a few fortunate persons who are equipped with high degree of moral refinements and power. S.B. Dasgupta writes, "If *Yoga* and *Tantra* are made the common property of all, as it was made by the Buddhists of old, the whole routine of life is upset, and abuses of all tenets follow a matter of course. It is not necessary to state that this psychic culture appealed to men with striking force, particularly when the masters of *Tantra* could perform prodigious feats and miracles, and, as such, in the time of the *Siddhācāryas* the *Tantras* attracted almost every men without exception, and most of them must of necessity have had to be content with the shadow rather than the substance of *Tantra*. And, as a matter of fact, owing, to the great influence of *Tantras* in earlier days, even at the present time there are very few Hindus in India who are not following the Tāntric practices in some form or other.[63]

Philosophers and scientists of every age and country have visualized the presence of great energy behind the Cosmic structure. It has been named as God Spirit or *Śūnya*. According to Buddhist Tantra individual soul is called *Bodhicitta* and the supreme reality is called *Śūnyata*. The *Bodhichitta* is composed of *Śūnyatā* and *Karuṇā*, the realization of this brings about *Mahāsukha*. S.B. Dasgupta writes, "When the *Bodhicitta* moves still more upwards, a transcendental knowledge and realization is produced and it is called the *Mahāmūdrā*. It is described as essenceless, free from the veils of subjectivity (*Jñeyā-varaṇa*) and of the passions (*Kleśā-varaṇa*); it is like the clear mid-day sky of the autumn, the origin of all wealth, the unity of *Bhava* and *Nirvāṇa*, a supportless body of compassion, —the embodiment of *Mahāsukha*. The *Samaya-mudrā* (the *Mudrā* of knowledge) is the *Mudrā* par excellence—it is perfect bliss, perfect knowledge. We have seen that in the *Samputikā* as well as in the *Hevajra-pañjikā Karma-mudrā* has been placed in the *Nirmāṇa-cakra*, *Dharma-mudrā* in the *Dharma-cakra*, *Mahā-mudrā* in the *Sambhoga-cakra* and *Samaya-mudrā* in the *Mahāsukha-cakra*.[64] From this it spears that *Karma-mudrā* represents the totality of the process and the resulting bliss and knowledge when the *Bodhicitta* remains in the *Nirmāṇa-cakra*, *Dharma-mudrā* is similarly the process, resulting bliss and knowledge when the *Bodhicitta* is raised to the *Dharma-cakra*, *Mahā-mudrā* similarly refers to the *Bodhicitta* in the *Sambhoga-cakra* and *Samaya-mudrā* to the *Bodhicitta* in the *Mahāsukha-cakra.*[65]

According to *Śekoddesa-ṭīkā* there are four kinds of bliss, *i.e. Ānanda, Paramānanda, Viramānanda* and *Sahajānanda.* The first state of *Ānanda* is the bliss when the *Bodhicitta* is in the *Nirmankāya,* second state of *Paramānanda* is when *Bodhicitta* is in the *Dharmacakra,* third state of bliss (*Virmānanda*) is when Bodhicitta is in the *Sambhog-cakra* and *Sahajānanda* is in the state if *Mahāsukha-kāya* a *Vajra-tantra* says that *Ānanda* means ordinary pleasure, *Parmānanda* is more intense, *Virmānanda* refers to detachment from the transient pleasure and *Sahajānanda* is a state of *Mahāsukha.* Corresponding to the four stages of *Ānanda there* is the four states of mind, *Jāgrat* (wakefulness), *Svapna* (dream), *Suṣupti* (deep-sleep) and *Turīya* (*samādhi*). Again it refers to four kinds of elements, *i.e. Kāya* (body), *Vāk* (speech), *Citta* (mind) and *Jñāna* (knowledge).

Mind cannot subjectivise *Bodhicitta,* because it is a supreme subjectivity. *Kālacakra Tantra* is the mystic process of transforming the being and existence into *Bodhicitta.* With the unification of *Kālacakra* with *Viśvāmatā* or *Prajñā* and *Upāya* mind is merged and dissolved into Buddhahood. Supreme perfection issues from this esoteric unification of *Kālacakra* with *Viśvāmatā* or *Prajñā* with *Upāya.* It is the course of liberation.[66] The state of Buddhahood is not death but spiritual perfection. It is a perfection of knowledge, where there is no impurity to obscure. It is fullness of life and richness of being and existence. Life dies into the divine fullness.

REFERENCES

1. George N. Roerich, *The Blue Annals* (Delhi: Motilal Banarsidass, rpt. 1979), p. 754 n.l. Dhanyakataka is also identified as being three days travel across the sea from Bengal in eastern India; see *The World* of *Tibetan Buddhism* (Japan: Gyosei Ltd., [1984]), p. 96.
2. The *Kālacakra-Tantra* and other texts, volume 1, edited by Prof. Dr. Raghu Vira and Prof. Dr. Lokest Chandra, (New Delhi: International Academy of Indian Culture, 1966), I. lc, Sanskrit, p. 332; Tibetan, p. 53.4
3. *Sanatan Sadhan Ki Gupt Dhara,* University, Varanasi, II edition, 2002, p. 61.
4. *The Cultural Heritage of India,* vol. IV, p. 270.
5. *Ibid.,* p. 271.
6. *The Cultural Heritage of India,* vol. IV, p. 271.
7. *Philosophy of Gorakhnath,* Prefatory Note, p. xxvi.
8. *Taking the Kālacakara Initiation* by Alexander Bergin, p. 27.
9. *Taking the Kālacakra Initiation,* Alxender Berzin, Snow Lion Publication, Ithaca, New York, 1997, p. 30
10. *Sri Kālacakratantra-Rāja,* Biswanath Banerjee, Pub. 1985, rpt. 1993, New Asian Printers, Calcutta, p. xiii.
11. काकारात् कारणे शान्ते लकाराच्च लयोऽत्र वै ।
चकाराच्चलचित्रस्य क्रकारात् क्रमबधनात्।।
कालोऽसरसुखं ज्ञानमुपाय: करुणात्मक:।
ज्ञेयाकारं त्रगच्चक्रं श्रीप्रज्ञाशून्यतात्मिका।।

करुणाशून्यतामूर्तिः कालसंवृतिरूपिनी।
शून्यताचक्रमिव्युक्तं कालचक्रोऽदयो मतः।।
Śrī Kālachakratantra, Rāja. p. xiii.

12. *Kālachakratantra Rite of Initiation*, Tenzin Cyatso, The Dalai Lama, Jeffery Hopkins, Wisdom Publication, Boston, USA. 1985, p. 49.
13. *Gautama, the Buddha*, p. 59
14. *Indian Philosophy*, vol. I, pp. 682-3.
15. *Majjhim Nikāya*, translated by Chalmon, pp. 495-96.
16. *The Hevajrā Tantra*, Part I, p. 20.
17. *Kālacakra Tantra, Rite of Imitation*., p. 57.
18. *Ibid*., p. 212.
19. *Ibid*., pp. 212-13.
20. *Tantra in Tibet*, H.H. The Dalai Lama, Tsong-ka-pa and Jeffrey Hopkins, Snow Line Publication, 1987, New York, USA, p. 107.
21. *Prumanavārttika*, Acharya Dharmakirtti, Varanasi: Buddha Bharati, 1968, vol. III, 73.1.
22. *Kālacakra Tantra: Rite of Initiation*, Tenzin Gyatso, The Dalai Lama and Jeffrey Hopkins Wisdom Publication, Boston, USA, 1985, p. 15.
23. *Ibid*., p. 18.
24. *The Cultural Heritage of India*, vol. IV., p. 271.
25. *Philosophy of Gorakhnath*, Prefectory Note, p. xxvi.
26. *Nameste Kāla-cakrāya sarva-varṇa-kanaye*
    Paramā-kṣara-sukha-pūrṇa jñāna-kaya namo (sic) *stute*
    Śūnyatā-Karuṇā-bhinnaṁ bodhi-cittaṁ bad akṣaram
    Tena sekena me nātha prasādaṁ kuru sampratun, p. 24.
27. *Kṣāraṁ pradhanamamtasaruṁ haraḥ*
    Kṣaratmanvisate deva ekaḥ
    Tasyabhidhyānāda yojanāt tattābhavad
    Bhū-yaścate viśvamaya nivṛttiḥ— Ibid.
28. *Lamaism*, by Waddell, p. 15.
29. *Ibid*., p. 131.
30. *Modern Buddhism*, etc., intro., p. 8.
31. Preserved in the Cambridge University Library (Cambridge Ms. Add. no. 1364)
32. Ms. (Cambridge Add. No. 1364) p. 1(B).
33. G. O. S. ed. by Mario E. Carehli, D. Litt.
34. *Śekoddesaṭīkā*, p. 3.
35. As for the unification of *prajñā* and *upaya* see *infra*.
36. *Kakrat kāraṇe sante lakaral layo'tra vai*
    Cakarac cala-cittasya krakarat krama-badhanaiḥ
    (—naṃ)?— *Ibid*., p. 8.
37. *Kālacakra Tantra : Rite of Initiation*, Tenzin Cyatso, The Dalai Lama, Jeffery Hopkins, Wisdom Publication, Boston, USA. 1985, pp. 13-14.
38. *Pramanavārttika* of Achārya Dharmakirtti, Varanasi, Bauddha Bharati, 1968, vol. 3, 73, I.
39. *Kālacakra Tantra, Rites of Initiation*, p. 18.
40. *Studies in Mahāyāna*, p. 45.
41. Such is the description of ultimate reality in Buddha's utterances. See Origins of Buddhism, pp. 173 75.
42. The following description is taken from the Seventh Dalai Lama's means of Achievement of the complete Mandalla of Exalted Body, Speech, and mind of the supramundane victor, the Glorious *Kālacakra*: the sacred word of scholars and Adepts (becom idan 'das dus kyi sgrub thabes mkhus grub zhal lung), [n. d. in the same volume as kay-drup's man-dala Rite], 86, 1-87.7)

43. The painting of *Kālacakra* on the 1984 calendar of the Tibetan Medical Centre in Dharamsala shows three arrows, but the picture in the Madison booklet shows a single arrow. The word in Tibetan Dictionary by Geshe Chosdag identifies this as phyag males' which we presume to be just the honorific of "arrow" and not "hard arrow." Since, as will be seen, *Kālacakra* is also holding a bow. The term may mean that the arrow has the capacity of fire. 87-7-88-2.
44. *The Hevajrā Tantra: A critical study*, by D.L. Snellgrove, Part I, Introduction and translation, p. 22.
45. *Tantra in Tibet*, H. H. Dalai Lama, Tsang-ka-pa and Jeffery Hopkins, Snow Lion Publication, New York, USA, 1977, p. 51.
46. The six branches as set forth in the *Kālacakara Tantra* are withdrawal, concentration, vitality and exertion, holding, mindfulness, and meditative stabilisation (*Pratyāhāra, dhyāna, prāṇāyāma, dhāraṇā, anuṣmṛti, and samādhi*).
47. *Tantra in Tibet*, H.H. Dalai Lama, Tsang-ka-pa and Jeffery Hopkins, Snow Lion Publication, New York, USA, 1987, p.107.
48. *Vimal Prabhā*, vol. III, p. 12.
49. *Ibid.*, pp. 21-22
50. Lokesh Chandra's *Introduction to the Kālacakara-Tantra and Other Texts*, vol. I, p. 6.
51. See, *The Blue Annals*, p. 754-55.
52. Helmut Hoffman, *The Religions of Tibet*, pp. 127-128.
53. Helmut Hoffman, *The Religions of Tibet*, p. 126; Lokesh Chandra's *Introduction to the Kālacakra-Tantra and other texts*, vol. I, p. 7.
54. *The Blue Annals*, p. 755.
55. *An Introduction to Buddhist Esoterism*, p. 49.
56. *Kālachakratantra Rite of Initiation*, Tenzin Cyatso, The Dalai Lama, Jeffery Hopkins, Wisdom Publication Boston, USA, 1985, p. 209.
57. शिवशक्तिसमायोगा योग एव न संशयः। *Śakti and Śākta*, p. 607.
58. यथा ध्यानस्य सामर्थ्यात् कीटोऽपि भ्रमरायते।
    तथा समाधिसामर्थ्याद्ब्रह्मभूतो भवेन्नरः।।16।। *Ibid.*, p. 238
59. *Kulārṇava Tantra*, ch. XIII.
60. *Ibid.*, pp. 293-94.
61. उत्तिष्ठत जाग्रत प्राप्य वरान्तिबोधत।
    सुरस्य धारा विशिता दुरत्यया दुर्गं पथस्तत्कवयो वदन्ति।।14।। —I. iii. 14.
62. Śvetāśvatara Upaniṣad, i. 15.
63. *An Introduction of Buddhist Esoterism*, Benoytosh Bhattacharya, Vidya Vilas Press, 2nd ed., Varanasi, 1964, p. 168.
64. Vide Samputika, MS. [R.A.S.B., No. 4854, p. 10(A)]
65. *Cf.* also *Śekoddesaṭīkā* (G. O. S.), p. 62, *et seq.*
66. ज्ञानं मोक्षैककारणाम्। *Tantrāloka*, vol I. p. 192.

6 Tantra Sādhanā

According to Buddhist Tantra *Prajñā* and *Upāya* constitute transcendental reality which is known as Bodhicitta. The reality is neutral by nature. The *Prajñā* and *Upāya* can be rendered as transcendental and immanent, dynamic and static or positive and negative. *Prajñā* and *Upāya* or *Śūnyatā* or *Karuṇā* are two aspects of the *Bodicitta*. *Prajñā* is pure knowledge or consciousness and *Upāya* is means. However, neither *Prajñā* nor *Upāya* is the transcendental reality, they are inseparable. *Boddicita* is the state of neutrality produced through the unification of *Prajñā* and *Upāya*. The mystic unification of *Prajñā* and *Upāya*, under one condition produces the highest state of *Mahāsukha*, and under another, the manifest world or phenomenal process as a whole. The association of *Upāya* with his consort *Prajñā* in realm of *Pravṛtti* is responsible for the creation of the world, but when *Prajñā*, in the form of *Herukā*, moves towards *Uṣṇīṣa-Kamala* in a process of introversion, there unification results in a state of infinite unity and supreme divinity. The metaphysical unification of *Prajñā* and *Upāya* binds and the mystic unification liberates.

The hallmark of Tantra Sādhanā is the happy and harmonious blending of *Bhoga* (enjoyment) and *Yoga* (salvation). In both Hindu and Buddhist Tāntric tradition *Sādhaka* sees the world as the manifestation of divine bliss. With the help of the esoteric process of gradual superimposition of divine ideation and incantation of the proper *mantra* under the proper guidance of a proper *Guru*, mundane activities become the means for liberation. Enjoyment becomes salvation. According to both traditions *Sādhanā* promises the *Sādhaka* not merely salvation but enjoyment also, not merely beatitude (*niśeyaṣa*) but also progress (*abhyudaya*). *Tantra* and *Yoga* are only esoteric techniques through which one can obtain liberation. It is shortest and surest route to the *summum bonum*. *Tantra* is based on esoteric and scientific principles. It is a positive method of overcoming the strong desires for sensuous enjoyment. However, Tantra Sādhanā and its higher values do not attract a parched up soul. The sentient beings who are elevated and wedded to the higher values can alone abstain from sensuous enjoyment and lead a spiritual life. However, *Tantra* does not condemn or adore sensuous enjoyment. Suppression and repression of instincts and sensuous desires lead to immorality. A man may suppress his instincts for a shorter duration but with the passage of time it is bound to result into a volcanic eruption. Immorality and sin in the garb of yellow robes in any religion is not a sign of moral health. The introduction of *Pañcmakāra Sādhanā* is directed towards the control over the sensuous desires. *Pañcamakāra Sādhanā* comprises of *madya* (wine), *māṁsa* (meat), *matsya* (fish), *mudrā* (grain) and *maithuna* (copulation). This *Sādhanā* is enumerated in all *Tantras* of both Hindu and Buddhist provenance. We have already discussed in detail the real meaning and significance of *Pañcamakāra Sādhanā* in obtaining liberation in the previous chapter.

We are all aware that Tantra Sādhanā is like walking on the razor's edge. One cannot succeed in its spiritual pursuits without the guidance and the blessing of a *Guru*. Hence, we would like to discuss the concept of *Guru* along with the concepts of *Mudrā, Maṇḍala* and *Abhiṣeka* which constitute Tantra Sādhanā.

Guru Tattva

The Guru occupies a pivotal role in Tantra Sādhanā. Without taking refuse in Guru sentient being cannot establish the harmonious relation between the enjoyment (*bhoga*) and salvation (*yoga*). Truly speaking the state of equanimity between the enjoyment and salvation is called *Jīvana-mukti* (liberated soul). According to the Āgamic tradition neither the *Kaivalya* of Sāṁkhya nor the salvation of Vedānta is real enlightenment. This had been accepted by both the dualistic and the non-dualistic Āgamic tradition. In Indian culture and tradition, the concept of *Guru* occupies an important place. The philosophical and esoteric knowledge has been preserved and propagated through the unbroken chain of *Gurus* and disciple. It is an impossibility to practice Tantra Sādhanā without getting proper *Abhiṣeka* from the proper Guru. In Tāntric Buddhism the position of *Guru* is paramount and supreme. He is the embodiment of the Buddha and Dharmakāya. In every Tāntric work there is evidence of the high esteem in which the *Gurus* were held,[1] and in many works the characteristics of the *Guru* and the disciple are enumerated.[2]

Unless one gets proper initiation (*Abhiṣekas*) from a proper *Guru* one cannot attain *Nirvāṇa*. The Vajrayāna literature has discussed in detail about the qualification and the characteristics of a true *Guru*. The task of *Guru* is very difficult. *Tantra* expounds the role of a *Guru*. According to *Tantrasāra*, it is the *Guru* who opens the eyes of the disciple and helps him in understanding the true meaning and signification of the *Mantra*. *Tantrasāra* says, "Guides the disciple through dark devious and dangerous practices to the realm of light and anoints sin as peer of the spiritual kingdom.[3] The initiation of *Guru* is mandatory for access to the esoteric meaning and significance of the *Mantra*. To attain the proper status and position of *Guru* is a difficult proposition, unless one qualifies and fulfills all the conditions laid down in *Tantra*.[4] The *Guru* imparts you the secret lesson on *Tantra* after getting full satisfaction from the *Sādhakas*. *Guru* gives the *Sādhaka* what he needs. Without the blessing and guidance of *Guru* one cannot tread the difficult path of *Tantra*. Book is no substitute for *Guru*.

The sentient being is enslaved in the cycle of perpetual birth and death because of his ignorance of his essentially pure nature. The task of *Guru* to create proper psycho-physical condition for the transformation from unit to cosmic consciousness. Lama Yeshe writes, "Completion, Buddhahood, totality, or whatever we want to call it—is not only a theoretical possibility but something that people like us can and do actually achieve. In the Buddhist Tāntric tradition the source of this inspiration is the *Guru* (*lama* in Tibetan) or teacher and spiritual guide. And the root of the Tāntric Path is unifying oneself with this source of inspiration through the practice of *Guru-yoga*.[5]

We need a proper *Guru* who could help us in under-standing the teachings of *Taṇtra*. The book could not help to understand the esoteric meaning and the significance of the Tāntric texts. Tāntric texts are written in *Sandhyābhāṣā* and hence its esoteric significance is hidden. It is a task of *Guru* to give us practical demonstration and the meaning and the information embodied in different Tāntric texts become meaningful and helpful in the path of the realization of *Bodhicitta*. The Tāntric texts are pregnant with profound mystical and philosophical imports. The *Guru* reveals and unfolds hidden treasures of the infinite possibility of knowing our own human consciousness. When we come across a person who have transcended the limits of mundane concern, while living in the world and who speaks from the depth of his being such persons are spiritually enlightened. Such enlightened person has the capacity and power to awaken the dormant divinity of sentient being. Only such person who has already awakened his own or her dormant divinity can alone energize and inspire the sentient being to live the life of spirituality.

In *Tantra*, there is an esoteric technique to awaken the dormant divinity (*Kuṇḍalinī*) or *Parā-Śakti* by *Guru* which is known as *Śakti-pāta*. We find the historical and the mystic evidence of *Śakti-pāta* in the life of Vivekananda. Swami Ramakrishna Parmahaṁsa by his mere mystic touch of his feet awakened the *Kuṇḍalinī* or the *Parāśakti* of youngman Narendra and with the *Śakti-pāta* performed by Ramakrishna Parmahaṁsa transformed the young Narendra into Swami Vivekananda. This esoteric technique is being practiced in the whole Zen Buddhist tradition even today. It is called transmission of light. Another technical language it is called empowerment. Many people have complete misunderstanding about this Tāntric empowerment. The empowerment is a esoteric process of making one realize the limitless potentiality and power of one's own being. However, the transmission of light and empowerment could act only if both the *Guru* and disciple fulfil the conditions laid down in the *Tantra*. The empowerment occurs only when both the Guru and the disciple are active participants in this spiritual process of enlightenment. The task of *Guru* is to conduct the act of empowerment in such a esoteric way that disciple's mind and the body receive the Tāntric initiation in proper perspective. It is the moral and the spiritual duty of the *Guru* to prepare the disciple for such initiation. Unless the disciple performs the Tantra Sādhanā for a long time and prepare his mind and body to receive the proper initiation, *Guru* does not impart the act of empowerment.

The essence of *Guru* is empowerment. The *Guru* is one who has attained the state of spiritual sublimity in which the realization of *Bodhicitta* and *Mahāsukha* are inseparably unified. His Holiness Dalai Lama writes, "Taking to mind the benefits of relying on a spiritual guide and the disadvantages of not doing so, and so forth, make a promise to rely properly on a spiritual guide by way of both thought and deed. This is the essence of how to rely on the spiritual guide and how to keep the pledges of Aśvaghoṣa's fifty stanzas on the *Guru*. Through reflecting on the good qualities of the Lama's exalted body, speech, and mind you should plant the supplication firmly with strong faith and respect, not just from the mouth but from the depths of the heart. Within that, repeat as much as possible the name-*mantra* of the *lama*, together with imagination of the descent of ambrosia and purification through it."[6]

Aśvaghoṣa has tried to analyze the concept of *Guru*. The objective of getting initiation from proper *Guru* is to maintain *Amoghasiddhi* pledge of offering and attain enlightenment with the realization of the emptiness of inherent existence. It is stated that love is the longing that all sentient beings have happiness. Compassion is the longing that all sentient beings be separated from suffering and causes of suffering and equanimity is the longing that all sentient beings remain in the state of equal happiness. For the attainment of enlightenment the cultivation of altruistic motivation is mandatory. This altruistic motivation and intention helps the sentient being in preparing the proper psychophysical conditions to receive initiation from *Guru*.

Tantra imparts the lesson that one should not get enamoured with the marvels of mundane existence. Rather one should cultivate the motivation for achieving the supreme aim of getting liberation from the cyclic existence and for this one needs to take refuse in qualified spiritual *Guru*. Without following the *Guru*, one cannot rid oneself from yoke of the cycle of birth and death.

M.M. Gopinath Kaviraj says that there are two kinds of *Guru*, *Akalpita* and *Kalpita Guru*.[7] *Akalpita Guru* is one who has attained enlightenment and all the *Siddhis* without taking initiation from any *Guru*. About such *Guru* scripture says,

"अछष्टमण्डलोऽप्येवं यः कश्चिद् वेत्ति तत्वतः।
स सिद्धिभाग् भवेन्नित्यं स योगी स च दीक्षितः।।
एवं यो वेत्ति तत्त्वेन तस्य निर्वाणगामिनी ।
दीक्षा भवेदिति प्रोक्तां तच्छीत्रिंशकशासने।।"[8]

The Buddha belongs to this category of *Akalpita Guru*. In the annals of human history the Buddha is one of the greatest *Akalpita Gurus* who attained *Nirvāṇa* without the help and initiation by any *Guru* and probably he is the only historical person who helped and made about five hundred of his disciples enlightened beings through the transmission of light and empowerment. The other category is known as *Kalpita Guru*. Kalpita *Guru* is one who attains enlightenment with the help of other *Guru*.

The place of *Guru* occupies important place both in *Āgama* and *Nigama*, Tāntric and Vedic traditions. *Guru* is one who by his blessings through touch and sermon could awaken the divinity in sentient being. When the *Herukā* (*Kuṇḍilinī*) is made to awaken with the grace of *Guru* and reaches the *Mahāsukha Cakra* one gets liberated from all kinds of impurities and defilements. According to *Yoga Vāśiṣṭha* the inherent esoteric power of liberating the disciples from the bondage is the chief characteristic of a *Guru*. *Guru* through his *Kriyā Śakti* and touch and another techniques initiates the disciples to attain liberation.[9]

In the Buddhist Tantra the status of *Guru* is paramount. He becomes embodiment of the Buddha and Sugat. He is considered as *Dharmakāya* and the bestowal of enlightenment. He is omniscient. Without the blessings of *Guru* one cannot attain liberation. *Prajñopāya Viniścayasiddhi* holds *Guru* in a very high esteem.[10] The another Tāntric text *Jñānasiddhi* enumerates in detail the characteristic of the *Guru* and the disciple.[11]

There is some controversy regarding the qualifications of true *Guru*. After analysing the different qualifications and characteristics of different kinds of *Guru*, *Mālani-Tantra* says that for the seeker of salvation one should accept self-realized and enlightened one as his *Guru*. It says that person having the knowledge and the experience of divine effulgence and transcendental reality is real *Guru* and not the *Yogi*. However, the *Yogi* is also a *Guru*. In comparison to an ordinary *Yogi* the enlightened one is the best. When one should take refuse in *Yogi Guru* and when one should accept the *Jñāni Guru* enlightened *Guru* Ācārya Abhinavgupta has discussed this subject in detail. Those who are longing for salvation (*mokṣa*) and enlightenment (*Jñāna*) for them the self-enlightened *Guru* is a must. Even if one takes initiation from other *Guru* (preceptor) one will have to take refuse in self enlightened *Guru*.[12]

The *Guhyasamāja Tantra* says the *Guru* is one who initiates disciples in the *mantra* and guides and leads him to the path of liberation.[13] M.M. Gopinath Kaviraj says that the *Guru* who is not capable of imparting the knowledge of intuitional science he is *Guru* without any power. Those who are themselves ignorant how could they impart knowledge. Those who are longing for enjoyment (*bhoga*), salvation and intuitional science (*vijñāna*), he should accept self-realized and established in *Yogasiddhi* as his *Guru*. Those who are interested only in salvation (*mokṣa*) and intuitional science his *Guru* can be *Jñāni Guru*.

The *Śiva Sūtra* while enumerating the qualification of *Guru* says the *Guru* who has attained self-realization can alone help the aspirant in acquiring true knowledge.

Gururupāyaḥ

Guru is one who teaches the essential Truth. So, he is the means for leading one to the attainment of the potency of *mantra* and *mudrā*.

In *Mālinivijaya*, it has been said (Śiva addressing Pārvatī says) "One, who knows all the principles in their essentials, being able to throw light on the virility or efficiency of *mantras*, is a *guru* like myself." (II. 10).

In *Spandakārikā*, such matters being well known have not been treated. But in a way this matter has also been treated there in the last verse, which is as follows:

> "I offer my homage to that wonderful teaching of my *guru*, serving as a boat in crossing the fathomless ocean of doubts and full of such words as express wonderful, uncommon ideas. (IV.1).
> Or *guru* may be said to be the power of divine grace. As has been said in *Mālinīvijaya* "That (the power of grace) has been said to be the collective whole of *Śaktis*, that has been said to be the mouth of the *Guru*, *i.e.* the guru's power of grace."

In *Mantriśirobhairava* also, the same idea has been expressed in the following way :

> "*Guru*'s power of grace inherent in the mouth of the *guru* is greater than the *guru* himself." That power of grace affording a favourable opportunity to the aspirant is the means (to the unravelling of the secret of the *mantra*).[14]

According to Buddhism there is life beyond this life. Life is an unending stream of consciousness, it is a consciousness raised in the ocean of pure consciousness. This consciousness has many more consciousness behind it, and many more consciousness beyond it. In the ultimate analyses we came to the conclusion that there is a stream of pure consciousness.

This consciousness exists in every sentient being. It is called *Bodhicitta*. To understand and experience the stream of consciousness in its totality and to understand our life against this vast and unending stream of pure consciousness, there exists the inter-play of creation and dissolution. The metaphysics and the intuitional science (*Tantra*) have tried to understand the life and beyond this life as a stream of pure consciousness in understanding and experiencing this transcendental reality as a stream of pure consciousness. The *Guru* alone can be the guide and the pathfinder. Without taking refuse in *Guru* and getting proper initiation from him any effort to understand transcendental reality and infinite unity would be ludicrous efforts of emptying the ocean with the help of shell. We can understand the thrills of consciousness and we can hear the *Oṁkāra* and cosmic vibration of infinite unity within recess of our being and existence with the help of *Guru* only. It is *Guru* and *Guru* alone who can help us in transcending our being, our dimension, our time and our history and making us realise the totality and the sublimity of pure consciousness. This is called *Nirvāṇa*.

Mantra

The *Mantra* is the root concept of both Hindu and Buddhist Tantra. It is the life force of Tantra Sādhanā. *Mantra* is an esoteric formula that is to be practiced according to a strict Tāntric discipline. Each and every letter from 'अ' (*a*) to 'क्ष' (*kṣa*) of *Mātṛkā Varṇa* is living energy. They are acoustic roots of the different waves and the vibrations of the cosmos. These letters are the representative sonoric manifestation of the universe. According to Tantra *Śabda* is an expression of vibrational creative energy. When these letters are arranged after the Tāntric precepts a creative energy is generated which creates para-psychological wonders.

Mantra is the first principle of *Tantra*. There are lot of misunderstanding about *Mantra*. To understand the real meaning and significance of *Mantra* we have to understand the meaning and the significance of *Śabda* (sound). There is a great difference between the esoteric conception of sound and scientific concept of sound. The sound of physics is really the shadow of original sound. All empirical knowledge is inferential. Knowledge is nothing but the subjectivization of external objectivity. What we subjectivise is not real object but the different waves and vibrations. We subjectivise them with the help of our sensory organs. It is all vibrational play. These vibrations emanate from things and beings. They are characteristic essence of an act or thing. Among the vibrational manifestation of transcendental reality sound is the first and the subtlest. It is known as *Tanamātra*. The sonic *Tanamātra* is the first stage of manifestation. The musical notes of Beethoven are a supreme and sublime form of music. They are preserved in mute lines of a gramophone record or CD player. The sweet music is there, but one hears it only when the mute vibrational lines are transformed into sound waves. We hear different sounds only when the sonic *Tanmāntra* or waves are carried to the gates of our ear by ethereal or aerial vibration. What we hear is not 'sound as it is' but the shadow of the same. Physics deals with this 'shadow of sound' and not the original sound.

Swami Pratyagātmānanda says: "The real sounds or the sound as it is can be heard only by an absolute ear. 'The sound as it is' is the original sound. The sound which you, I, scientists and yogis hear is the distortion of the original form."[15] However, he has used the word '*Tanmātra*' in the Sāṁkhyian sense. According to Sāṁkhya, *Tanmātra* is beyond the reach of an ordinary person. Only a Yogi can have the perception of *Tanmātra*. But we differ from this Sāṁkhyian concept of *Tanmātra*. *Tanmātra* means the 'minutest form of that (objective)'. We receive and transmit *Tanmātra* according to our capabilities. The difference between our concept of *Tanmātra* and that of Sāṁkhya is conceptual. "The sonic *Tanmātra* can be heard by a yogic ear and the physical sound can be heard by the physical ear."[16] Hereby sonic *Tanmātra*, Swami Pratyagātmānanda means the sonic consciousness or *Śabda-Brahman* and not the sonic vibration.

Mantra Sādhanā is an esoteric technique to restore equilibrium or what is called *Sahajāvasthā*. In this state man goes beyond himself. He loses his own individuality. The sentient being attains enlightenment when he succeeds in establishing a parallelism between the rhythms of incantation, the rhythms of ideation and the rhythms of pulsation. With the help of constant ideation of the *Bodhicitta*, and an incantation of *Mantra* mind becomes pure and impeccant. Rāghava Bhaṭṭa defines *Mantra* as a mystic formula. 'The incantation of which brings the realization of cosmic consciousness (*Viśva-vijñānam*) and rid one of the bondage of worldliness is verily the *mantra*.'[17]

According to some indologists the *mantras* are development of *Dhāraṇīs* contained in works such as the *dharapiṭaka* Vidyā to which a reference has been given by Hiuan-tsang. According to Kern[18] the concept of *Dhāraṇīs* existed in Buddhism from its very inception. However, the *Mantra Sādhanā* has been introduced by Buddha himself.[19]

Attempt has been made to trace the origin of Tāntric mantra in Buddhism, while discussing the origin of *Mantra Sādhanā*. We are aware of the fact that all the great Tāntric treatises are in the form of Saṅgītis. The Buddha himself has introduced the Mantric system and other Tāntric practices in the assembly of Boddhisattvas. It is rightly believed that Buddha did not impart the secrets of *Mantra Sādhanā* to common mass because of the fact that the common mass were not qualified to receive the esoteric lessons of *Tantra*.[20]

The *Prajñāpāramitā Mantra* has been introduced and formulated by the Buddha himself. Great Buddhist Ācāryas Śāntarkṣita and Kamalaśīla are of the views that the Buddha is the originator of the concept of *Mantras, Maṇḍalas* and *Mudrās*.[21] *Mantra Sādhanā* is the main theme of *Tantra*. *Mātṛkā Varṇa* means methods of colours. There are innumerable waves and vibrations. Tāntric seers have divided them into fifty categories. The division is based on intuitive realization. These are fifty controlling sounds. The fifty letters are embodiments of fifty gross sounds. *Matṛkā Varṇa* is a causal matrix. All the letters are divided into two groups. Vowels are called *Bīja*, consonants are called *yoni*. Vowels are called *Bīja* because no compound can be made out of them. Consonants have the potentiality of making compound and addition (*Yogic*).

The Sanskrit alphabets are of Tāntric origin. They represent the different acoustic vibrations of the cosmos. The fifty letters are the fifty basic vibrations, which constitute the entire universe. They are the *Bījākṣara* of Tāntric esotericism. The word *'Mantra'* has been made from *man* + *trai* (*dhātu*) + i (suffix) = *mantra*, and means the incantation of which brings liberation from the trifarious bondage—physical, mental and spiritual. It creates an acoustic vibration in the psychic body of the *Sādhaka*, which awakens the *Kuṇḍalinī Śakti*. All *mantras* are words, but all words are not *mantras*. All words have originated from *Parā*, but only few words which have been originated from *Parā* are *mantras*.

Mantra is most potent weapon to cut asunder the trammels of nescience. The incantation of *mantra* is called *Praṇidhāna*. The incantation of the *Mantra* creates an acoustic vibration which awakens thè dormant divinity (*Kuṇḍalinī* or *Herukā*). According to *Tantra Mantra* are endowed with great mystic power. *Sādhanamālā* says if the *mantras* are incanted according to strict esoteric technique it could perform wonders and impossible task.[22] *Sādhanamālā* further says that through constant incantation of *Mantra* could generate so much power that the whole world could remain wonder struck.[23]

Mantras are powerful when they are applied strictly according to esoteric rules and formulations. The consciousness is the sole repository of the *Mantra*. Without the force of consciousness *mantra* is dead and useless. *Mantra-caitanya* is the *élan vita* of *Mantra Sādhanā*. It is an esoteric principles for unifying the internal ectoplasmic vibration with the cosmological vibration and lead on to the realm of spiritual sublimity. The adjustment between the individual ectoplasmic vibration and the cosmic vibration is the science and metaphysic of *Mantra Śāstra*. *Mantra* without consciousness force is of no consequence. *Mantras* which are alive with their life-force give all success.[24]

Bereft of this conscious-power *mantras* are combination of mere letters. They do not fructify. *Mantras* whose potency is asleep do not give any result. In the absence of the consciousness-force *mantras* become mere letters; even millions of incantations of such lifeless *mantras* do not give any fruit.[25]

The *Tantras* has formulated strict rules and discipline for the use of different *Mantras*. According to Tāntric formulation incantation of *Mantras* has to be performed with great care. According to *Sādhanamālā Mantra* should not be incantated either quickly or too slowly. The mind of the *Sādhaka* at the time of incantation of *Mantra* should be free from all kinds of impure reflection. Mind should be concentrated on each and every letter of the *mantra*. The *mantra* should be incantated so long as the *Sādhaka* does not become tired in his feelings and thoughts.[26]

Śiva Sūtra says, "*Mantra* is *citta*."[27] *Citta* means here cosmic consciousness. Bhāskara, the great commentator of *Śiva Sūtra* and author of *Śiva Sūtra Vārttika* says: "*Mantra* is that which is of the nature of the bringing intuitive realization of self."[28] The nature of *mantra* is consciousness.[29] The mantric power is not a mechanical force but a spiritual principle which awakens the dormant divinity.

Tantra enjoins upon every man and woman to awaken *mantra*. *Mantric* consciousness is the supreme state of evolution. It is a mystic technique for accelerating the process of enlightenment.

Śiva Sūtra further says, that the basis of knowledge is *Mātṛkā*.[30] *Mātṛkā* stands for the mystic sound corresponding to each letter of Sanskrit alphabet. This is called *Mātṛkā* (the mystic soniric power) because it produces the entire universe. The Sanskrit alphabet from 'अ' to 'क्ष' the mother of entire universe is a presiding deity. She is called *Mātṛka* because she is unknown. When the *Mātṛkā* is known she leads one to salvation. The different letters are being presided over by different deities.

1.	A varga; (the class of vowels)	Yogīśvarī or Mahālakṣmī
2.	Ka varga (ka, kha, ga, gha, ṅa)	Brāhmī
3.	Cavarga (ca, cha, ja, jha, ña)	Māheśvari
4.	Tavarga (ṭa, tha, ḍa, ḍha, ṇa)	Kaumārī
5.	Tavarga (ta, tha, da, dha, na)	Vaiṣṇavī
6.	Pavarga (pa, pha, ba, bha, ma)	Vārāhī
7.	Yavarga (ya, ra, la, va)	Aindrī or Indrāṇī
8.	Śavarga (śa, ṣa, sa, ha, kṣa)	Cāmuṇḍā

The *Guhyasamāja Tantra* which is the canonical literature of Buddhist Tantra discusses in detail about the *Mantra Śāstra*. While analysing and evaluating the concept of *Mantra Guhyasamāja* says that the *Mantra* is secret and the most powerful esoteric method to attain Vajrajñāna. By the incantation of *Mantra* alone one can attain salvation.[31] *Mantra* is an acoustic science, which brings the realization of inner psychic potentiality of man. Incantation of the Mantric formula creates an acoustic vibration which awakens the sleeping Kuṇḍalinī. This is most secret science of *Tantra*. The sole objective of *Mantra* is to attain liberation from the mundane, supra-mundane and spiritual bondage. The incantation of *Mantra* brings about the attainment of the four fold *Puruṣārtha* of life, *i.e. Dharma* (righteousness), Artha (wealth), *Kāma* (mundane happiness) and *Mokṣa* (liberation).[32]

The incantation of *Mantra* should always be associated with the ideation of transcendental reality. The ideational part of *Mantra* is the core of *Mantra Sādhanā*. M.M. Gopinath Kaviraj says: "According to the directive of Maharṣi Patañjali, in *mantra* incantation, the ideation of *mantra* is essential. Incantation and ideation are inseparable."[33] *Mantras* are innumerable. However, only *Siddha Mantras* are to be meditative. All *mantras* are acoustic. The acoustic vibrations of *Mantras* are flowing without any feeling both in the cosmos and in the sentient being. When through the esoteric process of Mantric incantation, one establishes parallelism between his unit ectoplasmic vibration and cosmic vibration, it is called *Mantra Siddhi*. The *Siddha-Mantra* is pregnant with divine consciousness and force. It comes from a perfect being or the *Guru*. It is a perfect *Mantra*. *Tantra* warns against the practice of *Mantra* heard by chance, seen by deceit and taken from some printed books; these lead to inevitable disaster.[34]

Man is dormant divinity (*Bodhicitta*) but due to impurities and defilements he has identified himself with lower manifestation. The bondage is in the form of different propensities and defilements of mind. Both the baser and benign propensities are the causes of bondage; one is a fetter of iron and other of gold but both are chains which keep man in bondage. *Mantra Sādhanā* is a esoteric process to purify the *Kāya, Vāk* and *Citta* of sentient being. *Guhyasamāja Tantra* says, that the *Mantra Sādhanā* brings about the purification of *Kāya, Vāk* and *Citta* and leads one to salvation.[35]

M.M. Gopinath Kaviraj has dealt in detail on the science of *Mantra*.[36] According to him one can awaken his or her *Kuṇḍalinī Śakti* through the incantation of *Mantra*. *Mahāmāyā* is also called *Kuṇḍalinī Śakti*. In every sentient being the *Kuṇḍalinī* resides. In the *Mahāmāyā* the consciousness force resides in the dormant state. The *Mantra Sādhanā* awakens the dormant divine power and makes one realise his own true being.

There are some confusion about the concept of *Mantra*. The Vedic hymns are not *mantra*. They are merely sublime poems. The Vedic hymns are not *mantra* because the chanting of Vedic hymns does not create that acoustic vibration which is necessary for the awakening of *Kuṇḍalinī Śakti*. The Vedic hymns may create a psychological climate for *Mantra Sādhanā*.

The *Mantra Sādhanā* should be performed under strict esoteric discipline. Adherence to principles of morality is pre condition for *Mantra Sādhanā*. Negligence on the part of sentient being in observing esoteric discipline and disobedience to moral principles obnubilate the sentient being.

While enumerating the importance of *Mantra*, *Śiva Sūtra* says that one after the blessings of the *Guru*, *Mātṛkā Cakra* accrues enlightenment.[37] According to *Śiva Sūtra* in unmanifest state *Kuṇḍalinī* is *Bīja, i.e.* the seed of manifestation and in the manifest state she is *jīva i.e.* life of all. The word *Kuṇḍalinī* means the divine creative Energy–Visarga-Śakti of Śiva's *I*-consciousness. It is coiled in three and a half folds. One fold represents the objective aspect (*prameya*) of the Supreme *I*–consciousness, another fold represents the *pramāṇa* or knowledge aspect, the third fold represents the *pramātā* or the subjective aspect; the remaining half represents *pramā* aspect which contains within itself both the subjective and the objective aspect in indistinguishable unity.

The *Sādhanā* of *Mātṛkā* is of profound importance. There is nothing beyond the science of *Mātṛkā* (letters).[38] The *Mantra Sādhanā* is the clear realization of the significance of *Mātṛkā Cakra*. This *Mātṛkā*, the realization of the power of *Mantra*, is the secret of *Tantra Sādhanā*. It liberates the sentient being from his pseudo *I*-ness, from his psycho-somatic self. It liberates sentient being from reified mind and leads him to salvation.[39]

Professor S.N. Dasgupta[40] is of the opinion that in transforming the different letters into *Mantra Tantras* have been greatly influenced by the *Mīmāṁsā* doctrine of *Śabda*. According to *Mīmāṁsā Śabda* is eternal. The meaning of *Śabda* is independent of any human agency. For the realization of the inherent meaning of the *Śabda* a special mystic power is required. *Śabda* being of the nature of the *Varṇa* the fifty letters of *Varṇa-mālā* are considered to be the totality of the presiding force of the basic fifty sonic sound.

M.M. Gopinath Kaviraj in his paper entitled *'Tantric Bauddha Sādhanā'* deals in detail about *Mantra Śāstra*. He says, that *mantranaya* is a profound esoteric practice. Unless one attains a high degree of qualification for performing *Tantra Sādhanā*, one should not be initiated into *Mantra Sādhanā*. The science of *Mantra* is practiced in India since ancient time. Because of its esoteric power which could be misused, *Mantra Sādhanā* was kept secret from the common masses. Everybody knows about the first *Dharmacakra Parivartana*. However, second and third *Dharmacakra Parivartan* is not very much known, but it is also authentic historical events. The profound philosophy of *Āgama* was propagated at the mountain Kailāśa and Meru by Śaṁkara and other Ācārya likewise the Buddha propagated the profound mystic practice of *Prajñāpāramitā* amongst his enlightened disciple at the Mt. Gṛidh Kutir near Rājagṛha.[41] Thus, the *Pārmitānaya* and *Mantranaya* are considered as the most profound philosophical and esoteric practice for the attainment of Buddhahood.

Maṇḍala

Maṇḍala is a mystic diagram. *Maṇḍala Sādhanā* is an important esoteric technique to awaken the *Kuṇḍalinī Śakti* and acquire different kinds of *Siddhis*. It stands for higher esoteric power. When one attains some kind of higher spiritual and moral power one is initiated into *Maṇḍala* worship. *Maṇḍala* means an esoteric apparatus by which *Sādhaka* attains both mystic powers (*siddhis*) and salvation.

Maṇḍala worship is a higher form of Buddhist Tantra. It is an esoteric technique to control the mind and fix it on the ideation of *Bodhicitta*. It helps the sentient being in overcoming the mundane desire which leads one to degeneration and moral degradation. *Maṇḍala* worship is invariably used in *Vajrayāna* and *Kālacakra Tantra*.

According to Buddhist Tantra there are different kinds of deities. The different deities have different *maṇḍalas*. The different *Mantras* are used for different deities and *maṇḍala* worship. *Maṇḍala* is of various kinds. It depends on the mode of worship. The proper selection of *mantras* and *maṇḍala* is one of the most difficult problems in *Tantra Sādhanā*. The *Guru* alone can help and guide in this intricate and complex problem of Tāntric esotericism. *Maṇḍala* is one of the cardinal principles of Tāntric esotericism. There is an integral and close relation between deity and the *maṇḍala*. *Maṇḍala* is the body and the deity is the soul. In *Hindu Tantra*, *maṇḍala* is called *Yantra*.

Maṇḍala worship is extremely sublime form of *Tantra Sādhanā*, because the worship of *Maṇḍala* and meditation on it leads to the eradication of defilement. It helps in eradicating the obstruction to liberation.

As we are aware that along with the *Mantra Sādhanā* the *Maṇḍala* worship has been introduced into Buddhist Tantricism. The *mantra*, *maṇḍala* and *mudrā* elements have a deeper significance in Buddhist Tantra. *Mantra* reveals the secrecy of the potency of *Śabda*. *Mudrā* reveals the secrecy of touch as associated with the potency of physiological system. S.B. Dasgupta writes, "With *Mantra* and *Mudrā* the element of *Maṇḍala* or describing the mystic circles was also introduced. Though this *Mudrā* element with the *mantra* element and some other esoteric practices may be traced back to the later Vedic practices, we have reason to think that in the evolution of *Mudrā* in esoteric Buddhism the different postures of the hands and fingers of Śākyamuni have something to do, and some of these postures do allude to some of the incidents of his life."[42]

Maṇḍala worship is though very profound it is very risky. It is not necessary that everybody should be allowed to perform this *Sādhanā*. Before practicing *maṇḍala* worship sentient being is required to purify his *Kāya*, *Vāk* and *Citta*. After getting initiation into *maṇḍala* worship *Sādhanā* is done with great care and restrained. According to both Hindu and Buddhist Tantra each deity has his own *maṇḍala* and thus the deity must be installed in his proper *maṇḍala*. If the *Sādhaka* is absent minded and commits mistake of installing another deity and invokes he is cursed by both the deities. John Woodroffe writes: "*Kaulavaliya Tantra* says that the distinction between *Yantra* and *Devatā* is like that between the body and the self. *Mantra* is *Devatā* and *Yantra* is *Mantra* in that it is the body of the *Devatā* who is *Mantra*."[43] *Yantra* is ensouled by *Mantra*. The deity is in the form of *Mantra*. The deity is immediately pleased if he is worshipped in the *Yantra*.[44] *Yantra* occupies a very important place in *Tantra Sādhanā*. It regulates and subdues (*niyantrana*) all misery arising from sex, anger and other failing. It is embedded in mysticism. As body is to the *Jīva* and oil is to the lamp, *yantra* is to the deities.[45] *Maṇḍala* is the mystic seat of all deities.

Maṇḍala is a mystic embodiment of the identity of *Nirvāṇa* and *Saṁsāra*. It is a mystic process of identification of *Saṁsāra* with *Nirvāṇa* which is considered as process of purification. The wrath is identified *Akṣobhaya*. Here the phenomenal existence is taken as none other than the aspect of absolute existence. D.L. Snellgrove writes, "To symbolize and to purify (in this sense) is essentially the same thing. The simplest form of *Maṇḍala* is that shown on diagram, where the five Buddhas, who embody the five transcendent wisdoms,[46] are equated with the five evils that lie at the root of phenomenal existence. This simple scheme is of great interest in that it illustrates so well the fantastic conclusions that extreme monism of this kind must arrive at, when its sole measure of what is real (*tattva*) is the mystic state. One identifies in fact those states, human passions and feelings and so on, which are now no longer experienced directly, with the blissful state of unity which is being experienced, and then when one emerges from this state, one envisages those passions and so on, now actually experienced, as so many aspects of the one mystic unity."[47]

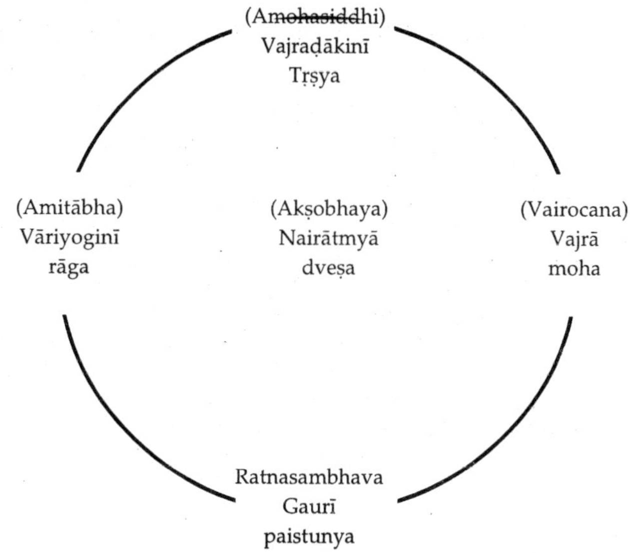

The Inner Circle of five Yoginīs *showing their sphere of purification and their correspondence with five Buddhas*

The purpose of *Maṇḍala* worship is to transform the phenomenal existence into a mystic absolute. Sentient being is considered as belonging by nature one of the five families each represented by one of the five Buddhas. The *Maṇḍala* suitable for every sentient being would have the Buddha installed at the centre of the *Maṇḍala*.[48]

Maṇḍala has been used in many senses in *Tantra*. One will have to be very careful in understanding the real meaning and the significance. It would not be out of place to mention that according to Wittgenstein the meaning of a word or sentence is understood only in a cultural context. There is no fixed meaning of any word. The meaning is determined by the use of different words in a different cultural contexts. Likewise the meaning of different symbols can be understood in the different esoteric contexts. Dalai Lama writes, The term '*Maṇḍala*' (dkyil khor, *Maṇḍala*) has many meanings. Our world is conceived as residing on *Maṇḍalas* or sphere of wind, water, and so forth; here '*Maṇḍala*' refers to the four elements. In a context such as "being directed towards entry to a path of the *Maṇḍala* (or spheres) of the bad transmigrations," '*Maṇḍala*' refers to birth-places. In "The *Maṇḍala* of the retinue of Boddhisattvas", "*Maṇḍala*" means the circle of a retinue. A drop of perfumed water can be called a "*Maṇḍala*" of perfumed water. A garland or series of light rays is called a *Maṇḍala* of light. The earth or the foundation, under a fence is called *Maṇḍala*. "Sun *Maṇḍala*" or "Moon *Maṇḍala*" just mean sun and moon but can refer to their round shape. In "Bow down with (the body) having five *Maṇḍala*", "*Maṇḍala*" refers to the five limbs-two arms, two legs and head. "*Maṇḍala*" also refers to an inestimable mansion that is the residence of deities, as well as to the resident deities. In addition, it can refer to the combination of divine residence and residents."[49]

The *Abhiṣeka* ritual of *Kālacakra* considers *Maṇḍala* as divine residence as well as mystic diagram of deities. Dalai Lama deals in detail about the concept of *Abhiṣeka* and *Maṇḍala* in his '*Kālacakra Tantra Rite of Initiation*'. For the realization of emptiness of inherent existence the deity *Kālacakra* is associated with *Kālacakra Maṇḍala*. *Kālacakra Maṇḍala* emits five colours—blue, red, white, yellow and green. *Kālacakra's* body is blue in colour. He has three necks and black in the centre, red to his right, white to his left. He has four faces. The black face in the centre symbolizes fears. If we walk round the *Maṇḍala* we could see the southern door of the mind *maṇḍala*. We see that his right face is red and it represents desire. His back face is yellow and it is observed in deep meditation. His left face is white and it symbolizes peace.

The quintessential characteristic of *Maṇḍala* is its geometrical regularity towards the various directions. In the *Yogini Tantra maṇḍala* is inhabited with famine deities. Even the centre is occupied by *Nairātamā*, the consort of *Hevajrā*. However, *Hevajrā* and *Nairātamā* are essentially one. The *Nairātamā* essentially represents the state of harmony and oneness (*Saṁrastā*). The purpose of the *Mantra* and the *Maṇḍala* worship is to have mystic experience of essential unity of *Nirvāṇa* and *Saṁsāra*. One may select his own divinity (*Īṣṭa Devatā*) and ideate upon it. But the whole purpose of ideation is to comprehend the existence in knowledge of its non-existence and likewise to conceive of *Herukā* in knowledge of his non-existence.

The mantra Hūṁ is the *Bīja Mantra* to awaken *Herukā* or *Kuṇḍalinī*. Sometimes we complicate the process by envisaging this *Vajra* by transforming itself at the centre of which *Hevajrā* is enthroned.[50] The basic function of *Maṇḍala* is to express the truth of emanation. It is considered as the centre of the Universe. Its core is Mt. Meru. It is considered as the Royal *Stūpa* and palace of universal worship and power. It seems that all these ideas and notions have been incorporated in Buddhist *Stūpa*. According to one school of thought *Maṇḍala* is primarily envisaged as *Stūpa*. D.L. Snellgrove writes, "One may envisage the final stage of emanation as the *Maṇḍala* of sixteen divinities, or one may envisage it as countless forms of *Hevajrā* filling space in a regularized order in every direction. Then one must realise the identity of oneself with the whole process by associating one's personality with the emanation, which is achieved by a strenuous act of belief : OM HERUKĀ–*svabhāvātmako* HAṀ—I am of the essence of Herukā.'[51]

G. Tucci has done a pioneering work on *Maṇḍala*. His book entitled '*Teoria*

Pratica del Maṇḍala' is a landmark in the study and understanding the mystic significance of *Maṇḍala*. According to him *Maṇḍala* is 'psychocosmogramme.' *Maṇḍala* worship is closely related with empowerment. The *Maṇḍala* visualized in ritual is three-dimensional world. It is made of a light ruby palace floating in a space at the centre of orbit protective spheres of lotuses and diamond hard *Vajra* forms the ground.

Maṇḍala is made of sand or paint forms the basis of meditation. The hallmark of *Maṇḍala* worship is the visualization. Bereft of ritual and visualization *Maṇḍala* is like an artifact from a lost civilization. R. Kohn writes, "In the *Maṇḍala* numerous metaphors merge. Some of these can be construed from the drawing itself. Most are revealed only by the ritual for which the *Maṇḍala* was originally created and by the literary and oral tradition that supports that ritual. One important metaphor is birth. The *Maṇḍala* string, homologized to semen impregnates the "Mother's sky". At the centre of the *Maṇḍala*, male and female symbols interpenetrate as the primal source. The deity within the *Maṇḍala* is born from a seed-syllable described as "The great drop of semen that causes the incarnated body". It is no wonder that the type of meditation to which the *Maṇḍala* belongs is called the Generation Creation or stage (*Tib, bskyed rim*); an equally valid, perhaps even better translation might be the 'birth process'.[52]

Maṇḍala is conceived sometimes as a reality. It is taken as the recreation of the world in a new image. This image is embodiment of harmony and peace. It is paradise. It gives a new perspective to visualize the mode of our existence as paradise. In our four doored *Maṇḍala* the new world is symbolized and conceived in various ways. The door and the centre of the *Maṇḍala* symbolizes the new world as paradise.

In preparing the *Maṇḍala*, a great care is taken of its geometrical articulation. The rituals of line and of the colours are the work of the teacher and the disciple. The teacher visualizes himself as the deity of *Maṇḍala*. The disciple considers himself as his consort. On the table the teacher and the disciple place five colours of thread. Both of them visualizing themselves as the master of *Maṇḍala* and his consort they project a complex visualization. In this process the creative force of the lines becomes one with the creative force of the deified participants. It conceives new reality in the womb of the space.

Samten Karmeya views that *Maṇḍala* symbolizes a notion of cosmology. He writes, "in rituals, it represents the divine residence, mentally created in accordance with the specifications prescribed in ritual texts, but it can also be made with materials, either on a temporary or a permanent basis, within the ritual premises. It can be a painting or made of coloured sand or a three-dimensional construction.

Just as its symbolical significance varies from one tradition to another, its philosophical interpretation also differs from one particular Tāntric sect to another within one school. However, its principal function lies in the notion of a mystic place where the officiating master communicates with the principal divinity and where the neophyte is admitted in order to receive the empowerment initiation. It is in this sacred sphere where the divinities are invoked to come down from their celestial residences, offered meals, made to listen to confession and requested to give blessings. However, another level, the mystic himself takes the place of the principal divinity in the *Maṇḍala*. In this state, which is beyond the spatio-temporal delimit, and where one was at the beginning of existence, the unity of all dichotomic notions such as *saṁsāra* and *nirvāṇa*, oneself and the other, and subject and object are realized in himself, and his divine residence symbolizes the reintegration of microcosm and macrocosm."[53]

Maṇḍala is mystic symbol. It stands for transcendental world that exists in the mind of every sentient being. The *Maṇḍala* drawn on the ground or as a painting does not represent true *Maṇḍala*. It is an ideational support for the realization of true *Maṇḍala*. In our mind is true *Maṇḍala*. It is symbolism which depicts esoteric structure of the universe with the Buddha. It stands for that which exists in our being. This is esoteric process through which a *Sādhaka* must travel in his pilgrimage back to his own centre, the locus of his indwelling *Nirvāṇa*. A. Snodgrass writes, "The formal *Maṇḍala* delineated on the ground can simultaneously depict both worlds, the inner and the outer, because of the strict analogy that exists between them. Each part of the universe is analogous to every other part and to the whole, so that the total cosmos is located at the centre of each mind. When the initiate enters the *Maṇḍala*, he is ritualistically traversing his inner states; in his innermost mind, he is crossing the flood of *saṁsāra*, tracing his way to the centre of the cosmos which is the *bodhi-maṇḍala*, the place where the Buddhas attain Enlightenment."[54]

The symbolism of *Yantra* is pregnant with profound mysticism. *Śrī Cakra* symbolizes the cosmos and its divine cause. There are two sets of triangles, one composed of four males (*Śiva*) triangles and other of five females (*Śakti*). From the macrocosmic point of view, the *Śakti* triangle stands for the five vital functions, the census of knowledge, the five census of action and the five subtle and five gross forms of matter and the mind. *Śiva* triangles represent the four higher *tattvas, i.e. Māyā, Śudhavidyā, Maheśvara* and *Sadāśiva*.

In the centre of *Śrī Cakra*, which is represented by a point (*bindu*), resides *Śiva* (*Kāmeśvara*) and *Śakti* (*Lalitā*) in an undifferentiated (*abheda*) union. Enclosing the *bindu* is an inverted triangle which symbolizes will (*icchā*), action (*kriyā*) and knowledge (*jñāna*) aspects of *Śakti*. The three *guṇas* and the deities preside over them. The other *cakras* are the *Aṣṭakoṇa* (eight triangles), *Daśāra-yugma* (two cakras, each of ten triangles), *Manvasra* (fourteen triangles), *Aṣṭadala* (eight lotus petals), *Ṣoḍaśadala* (sixteen lotus petals), *Vṛttatraya* (three circles and three squares). These nine *cakras* are ruled over by *yoginis* (divinities) presiding over forms of mind, sense and matter. *Yoginis* are called *Āvaraṇa Devatās* (veiling deities), because they veil the pure consciousness (*cit*) and create the appearance of the world of mind, sense and matter and limited and differentiated (apūrṇa). *Śrī Cakra* is the mansion of *Devī*. The realization of *Devī* (*Śakti*) and consequent bliss for the *yogi* comes from her *Mantra* which is the *Śrī-Vidya*."[55] The prescription for this *mantra* is given, and it is considered to be the most important esoteric item in *Śaktism*.

Maṇḍala Sādhanā is not important to everybody. It is employed for worldly gains also. After getting initiation into *Sādhanā* the *Sādhaka* draws *Maṇḍala* and meditates upon its esoteric form. The visualization and the empowerment are two potent esoteric techniques with the help of which *Sādhaka* succeeds in liberating himself from the various kinds of mental reifications which leads one to the attainment of Buddhahood.

Maṇḍala undoubtedly gets the primary support from the mind. The crude and sand *Maṇḍala* drawn on the ground for painting is not real *Maṇḍala*. It does give esoteric support for the visualization of the *Maṇḍala* through the process of Mantric ideation. It is a thought construct. It is spiritual structure symbolizing the mystic integration of microcosm and macrocosm. It is the locus of enlightenment, which resides in the recess of one's own being and existence.

Abhiṣeka

The language of *Tantra* is quite different from the language of literature. Like every branch of science *Tantra* has developed its own symbolism. Thus, the inner and the correct meaning can be understood only after getting initiation (*Abhiṣeka*) into the Tāntric esotericism. *Abhiṣeka* is the mystic technique of imparting the secret of *Tantra Sādhanā*. We cannot express the real significance and the depth of mystic experience in ordinary linguistic form. Wittgenstein after analysing the structure of language comes to the conclusion that there is limit of what is speakable and what is unspeakable. We are all aware of his famous statement that whereof we cannot sayeth thereof we must consign to silence. The experience of the transcendental reality is simply inexplicable (*avācya*). That is why *Tantra* and other philosophical treatises take the help of similies and metaphors. However, the word cannot correctly and properly communicate the higher spiritual experiences. That is why *Tantra* adopts varied symbolism to communicate the deep and profound mystic experiences of the intuitional science, at the same time it protects from the misuse of Tāntric esotericism. Angarika Govind writes: "In order to preserve its secret nature, they also had to use a language of symbolism which only the 'initiates' could understand. To the common people the words carried altogether different meanings. Unfortunately, a language of double interpretation was used by the writers of this school, 'as a sort of shock therapy'. The apparent meaning of these words gave a shock to common people, but to the 'initiates' they carried an altogether different meanings."[56]

His Holiness Dalai Lama says that there are seven kinds of initiation. He writes, "First, the students offer *maṇḍala*, after which they make a supplication for all seven initiations. Then, the Lama clears away any inauspiciousness and confers the seven initiations individually. In offering *maṇḍala*, imagine that, as before, you are outside the eastern door of the exalted body *maṇḍala*. Since today is the time of actually receiving initiation, you should be careful to perform the necessary imaginations for each part as to identify them".[57]

M.M. Gopinath Kaviraj making detail analysis and examination of *Abhiṣeka* says that without *Abhiṣeka* real knowledge of the transcendental reality cannot be obtained. Those who have not gone through the full process of *Abhiṣeka* such persons do not possess the qualification of becoming a *Guru*. The real essence of *Guru* iṣ to initiate the wheel of *Dharma*. The enlightened Buddha initiates the process of *Dharmacakra Parivartana* through the process of *Abhiṣeka*.[58]

According to Vajrayāna there are seven kinds of initiation. They are *Udakabhiṣeka, Mukutabhiṣeka, Pattabhiṣeka, Vajrabhiṣeka, Namabhiṣeka, Anujñābhiṣeka* and *Prañābhiṣeka*. The first two *Abhiṣekas* are for the purification of the body. Third and fourth purify the *Vāk* (speech) and fifth and sixth *Abhiṣeka* bring about the purification of mind (*Cittaśuddhi*) and the last *Abhiṣeka* brings about the purification of knowledge (*Jñānasiddhi*). Really speaking the seventh *Abhiṣeka* is a process to bring about the change in the wheel of *Dharma* which leads to the attainment of Buddhahood. In consideration of the different kinds of sentient begins the secrets of Vajrayāna have been divided into *Saṁvṛtti Sattva* and *Paramārtha Sattva*. With the purification of body, speech and mind through seven kinds of *Abhiṣeka* a sentient being becomes entitled to know and practice the secret of Tāntric esotericism.

The *Sādhanamālā* also while enumerating the concept of *Abhiṣeka* talks of the purification of body, speech and mind. It enjoins that after the purification of body, speech and mind and incantation of *Mantra* and meditation bring about the *Siddhis* and salvation.[59]

Sādhanamālā highlights the teachings of *Prajñāpāramitā* while discussing the process of *Abhiṣeka*. It enjoins that only after understanding the teachings of *Prajñāpāramitā* one should invoke all the Buddhas to get him initiated in *Vajrābhiṣeka Sādhanā*.[60]

We have already discussed above the different kinds of *Abhiṣeka* from the practical (*saṁvṛtti*) and transcendental considerations. *Abhiṣeka* is again of two kinds, *Saṁvṛtti* is of two kinds, *i.e. Lokasaṁvṛtti* and *Yoginisaṁvṛtti*. All the seven kinds of *Abhiṣeka* from *Udakābhiṣeka* to *Prajñābhiṣeka* are meant for the attainment of mundane *siddhis* (*Laukiksiddhi*). In Tantra it is called the former aspects of *Tantra Sādhanā*. The *Kumbhibhiṣeka, Guhyabhiṣeka* and the *Prajñābhiṣeka* belong to the *Yoginisaṁvṛtti Abhiṣeka*. Though, the *Abhiṣeka* comes under the *samvṛtti* but it is conducive to transcendental *Abhiṣeka* also.

Again, there are three kinds of transcendental *Abhiṣeka, i.e. Kṣara, Akṣara* and *Aspandana*. The transcendental *Abhiṣeka* is without any ideational and vibrational import. This is the higher kind of meditational practice where one meditates on the thousand petalled lotus. It brings about the experience of bliss in body, speech, mind and knowledge. The Buddhist Tantra also talks of thirty-two petalled lotuses and eight petalled lotus residing in *Anāhata Cakra*. Buddhist Tantra prescribes the meditation and visualization of *Vajramaṇi* that can be attained through piercing the different nerve plexus (*Padamas*). From the above enumeration of Buddhist esotericism without visualizing the *Bindu* residing at the centre of *Uṣṇīṣa-Kamala* one cannot attain the state of perfection and enlightenment. This is known as *Sahajāvasthā* the state of choiceless awareness.[61]

According to some Tāntric tradition one should approach the proper *Guru* for getting *Abhiṣeka* (initiation) into Tāntric esotericism after securing a proper *Prajñā* (women). The *Abhiṣeka* is an ancient rituals which is found in the early Buddhism also in the concept of *Pabbajjā* (vow of renunciation). In Theravāda Buddhism *Sādhaka* takes initiation to *Upasampadā*. The rite and the ritual of *Abhiṣeka* are found in all the schools of Buddhism. However, *Abhiṣeka* is mandatory and indispensable practice of Buddhist Tantra. It is stated that the Yogini who wishes to attain the Yogihood without proper initiation is like darting a blow at the sky with fists and drinking the water of mirage.[62]

Yogaratnamālā says that "Consecration is said to be fourfold for the benefit of living beings. One is sprinkled, that is to say cleansed and the consecration are distinguished as four". Thus it is said (in our text, II. *I*ii. 10) "the master, the secret, the *Prajñā* and then the fourth thus", in order that (the initiate) may progress far from evil *dharmas*. It is his 'bond' (*saṁvara*). The essential nature of the Master-Consecration is a conferment by means of the *Karmamudrā* and contains in essence the four moments and the four joys."[63]

According to *Śrī Cakra-Sambhāra-Cakra* there are six kinds of *Abhiṣeka, i.e. Abhiṣeka* with *Udaka* (water), *Mukuṭa* (crown), *Vajra* (indestructible), *Ghaṇṭā* (bell), *Nāma* (name) and *Ācāraya* (preceptor). These six *Abhiṣekas* are of the nature of six *Tathāgathas*. The initiation with *Udaka* (water) is the nature of ideal knowledge and it represents *Akṣobhaya*. The initiation with crown represents the equalizing knowledge (*Samatajñāna*) and it represents *Ratnasambhava*. Initiation with *Vajra* refers to discriminative knowledge. It stands for Amitabha. The initiation with *Ghaṇṭā* connotes the performance of duties and it represents *Amoghsiddhi*. The initiation with *Nāma* represents the knowledge of pure *Dharma Dhātu* and it represents *Vairocana*. And the last kind of *Kalasābhiṣeka* by Ācārya represents the pure knowledge (*Vajrajñāna*). These *Abhiṣekas* are followed by the *Guhyābhiṣeka, i.e.* the initiation into the secret of Tāntric esotericism. The quintessence of the *Abhiṣeka* is to impart the secret esoteric technique of Tantra Sādhanā to the *Sādhaka* through which he could experience the transcendental reality (*Bodhicitta*) with the unification of *Prajñā* and *Upāya*. S.B. Dasgupta writes, "After the *Guhyābhiṣeka* the preceptor explains to the disciples the void nature of the self (*pudgala*) as well as of all the objects (*dharma*), and also how this yogic process leads a man to the realization of that perfect knowledge (*Prajñā*). This part is, therefore, called the *Prajñābhiṣeka* or the *Prajñā-Jñānā-bhiṣeka*. But as *Vajra* is the ultimate adamantine reality and the ultimate principle of purity, the initiation ends with an initiation into the *Vajra-jñāna* called the *Vajra-jñānā-bhiṣeka*."[64]

According to *Advayavajrasmgraha* the *Abhiṣeka* is considered as cleansing away exterior dirt with water. The *Sādhaka* sprinkles water for washing away of ignorance. The rite of *Abhiṣeka* is sometimes compared with the Christian rite of Baptism. We feel that rite of *Abhiṣeka* is quite different from that of Baptism. According to *Mañjūśrīmulakalpa Abhiṣeka* refers to the esoteric process of initiation into mystic signification of the *Maṇḍala. Hevajrā Tantra* speaks of four kinds of *Abhiṣeka* (1) *Gurubhiṣeka*, (2) *Guhyabhiṣeka*,(3) *Prajñābhiṣeka*, and (4) *Abhiṣeka*.

Abhiṣeka is fourfold esoteric process for the benefit of sentient being. This *Abhiṣekas* confers four kinds of bliss.

1. Ānanda
2. Paramānanda
3. Virmānanda
4. Sahajānanda

There is some misunderstanding about the conferment of bliss through the process of *Abhiṣeka*. It is wrongly assumed that the bliss emanating from *Abhiṣeka* is fundamentally related with sexual experience. The four bliss are experienced at four successive movements. The relationship with the four kinds of *Abhiṣeka* is a complicated and complex process. The *Guru* concretion bestows joy in anticipation. The *Guhyabhiṣeka* bestows joy by the preceptor. In the *prajñābhiṣeka* joy is experienced directly. *Sādhaka* experiences in the process of fourth *Abhiṣeka* the bliss of innate joy (*Sahajānanda*). *Yogaratanamālā* says that first bliss is experienced in the first *Abhiṣeka* in the second and so on.[65]

Dalai Lama says that there is a difference between entering into *Maṇḍala* and receiving *Abhiṣeka*. But for both *Maṇḍala* practice and getting initiation generation of altruistic mind of enlightenment is considered as mandatory. His Holiness Dalai Lama is showing great concern about the non-adherence of generating altruistic motivation. Even without generating altruistic mind of enlightenment and not adhering to the moral norms and values by the *Sādhakas* and even then they are getting initiation into the secret science of *Tantra*. It could lead to degeneration and decline of Tāntric esotericism. His holiness writes, "In the past, entrance into a *maṇḍala* and granting initiation were used very carefully, discriminating between the two, but now-a-days Tibetans tend to initiate anyone. *Vajradhārā* set forth a complete system with different levels—those who could just enter a *maṇḍala*, those who could also receive the water and headdress initiations, and so forth. When it is done systematically, the Lama, prior to granting initiation, analyses the student to determine whether he or she can engage in the three trainings (ethics, meditative stabilization and wisdom) and keep the vows. He allows those who are not qualified but who have great faith to enter a *maṇḍala* but does not allow initiation. These systematic restrictions, which when followed make initiation effective and practical, are often not followed now-a-days, causing trouble for both Lama and initiate."[66]

His Holiness Dalai Lama has discussed this theme in his book *Kālacakra Tantra and Rite of Initiation* and he has analysed the process of *Abhiṣeka* in detail. According to him the water and crown initiation are meant for purifying the body. After the water and crown initiation the *Sādhaka* is initiated into internal initiation. Detailed process has been enumerated. In the internal initiation the student is drawn into the body of Lama who stands for the principal deity enthroned the body of Lama and *Sādhaka* enters into the womb of the consort and gets dissolved into emptiness. The *Sādhaka* reappears as deity in this *Abhiṣeka*. All the male and female deities and Boddhisattvas are invoked and invited. The male and female consorts becomes attracted to each other and get united and melt into an entity of ambrosia, which is called the mind of enlightenment. His Holiness writes, "The ambrosia enters the body of the Lama, who is the principal deity and passes through his body, conferring initiation on the students who are, as mentioned just above, in the form of Vajra Body deities in the womb of the consort. Then, the students emerge from the womb of the consort and are set on the initiation seat. This procedure is the same for the remaining initiations.

> With the six syllables *[oṁ āḥ huṁ haḥ haṁ kṣaḥ]* and
> Water from the conch, [obstructors] are cleared away.

Rays of light from *huṁ* at the heart of the Lama who is not different from the principal deity draw you in; you enter his mouth, pass through the centre of his body, and through the Vajra path enter the Mother's lotus and melt into a drop which turns into emptiness."[67]

The *Guhyasamāja Tantra* writes that there are four kinds of *Abhiṣeka: 1. Kalasābhiṣeka* (*jada*); 2. the *Guhyabhiṣeka* (secret); 3. the *Prajñābhiṣeka;* and 4. *Abhiṣeka* which is secret of all secrets because it reveals the secret of *Mantra Sādhanā* to the *Sādhaka* and the practice of which brings about the purification of speech (*vāk*), body (*kāya*) and mind (*citta*). This fourth kind of *Abhiṣeka* leads to the attainment of *Paramapada* (transcendental reality).[68]

Buddhism is a philosophy of mind. According to Buddhism mind is never polluted by defilements and afflictions because it is of Buddha nature. The Buddhahood cannot be achieved from any external agency. Buddhist Tantra says the fundamental innate mind is a transcendental reality and it is called Buddha nature. The moment the sentient being understood and experienced that his innate nature is of clear light and of Buddha nature he would attain *Nirvāṇa*. This is the *Sahajāvasthā* of every sentient being. The purpose of *Abhiṣeka* is to make the sentient being realise his own innate mind of clear light and Buddha nature which is the essence of everyone's being and existence.

In Hindu Tantra *Dīkṣā* occupies an important place. According to *Śāradā Tilaka* the process of initiation is the giver of spiritual knowledge and a means to annihilation of *Saṁsakāra*. The initiation is an esoteric process of unfolding the mysteries of *Mantra-Śāstra*. It directs the *Sādhaka* to make proper use of *mantra* for awakening the *Kuṇḍalinī*. Abhinavagupta, the chief exponent of Kashmir *Śaivism*, speaks very highly of initiation. He says: "The initiation is a process of purification of *Tattvas* and a means to attain Śivahood."[69]

The objective of *Dīkṣā* is to rid oneself from principles of obscuration and to expose what it veils and thus enables the *Sādhaka* to attain self recognition (*Pratyābhijñā*). Abhinavagupta defines *Dīkṣā* as 'a process of imparting Real Knowledge (*Jñāna*) and a preceptorial instruction which removes the bondage of *Pāśa*. Such kind of benediction and benevolent act is known as *Dīkṣā*.[70]

Abhiṣeka or *Dīkṣā* has been taken to be the secret practice of Tantra Sādhanā. The Tāntric mysteries are revealed only to the initiates. It is an esoteric technique. Both according to Hindu and Buddhist Tāntric tradition through initiation the *Guru* imparts the practical lesson to disciple to make use of *Mantra* and *Maṇḍala* (*Yantra*). *Mantra* is imparted during initiation. *Mantra* that is not imparted from proper *Guru* does not bear any fruit. That is why the whole *Tantra Sādhanā* has been kept secret and it forbids the use of *Mantra* and *Maṇḍala* without proper *Abhiṣeka*.

REFERENCES

1. *Two Vajrayāna Works*, G.O.S. no. 44, p. 12, verses 9-16, where the *guru* is eulogized by the disciple.
2. *Ibid.*, p. 71 ff.
3. *Tantrasāra*, (1.49-52).
4. *Two Vajrayāna Works*, G.O.S. no 44, p. 12, verses 9-16, p. 72.
   अन्ये च मुखः ख्याता मिथ्याज्ञानाभिमानिनः।
   लोभादर्थे प्रकुर्वन्ति धर्मस्य देशनां पराम्।।
5. *Introduction to Tantra: A Vision of Totality*, Lam Yeshe, p. 95.
6. *Kalacakra Tantra: Rites of Initiation*, p. 398.
7. *Bhāratīya Saṁskṛti aur Sādhanā*, vol. I., p. 258.
8. *Ibid.*, p. 258.
9. दर्शनात् स्पर्शनाच्छब्दात् कृपया शिष्यदेहके।
   जनयेद् यः समावेशं शाम्भवं स हि देशिकः।। निर्वाणप्रकरण, 1/128/161.
10. *Prajñopāya Viniścayasiddhi*, GOS, p. 12, ślokas 9-16.
11. *Jñanasiddhi GOS*, chapter 13 and 14, on p. 71ff.
12. आमोदार्थी यथां भृङ्गः पुष्पात् पुष्पान्तरं व्रजेत्।
    विज्ञानार्थी तथा शिष्यो गुरोर्गुर्वन्तर व्रजेत्।।
    Bhāratiya Saṁskṛti aur Sādhanā, p. 263, vol. I.
13. गुरुणा मन्त्रमार्गेण शिष्याणां परिपाचनम्।
    सुव्रतस्याभिषिक्तस्य सुशिष्यस्य महात्मनः। *Guhyasamāja Tantra*, p. 153.
14. गुरुः = the spiritual director

उपायः = means.

गृणाति उपदिशति तात्त्विकमर्थमिति गुरुः य सोऽत्र वयाप्तिप्रदर्शकत्वेन उपायः। तदुक्तं श्रीमालिनीविजये

'स गुरुर्मत्समः प्रोक्तो मन्त्रवीर्यप्रकाशकः।

इति। स्पन्दे तु एवमादिप्रसिद्धत्वात् न संगृहीतम्।

'अगाधसंशयाम्भोधिसमुत्तरणतारिणीम्।
वन्दे विचित्रार्थपदां चित्रां तां गुरुभारतीम्।।

इति-पार्यन्तिकोक्त्या च एतदपि संगृहीतमेव।

गुरुर्वा पारमेश्वरी अनुग्राहिका शक्तिः। यथोक्तं श्रीमालिनीविजये
'शक्तिचक्रं तदेवोक्तं गुरुवक्त्रं तदुच्यते।'

इति। श्रीमन्त्रिशिरोभैरवेऽपि

'गुरोर्गुरुतरा शक्तिर्गुरुवक्त्रगता भवेत्।

इति। सैव अवकाशं ददती उपायः।। 6।।

Śiva Sūtra, The Yoga of Supreme Identity, Motilal Banarsidass Publishers, pp. 102-3, Delhi, 1979.

15. *Japasūtram* (1st ed.), p. 17, Bharatiya Vidya Prakashan, Varanasi, 1966.
16. *Ibid.*, p. 18.
17. मननं विश्वविज्ञानं त्राणं संसारबन्धनात्।
    यतः करोति संसिद्धो मंत्र इत्युच्यते ततः। *Śāradā Tilakam*, p. 126.
18. *Mannual of Buddhism*, p. 6.
19. प्रज्ञादिसाधनमिदं सुगतोपदिष्टं
    आख्याय नः सुविपुलं कुशलं यदासीत्।
    तेनाशु विस्मयकरं च निरूत्तरं च
    सर्वज्ञताऽपि पदमस्य जनस्य भूयात्।। *Sādhanamālā*, vol. I., p. 334.
20. अथ वज्रपाणिः सर्वतथागताधिपतिः तान् सर्वतथागतान् बोधिसत्त्वांश्चमन्त्रयते स्म। भूतपूर्वं भगवन्तः सर्वतथागता अनभिलाप्यानभिलाप्यबुद्धक्षत्रसुमेरूपरमाणुरजः समाः कल्पाः क्षीणा यावद् भगवक्तो दीपङ्करस्य तथागतस्यार्हतः सम्यक्संबुद्धस्यातिक्रान्तस्य काश्यपस्यापि महामुनेरभिसंबुद्धस्य व भाषितम्। तत्कस्मात् हेतोः। अभव्या भगवन्तः सत्त्वा अस्य महागुह्यपदार्थस्य तेन कालेन तेन समयेन मया न भाषितम्। अपि तु भगवन्तः सर्वतथागता अस्मिन् गुह्यसमाजे बुद्धबोधिं जणलवमुहूर्त्तेनैव निष्पादयन्ति। यदनैवकैर्गङ्गानदीबालुकासमैः कल्पैः घटयन्तो व्यायच्छन्तो बोधिसत्त्वा बोधिं न प्रान्पुवन्ति। तदिहैव जन्मनि गुह्यसमाजाभिरतो बोधिसत्त्वः सर्वतथागतानां बुद्ध इति संख्या गच्छति।
    Guhyasamāja, G.O.S., chap XVII, p. 144.
21. *Tattvasaṁgaraha*, p. 905. Kamalaśila says : योगः समाधिः। आदिशब्देन मुद्रामण्डलादिपरिग्रहः।
22. षाएमासात् सिद्धिराख्याता कर्त्तव्यो नात्र संशयः।
    किमस्त्यसाध्यं मन्त्राण योजितानां यथाविधि।। *Sādhanamālā*, vol. II, p. 575.
23. तस्मादिष्टफलाशंसी सम्पूर्णविधिमाचरेत्।
    विश्वविस्मापने शक्तिरस्मादस्योपजायते।। *Ibid.*, vol., p. 334.
24. मन्त्राचैतन्यसंहिताः सर्वसिद्धिकराः स्मृताः।
    Kulārṇava Tantra, ch. 15, ver. 60, p. 326.
25. चैतन्यरहिता मंत्राः प्रोक्ता वर्णास्तु केवलम्।
    फलं नैव प्रयच्छन्ति लक्षकोटिजपादपि। *Ibid.*, ver. 61.

26. ततः सर्वबुद्धबोधिसत्त्वप्रणामालम्बनजापमभ्यसन् यथाभिलषितं मन्त्रं न द्रुतं न बिलम्बितं असत्सङ्कल्पवर्ज्जितं मन्त्राक्षरगतचितं तावज्जपेत् यावन्न खेदो भवति। तत उत्थायार्य्य गण्डव्यूहादिसूत्राणि तथागतहृदयं सकृदवुस्मृत्य वाचयेत्।
Sādhanamālā, vol. I, p. 10.
27. चितं मन्त्रं ।।1।। *Śiva Sūtra*, ch. II. ver. I.
28. *Śiva Sūtra Vārttika*, p. 30.
29. *Ibid.*, p. 31.
30. ज्ञानंधिष्ठानं मातृका ।।4।। *Śiva Sūtra*, chap IV., ver. 5. p. 25.
31. संस्फरेद् विश्ववाद्वश्वं त्र्यध्वबीजेन तं जयेत्।
जयं जल्पंनमाख्यातं सर्ववाङ्मन्त्रमुच्यते।।
मन्त्रं मन्त्रमिति प्रोक्तं तत्त्वं चोदनभाषणम्।
यथैव हृद्यधिष्ठानं समाधिं च तथैव च।। *Guhyasamāja Tantra*, 157, vol. LIII.
32. शृणु देवि प्रवक्ष्यामि यन्मां त्वं परिपृच्छसि।
तस्य श्रवणमात्रेण मन्त्रतत्त्वं प्रकाशते।।
जपयज्ञात परो यज्ञो नापरोऽस्तीह कश्चन।
तस्माज्जपेन धर्मार्थकाममोक्षांश्च साधयेत्।।
33. *Tāntrika Vāṅgamya Mein Śāktadṛṣṭikoṇa*, p. 286.
34. *Ibid.*, p. 15.
35. कायवाक्चित्तनिध्यप्तेः स्वभावो नोपलभ्यते।
मन्त्रमूर्त्तिप्रयोगेण बोधिचित्ते च भावना।।
विचार्यैदं समासेन कायवाकचित्तलक्षण।
भावयेत् विधिसंयोगं समाधि मन्त्रकल्पितम्।।
Guhyasamāja Tantra, vol. LIII, p. 24.
36. *Bhāratīya Saṁskṛti aur Sādhanā*, p. 323.
37. मातृकाचक्रसम्बोधः, *Śiva Sūtra* : 7 ch. II, V. 2.
38. न विद्या मातृकापरा। *Svacchanda Tantra, Paṭala* 16 ver. 199.
39. मन्त्र दद्यात् तदा तस्य मन्त्रचोदनभाषितैः।
समाधिं मन्त्रराजस्य दत्वा गुह्यां समारभेत्।।
Guhyasamāja Tantra, vol. LIII, p. 120.
40. *General Introduction to Tantra Philosophy*, by Prof. S.N. Dasgupta, collected in his philosophic essays.
41. *Bhāratīya Saṁskṛti aur Sādhanā*, vol. I, p. 526.
42. *An Introduction to Tāntric Buddhism*, p. 62.
43. यंत्र यंत्रममत्रम् प्रोक्तं मंत्रामा देवतैव हि
देहात्मनोर तथा वेदो यंत्रदेवतयोसतया। *Śakti and Śakta*, p. 548.
44. यंत्र मंत्रमयं प्रोक्तं देवता मंत्ररूपिणी।
यंत्रे सा पूजिता देवि सहसैव प्रसीदति।।85।। *Kulārṇava Tantra*, p. 208.
45. शरीरमिव जीवस्य दीपस्य स्नेहवत प्रिय।
सर्वेषामणि देवानां तथा यन्त्रं प्रतिष्ठितम्।।87।। *Ibid.*

46. See p. 129 and I. viii, 6-7, where the terms are translated. See also *Mahāyānasūtrālaṅkāra*, ed., S. Levi, ix. 67-76. For other references see La Siddhi de Hiuan-tsang (transl. By de la Vallee Poussin, Paris 1928-9), p. 681. The full five are listed in MVP, p. 8.
47. *Hevajrā Tantra*, Part I, p. 29.
48. Concerning these families see *Buddhist Himālaya*, pp. 64-67, 74-75.
49. *Kālcakra Tantra: Rite of Initiation*, Dalai Lama, p. 75.
50. See Tucci, *Teoria Pratica del Maṇḍala*, p. 31.
51. *Hevajrā Tantra*, Part I, pp. 32-33.
52. *The Ritual Preparation of Tibetan Sand Maṇḍala*, Maṇḍala and Landscape, ed. A. W. Macdonald, D. K. Print World Pvt., New Delhi, 1997, p. 398.
53. Samten G. Karmey, *Secret Visions of the Fifth Dalai Lama*, London, Serindia Publication, 1988, pp. 71-72.
54. A. Snodgrass, *The Symbolism of the Stūpa*, Ithaca, Cornell University, Southeast Asia Program, 1985, p. 107 and *passim*.
55. *Saundaryalaharī*, p. 9.
56. 2500 years of Buddhism (second Reprint), p. 313. Publication Division, Government of India, New Delhi, 1964.
57. *Kālacakra Tantra: Rite of Initiation*, p. 257.
58. *Tantric Sādhanā aur Siddhānta*, Bihar Rastrabhasa Parishad, Patna, 1994, pp. 276-77.
59. तत्र दशाक्षराणि–ॐ तारे तुतारे तुरे स्वाहा। तथा चित्रवाक्कायाधिष्ठानाभिषेक– बिन्दुसूक्ष्मयोगजाया दयोऽपि ध्याततव्या इति

    एतन्मन्त्रवरं श्रेष्ठं सर्वबुव्डैर्नमस्कृतम्।

    पठितसिद्धिकरं दिव्यं वज्रपञ्चरभाषितम्।। *Sādhanamālā*, pp. 185-186.

60. तदुपरि वज्रतीक्ष्णं कनकवर्ण सर्वालङ्कारभूषितं दक्षिणे करे खड्ग वामे करे प्रज्ञापारमितापुस्तकं द्वीन्द्रियसमापत्त्या भावयेत्। ॐ वज्रतीक्ष्ण सुरतस्त्वं (त्वं) मनसा जपेत्। स्वदेवतामण्डलचक्रं प्रति भाषयेत्। मञ्जुघोषसमं (यं) इहैव जन्मनि भवति–ॐ शून्यताज्ञानवज्रस्वभावात्मकोऽहं, ॐ वज्राभिषेकं सर्वबुद्धा ददन्तु माम् ।

    ।। वज्रतीक्ष्णभट्टार कस्य साधनं समाप्तम्।। *Sādhanamālā*, p. 148.

61. *Tantric Sādhanā aur Siddhānta*, p. 278.
62. *nā'bhiṣikto hi yo yogā yogitvam abhivāṇachati* |
    hanyate muṣṭinā' kāśaṁ pivet ca mṛga-tṛṣṇikām | |
    — Quoted in the *Kriyā-Saṃgraha Pañjikā*, MS. p. 5(A).
63. *Yogaratnamālā* by Kāṇha belonging to Cambridge University Library, Add. 1699, vol. II, p. 107, 1.24ff.
64. *An Introduction to Tāntric Buddhism*, p. 161.
65. *Yogaratanamālā*, vol. II, p. 32.
66. *Tantra in Tibet*, p. 77.
67. *Kālacakra Tantra: Rite of Initiation*, p. 265.
68. अभिषेकं त्रिधा भेदमस्मिन्तन्त्रे प्रकल्पितम्।

    कलशाभिषेकं प्रथमं द्वितीयं गुह्याभिषेकतः।

    प्रज्ञाज्ञानं तृतीयं तु चतुर्थं तत् पुनस्तथा।।

    मन्त्रयोग्यां विशालाक्षीं सपुष्पां शुक्रसम्भवाम्।

    गुह्यगुह्याभिषेकं तु दद्यात् शिष्यस्य मन्त्रिणः।।

    खधातुमध्यगतं कृत्वा विण्मूत्रमज्जसंयुतम्।

    वज्रपदंप्रयोगेन सर्ववज्रान् समाजयेत्।।

सर्वांस्तान् हृदये पात्या कायवाक्चित्तवज्रतः
उत्सृज्य वज्रमार्गेण शिष्यवक्त्रे निपातयेत्।।
इदन्तत् सर्ववज्राणामाभषेकयदं परम्।
सिद्ध्यन्ति सर्वमन्त्राणि कर्माग्रप्रसराणि च।।

Guhyasamāja Tantra, vol. LIII, p. 160.

69. तत्त्वशुद्धिशिवयोजनारूपाया दीक्षाया इति।
Tantrasāra, p. 3, Kashmir Series of Texts and Studies, Srinagar, no. XVII, 1918.

70. दीयते ज्ञानसद्भावः क्षीयते पशुवासना।
दानक्षपणसंयुक्ता दीक्षा तेनेह कीर्तिता।।
Tantrāloka, vol. I, p. 80. Kashmir Series of Texts and Studies, Srinagar, 1918.

7 Conclusion

Buddhism is a philosophy of the mind (*Cittādarśana*). *Theravāda* reduces the mind into a set of thoughts and feelings and seeks deliverance from nescience through detachment. On the other hand, *Mahāyāna* especially the *Buddhist Tantra,* view mind as the seed of enlightenment (*Bodhicitta*). Through esoteric practice Buddhist Tantra achieves enlightenment. Mind is considered as *Kalpa-vṛikṣa* and *Cintāmaṇi.* The goal of Theravāda is to attain the state of eternal quiescence whereas the objective of Mahāyāna and Tantra Sādhanā is to transform mind into eternal emptiness. This eternal emptiness is called *Bodhicitta. Bodhicitta* is bereft of all existence. The Buddhist Tantra reveals the real nature of *Bodhicitta.* According to *Tantra, Bodhicitta* can be experienced only through the esoteric practice of *Mantra, Maṇḍala* and *Herukā* (*Kuṇḍalinī*). The practice of Buddhist esotericism unfolds the experience of spiritual perfection and the infinite unity of *Prajñā* and *Upāya.*

Some of the spiritual experiences are transcendent and some are concerned with philosophical reflection and religious investigation. The basic principles of Buddhist Tantra is that the all sentient beings are of Buddha nature. The Buddha nature remains unpolluted and pure in spite of defilements and cravings. This Buddha nature is pure consciousness and infinite bliss (*mahāsukha*). It is an eternal process based on the unchanging law which operates through eternal recourse. The practice of esotericism leads to the control of mind and senses and takes man to the highest experience of the purest conception of Love and Compassion, *Prajñā* and *Upāya, Śūnayatā* and *Karuṇā.* Buddhism does not believe in the personal Self. However, its noble ideal is to awaken trust and confidence in Buddhahood as being one's true nature. It awakens the aspiration and longing to realise one's own true Buddha nature.

There have been two great streams of thought in Buddhism, that of the *Sūtra* and that of the *Tantra.* The *Sūtra* and its commentaries created the vast literature of Buddhism. This is known as Theravāda Buddhism of Pāli text. There is a general misunderstanding that the Tāntric culture which regulated the life in ancient time did not prove very helpful for Buddhism. This is because of the fact that *Mahāyāna Sūtras* and the Tāntric treatises and their commentaries were not only little known in the academic world before the end of the nineteenth century, but they have been grossly misunderstood because of their profound mysticism. The Buddha was aware of the antinomical character of reason and the interminable nature of metaphysical conflict and he was also aware that this conflict can be resolved only by the higher state of critique. This heralded the new era of questioning and dialectical reasoning and which led to the quest for the proper esoteric method that could take man to the realization of the Buddha nature. Buddha had great faith in meditation and esotericism. The Buddha himself was an exponent of *Tantra* and he was aware that the dormant spiritual energy (*Kuṇḍalinī*) can be awakened only with ideation and incantation of the *Mantra*. The incantation of *Mantra* reveals the mystery of *Bhūmi* (consciousness) and awakens the dormant divinity which is known in Buddhist Tantra as *Herukā, Vajratārā, Vajrayoginī* and *Vajracaṇḍikā*.

Pañcamakāra Sādhanā is practiced both in Hindu and Buddhist Tantra. It is an esoteric technique for the transformation and the sublimation of baser instincts and tendencies to the higher experience of Bodhicitta. Anger and sex are innate biological instincts. It is an established principle that suppression and repression makes a man neurotic. The principle behind the *Pañcāmakāra Sādhanā* is that man must rise with the help of that *Śakti*, which, if misused will cause his fall. The scientific proposition is that the poison which kills can be transformed into elixir of life if suitably treated and tested by wise physician. Man has to work out his own salvation, not by negating his desire and suppressing evil tendencies, but by so canalizing them and sublimating into them higher forms of spiritual life. Buddhist Tantra says that the sentient being has to find out his own enlightenment not by incorporating his desire and suppressing the biological instincts but by sublimating and channelising them into higher spiritual experience. During *Sādhanā*, man and woman sublimate their corporeal existence and realise that they are the true manifestations *Upāya* and *Prajñā*.

In the history of human civilization, different philosophical and scientific doctrines have made claim to explain the nature of truth. However, Aristotelian natural science collapsed under the theoretical scrutiny of modern physics. The question arises whether the mathematical concepts have grounding in objective reality. What we observe is not nature in itself but the nature exposed to our method of questioning. C.S. Peirce has rightly stated that the conclusions of science make no pretence to being more than probable. The nature does not speak itself. The world of experience is related to our mind. According to Buddhism, reality is in eternal flux. Our experience is only the point instant. Reality is in the state of flux. Existence is contingent. There is no logical foundation for the theoretical basis of natural science. The natural world is known in relation to our modes of experience. The mind is the only instrument through which we know mind and consciousness. Consciousness is a continuum flow. The duality of the physical and the mental does not exist in the state of pure continuum. This continuum is known as emptiness. *Prajñā* is the esoteric experience of emptiness. *Prajñā* is *Nirvāṇa*. It is a state of salvation and pure bliss. Buddhist Tantra after analyzing the doctrines of speculative metaphysics come to the conclusion that it is futile to attempt to comprehend reality through senses and mind, and hence, it recommends the practice of *Mantra, Maṇḍala* and *Kuṇḍalinī* for the realization of the unity of *Prajñā* and *Upāya, Karuṇa* and *Śūnyatā* which is known as enlightenment.

The unification of *Prajñā* and *Upāya, Śūnyatā* and *Karuṇā* manifests in creation. The universe is nothing but the thought projection of *Bodhicitta. Prajñā* and *Upāya* are inseparable, *i.e.* the existence of one is not possible in absence of the other. Vajrayāna, Sahajayāna and Kālacakra are the development of Tāntric Mahāyāna. There is no difference between Hindu and Buddhist Tantra. The awakening of the *Herukā* (*Kuṇḍalinī*) and the incantation of *Mantra* are the mystic techniques of creating the awareness and the experience of the *Vajrasattva*, the absolute of Buddhist Tantra. With the incantation of *mantra* and the ideation of *Bodhicitta*, the mind is gradually transformed into eternal emptiness. *Uṣṇīṣa-Kamala* is the abode of *Bodhicitta*. It is a thousand petalled lotus. *Vajrasattva* resides in it. It is known as *Mahābindu*. When the *Kuṇḍalinī* reaches *Uṣṇīṣa-Kamala*, it drinks the pineal nectar contained in it. The *Sādhaka* becomes divine intoxicated. He becomes one with transcendental reality. It is known as the unification of *Prajñā* and *Upāya*.

Mahābindu is the transcendental reality. The whole universe has emanated from this transcendental point. All the waves and vibrations have originated from it. The experience of *Parābindu* in the mystic unification of *Prajñā* and *Upāya* is the supreme state of spiritual sublimity and beatitude. The attainment of this transcendental experience is possible only after piercing the different *Cakras* by the *Kuṇḍalinī* and getting united in its infinite unity and pure consciousness.

The Vajrayāna, Sahajayāna and Kālacakrayāna are the metaphysical schools of Buddhist Tantra. According to Vajrayāna enlightenment cannot be attained by subjecting the mind and body to suffering. Enlightenment can be attained by enjoying the mundane pleasures and thereby exhausting all the metempsychosis which binds man to mundane existence. Buddha was against physical suffering and penance. The Hindu and Buddhist Tāntric treatises have been written in *Sandhyābhāṣā*. The *Sandhyābhāṣā* is a twilight language which is full of symbolism. For the layman, this symbolism is nonsensical words but for the initiates it is of great esoteric importance and significance.

The Buddhist Tāntric tradition belongs to Mahāyāna. There are conceptual difference between Therāvāda and Mahāyāna. However, both of them believe that the realization of *Śūnyatā* brings about the cessation of suffering. Therāvāda believes in personal salvation. According to Mahāyāna, if one attains personal salvation, one cannot know the transcendental nature of reality.

Mantra, Mudrā and *Maṇḍala* and the invocation of deities are the esoteric basis of Tantra Sādhanā from its very inception. Buddha revised and resuscitated the lost science of *Tantra*. The *Guhyasamāja Tantra* which is considered as the Bible of Buddhist Tantra introduced the concept of *Śakti*. According to Buddhist Tantra the transcendental reality does not get affected by adventitious ideas. The Vedānta also speaks in the same vein and says that *Ātmā* remains unaffected, ineffective by the good and bad deeds of *Jīva* because the transcendental nature of *Ātmā* does not undergo any change and transformation.

The *Guhyasamāja Tantra* introduced the concept of five Dhyānī Buddhas presiding over the five *Skandhas*. The five *Skandhas* are *Rūpa* (form), *Vedanā* (feelings), *Saṁjñā* (name), *Saṁsakāra* (impression) and *Vijñāna* (consciousness). The names of five Dhyānī Buddhas are Vairocana, Ratnasambhava, Amitābha, Amogha-siddhi, Akṣovyabhya. The female counterparts of the five Dhyānī Buddhas are *Locan, Vajradhātrīśvarī, Pāndārā, Māmaki* and *Tārā*. These five consorts of Dhyānī Buddhas belong to the five families of *dveṣa, moha, rāja, cintamaṇī* and *samaya*. The names of five Boddhisattavas of the Dhyānī Buddhas are Vajrapāṇī, Samant-bhadra, Padmapāṇī, Ratanapāṇī and Viśapāṇī.

According to *Vajrayāna, Prajñā* and *Upāya* reside within the body of the sentient being. *Upāya* resides in high plexus (*Uṣṇīṣa-Kamala*) and *Prajñā* dwells in the lowest plexus (*Mūlādhāra*). Tantra Sādhanā aims at to awaken *Prajñā* (*Herukā*) from the lowest plexus and making her proceed in an upward movement till she becomes united with *Upāya* in *Uṣṇīṣa-Kamala*. Man represents *Upāya* and woman represents *Prajñā*. The esoteric commingling of the two is the giver of supreme bliss (*Mahāsukha*).

Buddhist Tantra heralded a new era of spirituality and religion which is the meeting ground of *Bhoga* (enjoyment) and *Yoga* (salvation). According to Buddhist Tantra world is the manifes-tation of Buddha nature. The process of cosmic ideation and *Bhoga* (enjoyment) turns into *Yoga* (salvation). Tantra Sādhanā is not meant merely for salvation but also for enjoyment, not merely for beatitude (*niśreyaṣa*) but also for progress.

The generic idea of Buddhist Tantra is that *Śūnyatā* and *Karuṇā* constitute Bodhicitta. *Śūnyatā* is creation and recreation of the universe. There is some misunderstanding about the introduction of the principle of *Śakti* in *Tantra*. *Prajñā* resides in every woman, but it does not mean that *Tantra* recommends the wanton enjoyment of woman. *Prajñā* is the realization of *Śūnyatā*. The Unification of *Prajñā* and *Upāya* is like the commingling of water and milk. This is known as *Prajñopāya*. The *Prajñopāya* is the creative matrix of the cosmos and every thing has emanated from this principle of supreme creativity. It is called *Mahāsukha* also because this creative matrix is the source of all happiness.

Buddhist Tantra has incorporated all the best philosophical concepts and doctrines and because of this it has become very popular. It is one of the greatest contributions made by Buddhism to world civilization because of its adherence to the philosophy of spiritual perfection and esoteric technique of transforming a sentient being into Buddhahood.

Against the doctrine of Dhyānī Buddhas and their inumerable emanations a devotional school of Buddhist Tantra came into existence. This is known as

Sahajayāna. Sahajayāna is a philosophical and mystic development of Vajrayāna. The whole literature of Sahajayāna is primarily poetical. It is an expression of profound sensibility and devotional feelings. This is known as Siddha literature which covers the whole gamut of human life. Siddha literature is in *Apabhaṁśa* language, it expounds the philosophy and the devotional sensibility of eighty four Siddhācāryas. The Siddhācāryas were great mystic poets and their language is full of symbolism. The songs and *dohas* of Siddhācārya are full of lyricism and grace.

Like other treatises of *Tantra*, the literature of Sahajayāna has also been composed in *Sandhyābhāṣā*. The language of Siddhācārya is esoteric (*Guhya*) the meaning and the significance of which are revealed only to the initiates. The symbols of this language are sexual and have amatory connotations but their hidden meaning is related to the profound philosophy and practice of mysticism. Most of the symbols represent the woman of the low caste. *Prajñā* is addressed as *Jananī* (mother), *Nartakī* (dancing girl) and *Dombī* (*dome* girl). *Prajñā* is called *Jananī* because she is the cause of creation. She is called *Nartakī* because the universe is a cosmic dance of *Prajñā* and every object is in a dancing posture (*Nṛtaratā*). She is called *Dombī* because she is beyond the touch of human mind and senses.

Buddhist Tantra expounds the practice of different *Cakras* (nerve plexus). These *cakaras* are abodes of different mystical gods and goddesses who grant different kinds of mystic power (*Siddhis*), and are known as different places of pilgrimage. The central objective of Tantra Sādhanā is to cross these different *cakaras* and reach the *Mahāsukha Cakra*, the fountainhead of infinite bliss and enlightenment.

The quintessence of the *Tantra Sādhanā* is to attain the mystic unification of oneself with Bodhicitta. This state of mystic unification is both an enjoyment and salvation. *Tantra* rejects the philosophical doctrine of nihilism and pessimism. *Tantra Sādhanā* is a mystic practice to realize and experience the divine presence of *Prajñā* which puts an end to all physical, mental and spiritual sufferings and inspire the *Sādhaka* to live upto the ideal and glory of the Buddha. *Tantra* views world neither as illusion nor as reality.

The oneness with the infinite is called qualified and non-qualified state of Buddhahood. Spiritually speaking *Tantra* is a mystic practice to awaken one's own dormant divinity and attain enlightenment after conquering all the mental tendencies and the dispositions. A man is wrapped in *Avadiyā*. Unless he eliminates the positive effect of Avidyā, he cannot get rid of the defilement. One can retrace one's way against the positive force of Avidyā only with the help of some negative force. *Kiṇḍalinī* is the negative force of individuation. It is *Parāśakti* and spiritual force behind all mental and physical activities. It is called *Adhāraśakti*. It is the fundamental negativity. When *Kuṇḍalinī* is awakened it becomes one with consciousness by becoming unsubjectivated (*Nirādhāra*).

The *Kuṇḍalinī* remains in a sleeping state. When it is awakened through yogic practice, *Sādhaka* obtains intuitive power to experience and visualize the divine effulgence. According to *Tantra* this state of *Mahāsukha* is both transcendental and immanent. The transcendental aspect of *Mahāsukha* is *Śūnyatā* and the immanent part of it is *Karuṇā*. Both *Śūnyatā* and *Karuṇā* constitute the infinite unity. This eternal co-existence of the two is known as *Mahābindu*. The division of the two is the origin of the creation.

The objective of *Tantra* is to awaken *Kuṇḍalinī* and make it conscious. When the *Kuṇḍalinī* is awakened, it forces its passage through different *Padmas* (*Cakras*) and excites them to action. The *Bodhicitta* opens up all occult powers and mystic vision come to the *Sādhaka*. When it reaches *Uṣṇīṣa-Kamala,* he becomes free from all defilements. It cuts asunder the trammels of nescience and *Bodhicitta* becomes free from the bondage of individuation. The *Kuṇḍalinī* is neither a biological nor a psychic principle. It is an exoteric concept but it can be seen intuitively. It has the brilliance of thousand of suns.

Mahāsukha (infinite bliss) is the quintessence of transcendental reality. The transcendental reality is realized when we experience the *Bodhicitta* as *Māhasukha* (infinite bliss). In our ordinary life, the experience of the highest happiness is in the state of copulation. *Tantra* is not a sexo-yogic *Sādhanā* but it is a psychological and esoteric process of transforming the mundane experience into supra mundane and spiritual experience of *Mahāsukha*. When this state is attained the objective multiplicity is merged into the infinite unity and everything else dwindles into non-existence. The sentient being attains Buddhahood which is a totality of all beings and existences. This is known as *Sahajāvasthā*.

Tantra explains the whole creation as the organic functions of the body. It believes that there is an isomorphic relation between human body and the universe, between microcosm and macrocosm. Philosophically speaking the first step in the process of Tāntric practice is to identify the innately misconceived, the *I*, and the inherent existence. According to Sāṁkya and Vedānta the erroneous identification of *I* with non-self is the real bondage. According to Buddhism, there is no inherent existence. Everything is in a state of flux.

According to *Kālacakra Tantra*, our body exists not only at the physical level but also on a subtle level about which we are profoundly ignorant. The ordinary physical body which is composed of physical elements undergoes change, decay and death. But there exists a subtle body which is called *Vajrabody* in Buddhist tradition and *Kāraṇaśarīra* in Hindu tradition. The Vajrabody or the Kāraṇaśarīra does not undergo any decay and death, as it is indestructible. Our physical body is constituted of nerve system. The Vajrabody is constituted of *nāḍīs* which keep flowing *prāṇa* (vital energy) and *bindus* (drops) which are the source of our true being and pure bliss. The purpose of Tāntric meditation is to become aware and alive of this Vajrabody and to attain and experience the infinite unity and enlightenment.

Tantra Sādhanā is just like playing with high voltage electricity and little carelessness may either bring death or untold suffering. Because of this danger and risk, *Tantra* has laid down a detailed qualification and condition for the practice of Tantra Sādhanā. *Tantra* was opened only for few persons who were equipped with high degree of moral refinements and powers. State of Buddhahood is not oblivion but spiritual perfection. It is a perfection of knowledge where there is no impurity. It is the fullness of life and the richness of being and existence. Life merges into the divine fullness.

Tantra is primarily spirituality. It is not a religion in the ordinary sense of the term. The degeneration of humanity cannot be prevented by religion and hollow philosophy. It can be achieved only through spiritual regeneration. *Tantra* vibrates the material incrustations of the mankind. It aims at arresting the decline of moral values and *Dharmas* and enthrone them to the wills and minds of the people. *Tāntric mantras* are not mere words. They are the mass of divine energy.

The present civilization and culture is buffeted as never before by the foreboding waves of materialism and consumerism. Mysticism and the profound teachings of Buddhist Tantra hold hope and promise for a better tomorrow. The Yoga and Tantra can play powerful role in moulding and transforming the cultural, ethical and spiritual life of mankind. It may well be the salvation of the crisis ridden present civilization.

The crisis in civilization has become a cliché. This crisis is a result of changed and changing cultural environment, and the radically conflicting value systems. The philosophical and scientific contemplation of the future society poses the problem of change and the problem of meaning. The belief in man who would guide and direct history towards the goal of just society has unfortunately been shattered. Scientific advancements have forced man to ask the cardinal question; how and why the system has gone awry. Scientific and technological advancements are getting out of balance with our moral and social performances. However, if we examine ills of the modern society and try to find the solution of the failures of present civilization which would unlease course of history that would be self-destructive, then we would realise the historical necessity of harmonious blending of Science and Spirituality, Tantra and Yoga for the moral transformation of man and society.

The dangerous fissures that have occurred in our social system can be overcome only by the cultivation of love and compassion, truth and non-violence. The constituents of society are not individuals but their relations. In the absence of ethical and spiritual contents of human relations no society worth its name can be formed and survived.

The great civilizations like Greek, Roman and Egyptian were destroyed due to inner contradictions and fissures created in the absence of proper spiritual anchorage and vision and the lack of the commitment to higher values whereas Indian civilization and culture survived the pillage of time and plunder of history because of its spiritual moorings and adherence to ethical and spiritual norms.

Science without spirituality has a chance of making man monster and spirituality without scientific temper makes a man inert. We are living in the best of times and at the same time we are living in worst of times. If we fail to resolve the present crisis of civilization created by the misuse of scientific knowledge and power and lack of spiritual vision and commitment, there will be the inglorious end of mankind. And if we succeed in creating a harmonious blending between science and spirituality, Yoga and Tantra, between man and divinity, there will be ushered a 'new era of hopes and promises' and that would be the harbinger of twenty-first century as an era of spiritual renaissance

Buddhist Tantra is a mystic technique to invoke the spirituality of man and woman. *Prajñā* (*Śakti*) according to *Tantra* is all pervading. She is immanent in living and non-living creatures in the form of energy. Modern science has also to affirm this universal permeation of energy. This would bring science and spirituality closer. *Tantra* provides the philosophical and mystic meeting-ground for both of them. *Tantra* believes that spiritual development should be given priority over scientific advancement, if not, the human civilization will be doomed to destruction. Science should be utilized for the service and sanctity of mankind. Man with the spiritual vision and moral commitment should be at the helm of affairs, so that science is not used for maiming, mutilation and annihilation of mankind.

BIBLIOGRAPHY

Source Books

Abhinavagupta. *Tantrālokā,* 12 vols., Kashmir Sanskrit Texts and Studies, vols. 27-39, Kashmir Government Publications, Srinagar, 1921-38.

——. *Tantrasāra,* Kashmir Sanskrit Texts and Studies; vol. 17, Srinagar, 1918.

——. *Paramārthasāra,* Kashmir Sanskrit Texts and Studies, Srinagar, 1916.

Avalon, Arthur (Sir John Woodroffe). *Mahānirvāṇa Tantra* (The Great Liberation), 3rd ed., Ganesh & Co., Madras, 1953.

——. *Kulārṇva Tantra,* Ganesh & Co., Madras, 1965.

——. *Hymn to Kālī* (Karpuradi-stotra), 3rd ed., Ganesh & Co., Madras, 1965.

Bhaskara. *Śiva Sūtra Vārtika,* Kashmir Sanskrit Texts and Studies, Srinagar, 1916.

Bhattacharya. Benoytosh (ed.), *Guhyasamāja Tantra,* Gaekwad Oriental Series, Baroda, 1931.

——. *Sādhanamālā,* 2 vols., Gaekwad Oriental Series, XXVI & XLI, Baroda, 1925-28.

——. *Niṣpannayogāvalī of Abhayakar Gupta,* Gaekwad Oriental Series, no. 109, Baroda, 1949.

Bhattacharya, Jivananda Vidyasagar (ed.). *Rudra Yāmalam Uttaratantram,* Vacaspati Press, Calcutta, 1937.

Brown, W. Norman (ed.). *Saundaryalaharī,* Harvard Oriental Series, vol. 43, Cambridge, Massachusetts, 1958.

Kṣemarāja. *Svacchanda Tantrani,* 6 vols., Kashmir Sanskrit Texts and Studies, Srinagar, 1921-25.

Kaviraj, Dr. Gopinath (ed.). *Tripurā Rahasyam,* Saraswati Granthamala, vol. 15, Varanasi, 1965.

——. *Yoginihrdayam,* vol. 7, Saraswati Granthamala, Varanasi.

Lakshmanadesikendra *Śāradā Tilakam.* Chowkhamba Sanskrit Series Office, Varanasi, 1963.

Leidecker, Kurt F. (ed.). *Pralyabhijñāhṛdayam* (The Scent of Recognition), Adyar Library, Madras, 1938.

Ramanujacharya, M. D. (ed.). *Ahirbudhnya-Saṁhitā of the Pañcarātrāgama,* 2 vols., Adyar Library and Research Centre, Madras 20, 1966.

Rinpoche, Samdog. *Vimala Prabha*, vols. I, II and III. Central Institute of Higher Tibetan Studies, Saranath, Varanasi.

Shastri, Haraprasad (ed.). *Advayavajra Saṁgraha*, Gaekwad Oriental Series, no. XL, Baroda, 1927.

Shastri, Madhusudan Kaul (ed). *Sri Mṛgendra Tantram*, Kashmir Sanskrit Texts and Studies no. L, Srinagar, 1930.

——. *Mālinīvijayottara Tantram*, Kashmir Sanskrit Texts and Studies, Srinagar, 1922.

——. *The Śivadṛṣṭi*, Kashmir Sanskrit Texts and Studies, Srinagar, 1934.

Snellgrove, D. L. *The Hevjarā Tantra*, 2 vols., London Oriental Series Oxford University Press, London, 1959.

General Books

Abhinavagupta. *Tantrasāra*, Kashmir Sanskrit Texts and Studies, vol. 17, Srinagar, 1918.

——. *Paramārthasāra*, Kashmir Sanskrit Texts and Studies, Srinagar, 1916.

Amratanandanatha. *Yoginīhṛdaya Dīpikā*, Saraswati Bhavan Series, Varanasi.

Anandamurti. *Ānanda Sūtram*, Ananda Marga Pracaraba Samgha, Anandanagar, P.O. Bagiata, Purulia (W. Bengal), 1964.

——. *Subhāṣita Saṁgraha*, 4 vols., Anandanagar, P.O. Baglata, Purulia (W. Bengal).

Aurobindo, Sri. *Bases of Yoga*, Arya Publishing House, Calcutta, 1949.

——. *On the Veda*, International University Centre, Pondicherry, 1956.

——. *Synthesis of Yoga*, Sri Aurobindo Ashram, Pondicherry, 1955.

Avalon, Arthur (Sir John Woodroffe). *The Serpent Power*, Ganesh & Co., Madras, 1958.

Avalon, Arthur (Sir John Woodroffe).*Tantrik Texts*, 2 vols., Luzac & Co., 46 Great Russell Street, London, 1922.

——. *Śakti and Śakta*, 2nd ed., Ganesh & Co., Madras.

——. *The Garland of Letters* (Varṇamālā), Ganesh & Co., Madras, 1963.

——. *Kāma-Kalā Vilāsa*, Ganesh & Co., Madras, 1963.

——. *Principles of Tantra*, (Tantratattva), Ganesh & Co., Madras, 1955.

——. *Hymn to Kālī* (Karpūrādi-Stotra), Ganesh & Co., Madras, 1965.

——. *Hymn to Goddess*, Ganesh & Co., Madras, 1964.

——. *The Greatness of Śiva*, Ganesh & Co., Madras, 1963.

——. *Introduction to Tantra Śāstra*, Ganesh & Co., Madras, 1963.

——. *Tantrarāja Tantra*, Ganesh & Co., Madras, 1952.

Ayangar, S. Krishnaswami (ed.). *Paramasaṁhitā of the Pañcarātra*, Gaekwad Oriental Series, LXXXVI, Baroda, 1940.

Bagchi, P. C. *Studies in the Tantras*, University Press, Calcutta, 1939.

——. *Kaulajñāna-nirvāṇa and Some Minor Texts of the School of Matsyendranatha*, Calcutta Sanskrit Series 111, Calcutta, 1934.

Banerjee, Akshaya Kumar. *Philosophy of Gorakhnatha*, Mahant Digvijay Nath Trust, Gorakhnath Temple, Gorakhpur.

Banerjee, Biswanatha. *Sri Kalacakra Tantra Raja*, The Asiatic Society, 1, Park Street, Calcutta, 1993.

Basham, A.L. *The Wonder That Was India*, Sidgwick & Jackson, London.

Berzin, Alexander. *Taking the Kalachakra Initiation*, Snow Lion Publication, Ithaca, New York, 1997.

Besant, Annie. *Brahma Vidyā*, Theosophical Publishing House, Adyar, Madras, 1927.

Bhattacharya, Chintamani (ed.). *Matrikabheda-Tantra*, Sanskrit Series no. VII, Calcutta.

Bhattacharya, Śrī Jīvananda Vidyāsagar (ed.). *Rudrayāmalam-Uttaratantram*, Vacaspati Press, Calcutta, 1937.

Bhattacharya, B. *The World of Tantra*, Munshiram Manoharlal, Delhi, 1988.

Bhattacharya, B. (ed.). *Śaktisaṅgama-Tantra*, Gaekwad Oriental Series LXI, XCI, XIV, 3 vols., Baroda 1932, 1941, 1947.

Bhattacharya, Benayatosh. *An Introduction to Buddhist Esotericism*, vol. XLVI, Chowkhamba Sanskrit Series, Varanasi.

——. *Buddhist Iconography*, Oxford University Press, London, 1924.

Bharati, Agehananda. *Tāntric Tradition*, Rider & Company, London, 1965.

Bloomfield, M. *Atharva Veda evaṃ Gopatha Brāhmaṇa*, Chowkhamba Sanskrit Series, Varanasi, 1964.

Bose, D. N. & Haldar, H.L. *Tantras—Their Philosophy and Occult Secrets*, Oriental Publishing House, Calcutta, 1956.

Bose, Manindra Mohan. *The Post Chaitanya Sahajīya Cult of Bengal*, University Press, Calcutta, 1930.

Briggs, G. W. *Gorakhanāth and the Kānphaṭa Yogis*, Oxford University Press, London, 1938.

Carelli, Mario (ed.). *Sekoddeśaṭīkā of Nādapāda (Nāropa)*, Gaekwad Oriental Series, Baroda, 1941.

Chakravarti, Chintaharan. *The Tantras: Studies on Their Religion and Literature*, Punthi Pustaka, Calcutta, 1963.

——. *Srinivāsa, Saubhāgyasubhadaya*, Library of the Maharaja of Alwar, Rajasthan, no. 2445.

——. *Śrīvidyākhaḍgamātā*, Chowkhamba Sanskrit Series, Varanasi, 1963.

——. *Śrīvidyā-Nityāracanam*, Chowkhamba Sanskrit Series, Varanasi, 1962.

Chatterjee, J. C. *Kashmir Shaivism*, Research & Publication, Government of Jammu & Kashmir, Srinagar, 1962.

Chaudhuri, Pandit B. (ed.). *Śaktisādhanā*, Chowkhamba Sanskrit Series, Varanasi, 1963.

Chakravorty, P.C. *Doctrine of Śakti in Indian Literature*, General Printers and Publishers, Calcutta, 1940.

Coomaraswamy, A.K. *Elements of Buddhist Iconography*, Cambridge, Massachusetts, 1935.

——. *The Dance of Śiva*, Noonday Publication, New York, 1957.

Cowell & Mitra. *Principal Upaniṣads*, 3 vols., Theosophical Publishing House, Adyar, Madras, 1932.

Dampier, Sir William Cecil. *A History of Science and its Relations with Philosophy and Religion*, Cambridge University Press, 1961.

Das, Sudhendu Kumar. *Śakti on Divine Power*, Calcutta University, Calcutta, 1934.

Dasgupta, Surendranath. *Yoga Philosophy and Religion*, Kegan Paul, London, 1924.

——. *History of Indian Philosophy*, 5 vols., Cambridge University Press, 1963.

Dasgupta, Shashi Bhushan. *Obscure Religious Cults*, 6/1 A, Banchharan St., Akrur Lane, Calcutta, 1946.

Dasgupta, S.B. *An Introduction to Tantrik Buddhism*, University Press, Calcutta, 1950.

——. *Obscure Religious Cults as Background of Bengali Literature*, University Press, Calcutta, 1946.

Dave, Sakratal Y. and Shastrī, A. Mahadeva, (eds.). *Paraśurā-makalpasūtra*, Gaekwad Oriental Series, XXII, Baroda, 1950

Dhargyey, Geshe Ngawang. *Kalacakra Tantra*, Library of Tibetan Works & Archives, Dharmashala, 1999.

Diksit, Pandit Ramanath (ed.). *Samatantra*, Chowkhamba Sanskrit Series, Varanasi, 1963.

Dikshitar, V.R. *The Lalitā Cult*, University of Madras, Madras, 1942.

Eliade, Mircea. *Le Yoga : Immortaliteet*, Paris, 1954. English version (trans.), W. R. Trask. *Yogi : Immortality and Freedom*, Bolligm Series, Pantheon Inc., New York, 1958.

Ernest Mackay. *The Indus Civilization.*

Evans-Wentz, W. (ed.). *Tibetan Yoga and Secret Doctrines—Seven Books of Wisdom of the Great Path*, Oxford University Press, London, 1935.

——. *The Tibetan Book of the Dead* (Bardo Thodol) (trans.), Oxford University Press, London, 1949.

——. *Tibet's Great Yogi Milarepa*, Oxford University Press, London, 1928.

Farquhar, J.N. *Religious Literature of India*, Motilal Banarsidass, Delhi, 1966.

Fitzerald, Edward. *The Religions of Tibet*, Allen & Unwin, London, 1958.

Foucher, Max-Pol. *The Erotic Sculpture of India*, Allen & Unwin, London, 1959.

Garfield, L. Joy. *The Fundamental Wisdom of the Middle Way*, Oxford University Press, New York, 1995.

Gambhirananda, Swami. *Eight Upaniṣads*, vols. 2, Advaita Ashram, Calcutta-14, 1963.

Geden, A.S. *Tantra's Entry in the Encyclopedia of Religion and Ethics*, J. Hastings, vol. XII.

Ghose, Atal Behari. *Śiva and Śakti*, Rajashahi, 1935.

Ghoshal, U.N. *Studies in Indian History and Culture*, University Press, Calcutta, 1955.

Glasenapp, H.V. *Buddhistische Mysterien*, Stuttgart, 1940.

Goddard, Dwight. *A Buddhist-Bible*, E.P. Dutton & Co; Inc., New York, 1952.

Gordon, Antoinette. *Tibetan Religious Art*, New York, 1952.

——. *The Iconography of Tibetan Lamaism*, New York, 1939.

Gordon, D.H. *The Prehistoric Background of Indian Culture*, N.M. Tripathi Pvt. Ltd., 164, Princess Street, Bombay-2.

Govinda, Lama Anagarika. *Foundations of Tibetan Mysticism*, Rider & Co., London, 1959.

Griffith, R.T.H. *Hymns of the Ṛg-Veda*, E.J. Lazarus & Co., London, 1920.

Guenther, H.V. *Yuganaddha—The Tāntric View of Life*, Chowkhamba Sanskrit Series, Varanasi, 1964.

——. *The Life and Teaching of Narapa*, Clarendon Press, Oxford, 1963.

Hoffmann, H. *The Religions of Tibet*, Allen & Unwin, London, 1961.

Hopkins, Jeffrey. *Tāntric Practice in Nying-ma*, Rider, New York, 1972.

——. *Tantra in Tibet*, Rider, New York.

Jacobs, H. *Western Psychology and Hindu Sādhanā*, Allen & Unwin, London, 1961.

Jaiswal, Suvira. *The Origin and Development of Vaiṣṇavism*, Motilal Banarsidass, Delhi, 1967.

James, William. *The Varieties of Religious Experience*, The Fontana Library, London, 1960.

Jhaveri, M.B. *Comparative and Critical Study of Mantra Śāstra*, Sarabhai Manilal Nawal, Ahmedabad, 1944.

Jñānānanda Paramahamsa. *Kāntāvalinirṇaya Tāntric Texts*, vol. XIV, Agamanusandhana Samiti, Calcutta, 1928.

Kaviraj, Gopinath. *Bharatiya Sanskrit aur Sādhanā*, vols. I & II, Bihar Rastrabhasa Parisad, Patna, 1996.

——. *Bharatiya Sādhanā ki Dhara* (Hindi), Bihar Rastrabhasa Parisad, Patna, 1984.

Kaviraj, Gopinath. *Tāntric Sādhanā aur Siddhanta*, 2nd edition, Bihar Rastrabhasa Parisad, Patna, 1994.

——. *Tantrik Vāṅmaya men Śāktadṛṣṭi*, 2nd edition, Bihar Rastrabhasa Parisad, Patna, 1994.

Kṛṣṇapriyacārya (ed.). *Maheśvara-tantram*, Chowkhamba Sanskrit Series, Varanasi, 1963.

Kṛṣṇamācārya, V. *Lakṣmītantram*, Chowkhamba Sanskrit Series, Varanasi, 1966.

——. *Lalitāśaraṇam* (Stotram), Vavillu Rāmasvāmī Sāstralu & Sons, Madras, 1955.

Lama, Dalai. *Kalachakra Tantra : Rite of Initiation*, Wisdom Publication, Boston, 1991.

——. *Tantra in Tibet*, Snow Lion Publication, New York, 1997.

Macdonald, A.W. (ed.). *Maṇḍala and Landscape*, D.K. Print World, New Delhi, 1997.

Macdonell, A. A. *Hymns from the Ṛg. Veda*, Oxford University Press, London, 1922.

Mādhavācārya. *The Sarva-Darśana-Saṁgraha*, Kegan Paul Trench, Trubner & Co. Ltd., Dryden House, Gerrard Street, London, 1908.

Maheśvarananda. *Mahārtha-mañjūśrī*, Kashmir Sanskrit Texts and Studies, no. XI, Srinagar, 1918.

——. *Maheśvarī-tantram*, Chowkhamba Sanskrit Series, Varanasi, 1963.

Majumdar, R.C. *An Advanced History of India*, Macmillan, London, 1958.

——. *Ancient India*, Motilal Banarsidass, Delhi.

Mallik, Kalyani. *Nāth-Sāmpradāyer Itihās*, University Press, Calcutta, 1950.

Marshall, Sir John. *Mohenjo-daro and the Indus Valley Civilization*, 41, Great Russell Street, London, 1931.

Max Müller (ed.). *Atharva-Veda, Sacred Books of the East*, vol. XXIX, Motilal Banarsidass, Delhi.

Minkowski Raum und Zeit. Physik, Zeitschrift.

Misra, Pandit Kanhaiyalal (ed.). *Yoginī-Tantra*, Gaṅgāviṣṇu Śrīkṛṣṇadās, Kalyan, Bombay, 1957.

Mitra, A.K. *Kulacūḍāmaṇi-nigaina*, Ganesh & Co., Madras, 1956.

Munshi, K.M. (ed.). *The History and Culture of Indian People*, Bharatiya Vidya Bhavan, Bombay, 1950.

Narayan. *Tantra-sāra-saṁgraha*, Chowkhamba Sanskrit Series, Varanasi,1963.

Nikhilnanda, Swami. *The Gospel of Ramakrishna*, Ramakrishna Math, Madras, 1950.

——. *Hinduism : Its Meaning for Liberation of the Spirit*, Allen & Unwin, 1958.

Oldenberg, Hermann. *Vedic Hymns*, Part II, *Sacred Books of the East*, Clarendon Press, Oxford, 1897.

Oman, J.C. *The Mystics and Saints of India*, T.F. Unwin, London, 1903.

Pande, G. C. *Studies in Mahayana*, Central Institute of Higher Tibetan Studies, Saranath, Varanasi, 1993.

——. *Foundations of Indian Culture*, vol. I, II & III, Motilal Banarsidas, Delhi, 1990

Pandey, K.C. *Abhinavagupta*, Chowkhamba Sanskrit Series, Varanasi, 1935.

Panigrahi, K. C. *Obscene Sculptures of Orissian Temples* in Proceedings of the Indian History Congress, VIII, 94-97.

Petech, L. *History of Madieval Nepal*, Serie Orientale Roma, Rome, 1960.

Piggot. *Pre-Historic India*, Harmondsworth, 1950.

Poleman, H. (ed.). *Tantra, Śaiva and Spanda: A Census of India Manuscripts in the United States and Canada*, American Oriental Society Monograph, vol. 12, 1938.

Pott, P.H. *Yoga en Yantra*, Leiden, 1946.

——. *Introduction to the Tibetan Collection of the National Museum of Ethnology*, Leiden, 1946.

Prasad, Durga (ed.). *Rājataraṅgiṇi*, Bombay, 1892.

——. *Kālikā-sahasranāma-stotram*, Sri Ram Press, Madras, 1957.

——. *Kālīvilāsa-tantra*, Chowkhamba Sanskrit Series, Varanasi, 1963.

——. *Kāmya-Yantroddhāra*, H.P.S., Calcutta, 1953.

Pratyagātmānanda, Swami. *Japasūtram*, Bharatiya Vidya Prakashan, Varanasi, 1966.

——. *Pāśupata Sūtra*, Trivendrum Oriental Manuscripts Library, University of Travancore, 1940.

Pūrṇānanda. *Śrītattvacintāmaṇī*, Calcutta Sanskrit Series, no. 19.

——. *Śyāmārahasya*, P.C. Paul & Bros., Calcutta, 1948.

Radhakrishnan, S. *Eastern Religion and Western Thought*, Oxford University Press, 1940.

——. *Indian Philosophy*, 2 vols., Macmillan, London, 1930.

Rājānakabhāskara. *Lalleśvarī-vyākhyāna*, Chowkhamba Sanskrit Series, Varanasi, 1963.

Ramanuja. *The Vedānta Sūtra* (Commentary), translated by George Thibaut, *Sacred Books of the East*, vol. XLVIII, Motilal Banarsidass, Delhi, 1962.

Ramcharan, Sri. *Mātṛ-sūpāsna*, Kalyan Mandir, Katra, Allahabad, 1949.

Rao, Gopinath. *Elements of Hindu Iconography*, 4 vols., Madras, 1914-16.

——. *The Naturalistic Tradition in Indian Thoughts*, University of Washington Press, Seattle, 1961.

——. *Rudrayāmala*, Anusandhāna Samiti, Calcutta, 1895.

Rele, Vasant G. *The Mysterious Kuṇḍalinī*, D.B. Taraporevala & Sons Co., Bombay, 1960.

Russell, Bertrand. *Religion and Science*, Oxford University Press, London, 1960.

Samkrityayana, Rahul. *Siddha Sarāhapāda Kṛta Donākaśa*, Bihar Rastrabhasa Parisad, Patna, 1957.

Santoshi, Sri. *Kaula-Kīrtana*, Chowkhamba Sanskrit Series, Varanasi, 1963.

Sarma, Paṇḍit Caturpal. *Anuṣṭhāna-prakāśa-mahānibandha*, Khemraj Srikṛṣṇadass, Bombay, 1951.

Shastri, K. S. Subrahmanya. *Descriptive Catalogue of Sanskrit Manuscripts*, vol. XX, Sri Vanivilas Press, Srirangam, 1951.

Shastri, R. Ananthakrishna. *Lalitā Sahasranāman*, Theosophical Publishing House, Adyar, Madras, 1951.

Shastri, Siva Sankar Avasthi. *Mantra Aur Mātṛkāon Kā Rahasya*, Chowkhamba Sanskrit Series, Varanasi, 1966.

Shastri, Pandit Raghunath (ed.). *Merutantra,* Laksmivenkatesvar Steam Press, Kalyan, Bombay, 1940.

Shastri, Pandīt Ganesa & Gokhle, R.R. (ed.). *Jñānāva-Tantra,* Anandashrama Sanskrit Series, no. 69, Bombay, 1952.

Shastri, Pandit T. Ganpati (ed.). *Maṇjuśrīmūlakalpa* (Arya), Trivendrum Sanskrit Series, Trivandrum, 1920.

——. *Mantramahārṇava,* Sri Laksmivenkatesvar Steam Press, Kalyan, Bombay, 1940.

——. *Mantrasiddhi Kā Upāya,* Chowkhamba Sanskrit Series, Varanasi, 1963.

——. *Mātrikābheda-tantra,* Chowkhamba Sanskrit Series, Varanasi, 1963.

Shastri, Haraprasad (ed.). *Advayavajra Samgraha,* Gaekwad Oriental Series, no. XL, Baroda, 1927.

Shastri, Hirananda. *Origin and Cult of Tarā,* Archaeological Survey of India, *Memoir* no. 20.

Shastri, Pandit Madhusudan Kaul (ed.). *The Siddhitrayī and the Pratyabhijñinạ-kāvṛti,* Kashmir Sanskrit Texts and Studies, XXXIV, Srinagar, 1921.

Shastri, Pandit Mukunda Rana (ed.). *Sitikaṇṭha Mahānsyaprakāśa,* Kashmir Sanskrit Texts and Studies, vol. XXI, Srinagar, 1918.

——. *Śrīvidyāstavamañjarī,* Chowkhamba Sanskrit Series,Varanasi, 1963.

——. *Śrīvidyāratnasūtra,* Sarasvati Bhavan Series, vol. XI, Banaras.

Satyānveśi. *Kaula Kīrtan,* Kalyan Mandir, Prayag.

Schietner. F.A. *Tārānātha's Geschichte des Buddismus in India,* Kaisseriche Akademic der Wissenschaften, St. Petersburg, Russia, 1869.

Shah, Priyabala (ed.). *Mudrā—vicāra-prakaraṇaṁ mudrā-vidhi,* Chowkhamba Sanskrit Series, Varanasi, 1963.

Shah, V.P. *A Peep into the Early History of Tantra in Jain Literature,* Bharata Kaumudi, vol. 11, Allahabad, 1947.

Sharma, Bhadra Shila. *Todala Tantram,* Kalyan Mandir, Prayag.

——. *Bhairavi Cakra-Pūjan,* Kalyan Mandir, Prayag.

——. *Kāmadhenu Tantra,* Kalyan Mandir, Prayag, Samvat 2021.

——. *Niruttra Tantra,* Kalyan Mandir, Prayag, Samvat 2017.

Sharma, D.S. *Hinduism Through the Ages,* Bharatiya Vidya Bhavan, Bombay, 1956.

Shastri, Har Prasad. *Bauddhagā Dohā,* Vāṇgiya Sāhityā Pariṣad, Calcutta, 1959.

Shastri Madhusudan Kaul. *Īśvarapratyabhijñā,* 2 vols., Kashmir Sanskrit Texts and Studies, Srinagar, 1921.

Shastri Madhusudam Kaul *Vāmkeśvarīmatam,* vol. LXVI, Kashmir Sanskrit Texts and Studies, Srinagar, 1945.

——. *Netra Tantram,* Kashmir Sanskrit Texts and Studies, Srinagar, 1939.

——. *Sri Mālinī Vijay Vārttikam,* Kashmir Sanskrit Texts and Studies, no. XXXI, Srinagar,1921.

Shastri, Mukunda Ram. *Parā-Triṁśikā,* Kashmir Sanskrit Texts and Studies, Srinagar, 1918.

Singh, L.P. Tantra : *Its Mystic and Scientific Basis,* Concept Publishing Company, N. Delhi.

Singh, Mohan. *Gorakhnatha and Medieval Hindu Mysticism,* Lahore, 1937.

Sivapadesundaram, S. *The Śaiva School of Hinduism,* Madras, 1934.

Snodgrass, A. *Symbolism of the Sūpta,* Ithaca Cornell University, 1985.

Stebbing, L. Susan. *Philosophy and the Physicists,* Dover Publication Inc., New York.

Subramanya, Cidānandanātha Brahmaśrī. *Śrīvidyā-nityāhnikan,* Chowkhamba Sanskrit Series, Varanasi, 1963.

——. *Śrīvidyā-mantra-bhāṣyam,* Chowkhamba Sanskrit Series, Varanasi, 1963.

Subramanyasastri, K.S. (ed.). *Mantraśāstra-mātṛkā-granthāṁ-vivaraṇātmikā śucikā,* Chowkhamba Sanskrit Series, Varanasi, 1963.

Sukla Ramadatt. *Hindi Tantrasāra,* Kalyan Mandir, Katra, Allahabad, 1958.

——. *Śyāmā-rahasyā-tantram,* Chowkhamba Sanskrit Series, Varanasi, 1963

Suzuki, D.T. *Laṅkāvatāra-Sūtra,* English translation, 1932.

Thakur, Devanath. *Mantrakaumudi,* Chowkhamba Sanskrit Series, Varanasi, 1963.

Thompson, E.J. & Spencer A.A. (ed.). *Bengali Religious Lyrics : Śākta,* Oxford University Press, 1923.

Tripathi, Lakshmi-Narayan. *Mantra Dīpikā,* Govind Mudranalaya, Varanasi.

Tucci. G. *Teoria epradica del Maṇḍala,* Casa Editrice Astrolabia, Roma, 1949.

——. *Tibetan Painted Scrolls,* vol. I, II & III, bibreo della stata, Roma, 1949.

Tucci, Giuseppe. *Theory and Practice of Naṇḍala,* Rider & Co., London, 1961.

Tucci, Giuseppe. *Tibetan Painted Scrolls,* Rome, 1949.

——. *Some Glosses upon the Guhyasamāja,* vol. III, 339-53, Brussels, 1934-35.

Underhill, Evelyn. *Mysticism,* University Paperbacks, Methuen & Co. Ltd., 36, Essex Street Strand, London, 1960.

Utpaladeva. *The Īśvara Pratabhijñā,* 2 vols., Kashmir Sanskrit Texts and Studies, Srinagar, 1921.

Van Manen, John (ed.). *Minor Tibetan Texts,* New Series, no. 1426, Calcutta, 1919.

Vasavada, A.V. *Tripura Rahasya,* Chowkhamba Sanskrit Series, Varanasi, 1965.

Vedantatirtha, Giriscandra (ed.). *Tarātantram,* Chowkhamba Sanskrit Series, Varanasi, 1963.

Viresvarananda, Swami. *Brahma Sūtra,* Advaita Ashram, Entally Road, Calcutta, 1963.

Vivekananda, Swami. *Rāja-Yoga,* Advaita Ashram, Entally Road, Calcutta, 1962.

Waddell, L.A. The Dhāraṇī Cuttin Buddhism Ostasiatische Zeltschrift. I. 155-95, Berlin, 1921.

——. *The Buddhism of Tibet or Lamaism,* London, 1895.

Wallace, B. Alan *Choosing Reality: A Buddhist View of Physics and Mind*, Snow Lion Publications, Ithaca, New York, 1996.

Wayman, Alexy. *Buddhist Tantras*, Samuel Weiser, New York, 1973.

Wellington, A.C. *The Mathematical Theory of Relativity*, University Press, Cambridge, 1960.

Yeshe, Lama. *Introduction to Tantra*, Wisdom Publication, Bostan, 1987.

——. *The Tāntric Path of Purification*, Wisdom Publication, Bostan, 1995.

Zimmer, H. *The Art of Hindu Asia*, Bollingen Series, New York, 1955.

——. *The Philosophies of India*, Meridan, New York, 1958.

——. *Zur Bedeutungdes Indischen Indeschen Tatitra-Yogo, Eranos* Tanrbuch, vol. 1, Zurich, 9-94.

Index